Inside Business Law

A Guide for Managers

David Field is Head of the Department of Law at Napier College, Edinburgh. After graduating with an honours degree in law from the University of Nottingham in 1967, he spent six years on the staff of Ealing Technical College specializing in the teaching of law to business and management students. In 1973 he crossed the border and qualified as a solicitor in Scotland, where he spent some years in private practice before taking up his current post in 1978. He does regular consultancy work for a variety of companies and has written several legal textbooks, including *Practical Club Law* and *Hotel and Catering Law*. A regular radio broadcaster on legal matters, he has also presented the occasional music programme. He is married and has two children.

David Field

Inside Business Law

A guide for Managers

Pan Books London and Sydney

First published 1981 by Pan Books Ltd,
Cavaye Place, London SW10 9PG
© David Field 1981
ISBN 0 330 26349 8
Printed and bound in Great Britain by
Richard Clay (The Chaucer Press) Ltd, Bungay, Suffolk

Contents

Throughout this book the law as stated is correct up to January 1981.

1 Law as a business regulator

Introduction

Every society which has the remotest claim to being advanced employs some sort of legal system to regulate its business and commercial life. The ancient civilizations all realized the importance of trade and the need for certainty and precision in the market place. The Romans, typically, sought to impose a universal code, the *jus gentium* on all races, in order that commerce might expand, to the greater glory (and profit) of Caesar. Maritime communities such as those in Rhodes and Barcelona perfected a law of the sea, which governed northern Europe for much of the later Middle Ages, and now the European Economic Community (EEC) seeks to 'harmonize' the commercial laws of all member states.

Britain has largely gone her own way, shaking off the effects of Roman occupation, unbowed by subsequent attacks by Spanish, French and German invaders, all of which might have led to the imposition of an early legal code upon her merchants. Even now, as a full member of the EEC, she is often the last to fall in line with Draft Directives designed to create one law for the entire Community.

The roots of English business law may instead be traced to those mercantile customs which, by the fourteenth century, were being administered in local merchant courts such as the 'Piepowder Courts' (a corruption of *pieds poudres*, referring to the dusty feet of the merchants who used them) and the 'Staple Courts' (in effect, local monopolies granted by royal patronage which controlled commodities such as wool, tin and leather). The mayors and burgesses who presided compiled their judgements on the basis of the customs – often local – which prevailed in the appropriate trade or commodity.

By the sixteenth century, the Common Law courts had grown jealous of the influence of local amateurs, and in successfully supplanting them, assimilated most of the mercantile customs upon which they relied. By 1800 or thereabouts, most mercantile custom had passed into the Common Law of England, and merely awaited codification. This began in the latter half of the nineteenth century, and statutes such as the Sale of Goods Act, 1893, the Bills of Exchange Act, 1882, and the Partnership Act of 1890, merely gave Parliamentary recognition to those rules which the merchants had known for centuries. The establishment of a special Commercial Court within the Queen's Bench Division of the High Court in 1894 was further evidence of the growing significance of business and commerce in the Common Law as a whole.

But this process produced merely a legal environment convenient for the entrepreneur; also, in the strict Victorian tradition of *laissez-faire*, it assumed that both parties to an agreement were equal in bargaining strength. Only after the Second World War did lawyers publicly acknowledge the truth, and the past thirty years or so have been marked by the tremendous growth in 'consumer law', that is, legislation designed to protect the individual consumer from the economic, and hitherto legal, strength of the producer and retailer. Notable milestones along this road have been the Consumer Credit Act, 1974, the Trade Descriptions Act, 1968, the Consumer Protection Act, 1978, the Supply of Goods (Implied Terms) Act, 1973, and the Unfair Contract Terms Act, 1977, all of which have their place elsewhere in this book.

So far have we gone along this road, in fact, that under certain sections of the Sale of Goods Act, 1893, there are different rules for someone who enters into a contract for the sale of goods as a 'consumer' than for someone who is a businessman. A long way from the Roman concept of one law for all.

At the same time, during the past ten years or so, the legal position of the employee has improved almost beyond recognition, and modern businesses have been forced to come to terms with concepts such as health and safety at work, unfair dismissal, time off for union duties and so on, which would have reduced to a state of speechlessness those of our Victorian ancestors who laid the foundations of modern business.

It has become traditional, when compiling the first chapter of any book with law as its subject matter, to examine the ways in which our laws may be classified. While this might provide an amusing academic parlour game for lawyers on long winter evenings, it is of little practical relevance to the business executive, who will instinctively classify the law into its various components according to the effect which they have upon him. On this basis, there is only one major division of law, that into *criminal law* and *civil law*.

Criminal law may be described as a code of conduct demanded from an individual (or partnership, or company, or nationalized industry) by society as a whole, championed by the government of the day. Breach of this standard results in *prosecution* either by the state direct (*Regina* or *Rex* or simply *R*. v. *Smith*) or through the agency of some public official such as a Health and Safety Inspector or a police officer (*Brown* v. *Smith*). If *convicted*, the person breaking this code may be *fined* or *imprisoned*, or both. Examples of criminal laws which relate directly to business are the Trade Descriptions Act, 1968, the Weights and Measures Acts, 1960 and 1979, and the Health and Safety at Work Act, 1974.

Civil law is the law which governs the relationships between individuals, and is enforceable only by the individual. If I break a contract with my employer, the only person with the legal right to take action on that breach is the injured employer; the state has no interest in my transgression unless I have at the same time infringed the criminal code. Whereas the criminal law *punishes* an offence against it, the civil law seeks to *compensate* the injured party at the expense of the wrongdoer. The person injured (the 'plaintiff') therefore sues the defaulting party (the 'defendant') for one of the remedies available (e.g. damages, injunction, specific performance). Again, this will be recorded as *Brown* v. *Smith*.

Since the two systems are so different, it is hardly surprising that there is a different network of courts for each of them, which we shall shortly examine in more detail. But first, we must complete our survey of the sources of business law.

Sources of law

The point has already been made that mercantile law owes much to the customs of the merchants themselves, and that historically, custom has therefore been an important source of English business law. Similarly, one may point to periods in our history in which our emerging legal system has been influenced by Canon Law (the law of the Catholic Church), Roman Law, and the works of authoritative early writers, whose expositions of the law as they found it are our only surviving link with the periods in which they wrote. Thus, names such as Glanville (twelfth century), Coke (sixteenth century) and Blackstone (eighteenth century) will live on for ever as vital historical sources of English law.

But none of these could be regarded as modern sources of business law; they may tell us where our law has come from, but they will be of no use to the manager or executive seeking to know what the law is on a particular matter now. For this information, you will need to turn to a modern source of law, of which there are basically only two, namely 'legislation' and 'judicial precedent' (or 'case-law').

Legislation

Legislation (the laying-down of rules of law by a body of persons authorized for this purpose) is without doubt the most powerful modern source of law, and any other potential source of law must take second place. Nothing can overrule or override the clear purpose and effect of an item of legislation; however much the judges may seek to interpret or distinguish one item of legislation from another, they must at the end of the day give effect to it, as the expressed will of those democratically elected to govern us.

Legislation may be truly described as a 'growth industry', and that growth, in the past half-century, has been phenomenal. Legislation has the advantages of being swift, comprehensive, democratic and responsive to change as compared with case law laid down by judges in individual cases heard before them. It has been the abused but willing tool of governments of all shades of political opinion for centuries, but it was in 1920 or thereabouts that the legislative explosion began. No modern government could survive to the end of the week without legislation.

The primary form of legislation is of course the Act of Parliament. Since Parliament is the supreme legislative body for the UK (with an arguable exception so far as EEC affairs are concerned – see below) it follows that an Act of Parliament (or statute) is the supreme source of law in this country. Once it has been subjected to the democratic process in Parliament (first reading, second reading, committee, report, third reading, and then on to the other chamber for a similar process), and been approved by the Queen, it becomes law on the day fixed for it to do so, and no one may stop it.

This does not of course mean that there are no institutional or legal controls on what is enacted by Parliament. Quite apart from the political checks inherent in the British Parliamentary system, the courts have certain weapons which they may apply against statutes which are unwise or unduly oppressive. The most powerful of these is the duty which the courts have of interpreting new laws which have never before been subjected to judicial scrutiny. In following this process, the courts can do much to alleviate hardship, oppression or sheer stupidity in the legislative process.

However, Parliament remains sovereign, and if necessary may enact legislation to counter the effect of a judicial decision. Thus, in 1965, the government of the day passed the War Damage Act in order to nullify the decision in *Burmah Oil Co. Ltd* v. *Lord Advocate* (1965), to the effect that compensation was payable from the public purse to those whose property had been deliberately destroyed in the retreat from the Far East during the Second World War. The Act was specifically drafted so as to take away the compensation already awarded to Burmah Oil by the House of Lords sitting in its judicial capacity.

Modern government is so complex that the somewhat ponderous system of legislation employed by Parliament can only be reserved for the most important matters. Many thousands of fairly routine legislative duties are delegated by Parliament to a variety of nominees, chief among whom are Secretaries of State enacting statutory instruments to cover matters handled by their departments, local authorities passing by-laws for the control of their areas, and various official bodies laying down rules to govern themselves and their members (e.g. Law Society, General Medical Council and Church of England).

This 'delegated legislation', as it is called, is not allowed to exist without considerable control from several quarters. For example, most forms of statutory instrument have to lie on the table of House of Commons for a given number of days, during which they may be challenged, while local authority by-laws and the autonomic legislation of bodies such as the Law Society normally require ministerial confirmation before they become law. In addition, since all such legislative power can itself only be delegated by some legislative process (as for example where an Act of Parliament gives a Secretary of State the power to enact statutory instruments), the courts are in a position to veto any item of delegated legislation by ruling it *ultra vires* ('beyond the powers' conferred by the statute).

There can be little doubt that without delegated legislation, modern Britain would grind to a halt. Parliament does not have time to debate every tiny matter, and it does not always have the technical expertise available to a Government minister. It cannot deal with a matter as swiftly as can delegated legislation, and it cannot be as flexible.

Until 1973, it could have been asserted with confidence that Parliament was supreme, a sovereign law-making body with no rivals. From 1 January 1973, the effect of the European Communities Act, 1972, was to incorporate into English law without any further legislative process, many regulations, directives and decisions of the Council or Commission of the EEC. Not only can the UK Parliament not prevent these from becoming part of UK law, it is prohibited by the same Act from enacting any law which is inconsistent with such EEC regulations, directives or decisions.

It is arguable (and the anti-EEC lobby is still using the argument) that Parliament has, by this process, lost at least some of its supremacy over legislation affecting the UK. While this is probably true, it should also be remembered that EEC legislation on the whole is confined to EEC matters, and that our own courts of law still have the power to 'interpret' it, except where such duties are expressly reserved for the European Court.

Thus, although Britain may not have a legal 'code' in the sense understood by German or American lawyers, it has the next best thing – a network of different statutes which together cover most eventualities. All legislation remains in force until repealed or amended by subsequent legislation.

As you move through the chapters which follow, you will soon appreciate just how much of the general business law which concerns you is statutory in origin, and just how well certain of these statutes have stood the test of time. Day to day details (on, for example, the price of bread, the minimum wage an employer must pay to an employee, or the prevention of accidents arising from the use of lifts and hoists) are to be found in statutory instruments, those most versatile of regulators. Legislation, in all its forms, provides the scaffolding in the legal framework of business.

Judicial precedent

If legislation is the scaffolding, then judicial precedent supplies the bricks which, piled carefully one upon another, give substance and form to the outline prepared by legislation. As has already been pointed out, legislation can go only so far in laying down a legal code – sooner or later, it is necessary for someone to define the limits of a particular provision or apply to it a novel situation. That 'someone' will usually be a judge in a court of law.

Since the reign of Henry I, when judges first began to travel the country dispensing royal justice, it has been recognized that judges have a limited power to 'make' law themselves whenever they come across a novel point which requires clarification or elucidation. It may be a point on which there simply is no law (an increasingly unlikely prospect), or, commonly, a judge may be required to interpret and apply a section of a statute to a new set of facts.

Whether one believes that in doing so the judge makes law, or one clings to the traditional view that he is merely discovering something which was there already, the practical effect is the same. A ruling has been given, a point has been clarified. Should that same question arise again in the future, then in an ideal world, one could say that the answer has already been supplied. However, the human capacity for hair-splitting being almost infinite, it is likely that one or other of the parties will claim that the previous ruling was based upon facts different from those in the present case, a process known as 'distinguishing'.

However, the principle is valid enough. A point of law, once decided by a court, may become a precedent for the future. Hence the phrase 'judicial precedent', or 'case-law' as it is sometimes called. Combine together a thousand or so such precedents in a small enough area of the law, and you have a legal 'code' every bit as comprehensive as a statute, and arguably more so, in that it arises from experience.

There are two types of precedent; those which are 'binding' on later courts (i.e. they must be followed) and those which are merely 'persuasive' (i.e. to be treated with respect, but not necessarily followed). Whether or not a particular precedent will be regarded as binding will depend upon the following factors.

(1) The facts of each case
It goes almost without saying that if the facts of the second case are not the same as the facts of the first one, then the

former case will not set a binding precedent for the latter. Much legal ingenuity is frequently displayed in an effort to distinguish one case from another, not least from the Bench itself.

(2) The points at issue in each case

One case can only set a binding precedent for a later case if the essential point at issue is the same in each case. If for example the crucial question in Case One was whether or not one must pay for goods delivered ten days late, but the judge also went on to make comment about the legality of delivering the wrong quantity on the correct day, then that judgement will not be binding in Case Two where delivery of the wrong quantity is made. This is because the question of incorrect quantity was not essential to the final judgement of Case One. Every judgement may be divided into the *ratio decidendi* (the vital ruling of law which led to the judgement in the case) and the *obiter dicta* (all the other matters dealt with in the judgement which were not directly relevant to the case in hand). It is only the *ratio decidendi* which can give rise to a binding precedent.

(3) The relative status of the two courts

A court will never be bound by an earlier decision of a court *below* it in the hierarchy of courts. On the other hand, it will be always bound by the decision of a court *above it*. The only variable factor is whether or not a particular court will be bound by its own previous ruling (assuming that it was the ratio of the case, and that the facts are identical), and this seems to vary from court to court.

The hierarchy of courts is described in the next section, and on the civil side consists basically of, in descending order of seniority, the House of Lords, the Court of Appeal, the High Court and the County Courts. The judgements of the House of Lords are binding on all other courts and even on itself, except where it feels that there is good reason for not following an earlier precedent. It follows from this that a House of Lords precedent is the most powerful and influential of all; often, the only way around such a precedent is to enact a new Act of Parliament to cancel it out (as in the case of the War Damage Act in 1965, as described above).

The Court of Appeal (Civil Division) is bound by House of Lords decisions, and also its own, except where there are conflicting rulings to choose from, or the earlier judgement is suspect because of some legal principle which was not considered. It also lays down precedents which will be binding upon all the courts below it.

The High Court is bound by judgements of the House of Lords and the Court of Appeal (Civil Division) as well as decisions arrived at by one of its own divisional courts (see below). One High Court judge sitting alone has no power to create binding precedents, nor do any of the lower civil courts such as the County Courts or the magistrates courts.

A similar system of precedent operates within the hierarchy of the *criminal* courts (House of Lords, Court of Appeal (Criminal Division), Crown Courts, Magistrates Courts).

Again, this reasonably clear 'pecking order' is subject to the overriding influence of the Court of Justice of the European Communities (usually simply called the 'European Court'), whose decisions, in all matters within its jurisdiction, are expressly binding on all English courts, even the House of Lords. However, the Court does not regard itself as bound by its *own* previous rulings.

The whole concept of judicial precedent is open to major criticisms, not the least of which is that it is hardly democratic to allow one man (or possibly three, five or seven men, as would be the case in the Court of Appeal or House of Lords) to 'make' law. In addition, one cannot lay down law for the future by the system of judicial precedent unless and until a suitable case arises, whereas legislation can be 'instant'. A case law system also tends to be bulky, and depends for its very existence on an efficient system of law reporting.

But case law has the advantage of being practical in origin, and designed to meet actual needs. It is 'enacted' by highly experienced legal practitioners and it can be used to fill in the gaps which inevitably appear in any statutory system, however comprehensive it is intended to be.

The inter-reaction of case law and legislation

The modern businessman seeking an answer to a particular problem (or, more realistically, the solicitor employed to find it for him) will almost certainly start his search by reading a section or sections of a statute, and possibly a set of Regulations made under it. He may *think* he knows what it means, but he would be well advised to continue his search in the Law Reports (of which many volumes now appear each year), in case the point has been interpreted or clarified in some recent judgement, bearing in mind that in the event of his finding two apparently conflicting judgements, he must apply the 'binding precedent' tests outlined above.

In short, the search for the law on a particular point will involve the searcher in a subtle game involving both major modern sources of law, statute and case law. Statute can be used to eliminate bad case law, but in its turn, every piece of legislation must run the gauntlet of the courts, whose judges can turn the tables on the legislators with their interpretations. It is probably for this reason that no written code could ever satisfactorily define the law as it applies to business, or any other human activity.

The civil courts of law

Enough has been written already about judicial precedent for you to have formed your own impression of the importance of courts of law. From the days of King Alfred, it has been recognized that mankind will always become involved in disputes, and that it is better for society as a whole that these be resolved in a civilized fashion, by a court or an arbitrator, rather than by more physical means. A system of courts for the settlement of grievances and disputes also creates the sort of confidence in society which is essential for the development of commerce. In short, although the businessman may never actually find himself inside a court of law, he owes the stability of his business at least in part to their existence.

Just as there is on the one hand the civil law, and on the other the criminal law, so there are two 'hierarchies' of courts to administer the two separate systems. Since the vast majority of business law is to be found on the civil side, we will concentrate on the civil courts to the exclusion of their criminal counterparts.

Our civil courts were drastically reorganized during the period 1873–75, and have remained basically the same ever since, although the types of business which each is authorized to handle change from time to time. The *plaintiff* in a civil action (i.e. the one who is bringing the action) has a choice between having the case tried locally, and less expensively, or tried at considerably extra expense (possibly to him) in the High Court.

The two local civil courts are the magistrates courts and the County Courts, and we may examine these first.

The magistrates courts

The main function of the magistrates courts is to administer criminal justice at a local level, and their civil jurisdiction is limited. Nevertheless, they are used extensively for the recovery of debts such as income tax, national insurance, and gas and electricity bills; they also grant liquor licences and enforce rate demands. Their main civil function is in the sphere of family law, where they deal with matters such as adoption orders, affiliation orders and separations, none of which is of direct relevance to a business.

Magistrates are most usually 'laymen' (i.e. not legally qualified) sitting in groups of between two and seven, although a 'stipendiary' magistrate may sit alone, since his is a full-time appointment and he is legally qualified. The jurisdiction of a magistrate does not extend beyond the narrow limits of his own district.

The County Courts

The modern County Courts were established in 1846 to deal with modest civil actions at a local level, thus saving the parties the trouble and expense of travelling to the High Court in London. This has remained their function, although the financial limits have changed with inflation; today, the County Courts may hear any normal civil action which involves a claim of no more than £2,000, a sum which may be increased for special cases (e.g. £120,000 in the case of the share capital of a company in liquidation, and £15,000 in cases involving trusts or mortgages). In addition, the County Courts may be designated by statute as the appropriate courts for the hearing of particular actions, regardless of the amount claimed (as with bankruptcies and cases referred under the Race Relations Act, 1976, the Consumer Credit Act, 1974, and the Rent Acts).

The parties may also, by agreement, refer a case involving any amount to the County Court for a hearing; if there is no such agreement, and the claim is 'over the limit', then it must be raised in the appropriate division of the High Court (see below). It is, of course, theoretically possible for a case under the County Court limit to be raised in the High Court, but various procedural devices exist to discourage this.

There is another important limitation on the jurisdiction of the County Courts, and this a geographical one. There are well in excess of three hundred County Courts in England and Wales (thus making the term 'County Court' a serious misnomer), and they are grouped into 'circuits', each of which is headed by a Circuit Judge. A Circuit Judge may hear any case which is within the jurisdiction of a court within his circuit (i.e. if the defendant either resides or has a place of business within the district, or the cause of action arose there). In addition, each court will have permanently attached to it a 'Registrar', who acts as its chief administrative officer, and also has the power to hear cases himself, where the amount claimed does not exceed £200, or the parties agree that he may hear the case.

An *ordinary* action in the County Court will commence

when the plaintiff or his solicitor fills in a form called a 'summons' (containing details of the parties and particulars of the claim) and files it with the Registrar. These are copied and served (normally by a bailiff) on the defendant, who is notified of the 'return day', i.e. the latest date on which the defendant must put in an 'appearance' if he intends to dispute the claim. Alternatively, he may admit liability on an earlier date, and make arrangements through the Registrar for the amount due to be paid. The approved procedure for a defendant wishing to defend an action is in fact for him to enter a formal 'defence' within fourteen days; copies of this will be served on the plaintiff.

The first stage in court will be the 'pre-trial review', in which the Registrar will attempt to get the issues in the case reduced to as simple a form as possible, and fix a date for the trial. If the defendant fails to appear at this stage, judgement may be entered for the plaintiff. It is at this stage that many cases are settled 'out of court'; alternatively, the Registrar may refer any case of less than £200 either to an independent arbiter, or to himself.

Assuming that none of these things happens, the trial will proceed on the day fixed for it. Failure of either party to appear can result in the case going against him in his absence. Very rarely, trial is by jury, although this is unlikely to happen in a commercial case. The usual rule of procedure is that it is for the plaintiff to prove his case on a balance of probabilities.

'Ordinary' actions cover matters such as breach of contract, claims for damages for negligence, and failure to fulfil hire-purchase obligations, in fact anything other than 'default actions' (which are simply for the recovery of a specified debt) and 'rent actions' (involving landlord and tenant). Special procedures apply in these cases.

The usual outcome of any trial in the County Court, assuming that the plaintiff is successful, is the award of damages, to the limits indicated above. The successful party may also normally expect to recover his costs from the other side. There is a right of appeal against County Court judgements to the Court of Appeal (Civil Division) on a question of law or evidence where the claim exceeds £20, and a question of fact where it exceeds £200. Bankruptcy appeals go to the Chancery Division of the High Court, and some matrimonial appeals to the Queen's Bench Division of the same court.

The High Court

Until 1971, the High Court sat almost exclusively in London, with occasional forays into the country on the old Assize circuits. Today, although its principal centre of operation is still the High Court Buildings in The Strand, it is empowered to sit in any of the 'first tier' Crown Court towns, or anywhere else authorized by the Lord Chancellor. The County Courts are therefore no longer the only local civil courts of any authority; but they are still the most convenient, since delay may still occur in bringing a case before the next sitting of the High Court.

There are three divisions of the High Court, namely

(1) Chancery
This division deals primarily with matters involving estates, trusts, mortgages, partnerships and land contracts. It also deals with revenue cases, planning appeals, probate matters and disputes involving landlord and tenant. Appeals are also heard by the Chancery Division in tax and bankruptcy cases from the County Courts.

(2) Family Division
This, as its name suggests, deals primarily with cases involving divorce, nullity of marriage, adoption, legitimacy and guardianship. It also handles probate cases in which there is no dispute between the parties. This Division also hears appeals in such matters from lower courts.

(3) Queen's Bench Division
The jurisdiction of the Queen's Bench Division is wider than that of the other two divisions, taking in all actions arising

from contract or 'tort' (civil wrongs such as negligence). Within the Division is the Commercial Court, which sits in Liverpool, London and Manchester, and deals exclusively with cases arising from business transactions such as insurance, banking and agency. Also within the Queen's Bench Division is a separate Admiralty Court, hearing actions arising from collisions at sea and carriage by ship.

Its appellate jurisdiction is also wide, hearing appeals from both County Courts and magistrates courts on matters within its subject areas.

Obviously, this is the most important of the Divisions from a commercial point of view, and its forty or so judges, headed by the Lord Chief Justice, resolve a wide variety of cases in the course of a working year. Procedure within the Division is governed by the Rules of the Supreme Court, which prescribe four different ways of commencing an action in the Queen's Bench Division of the High Court. The most common by far is the Writ.

A Writ is a standard-form document which specifies the identities of the parties, and in the Queen's name commands the defendant to 'enter an appearance' within fourteen days of receipt of the Writ, on pain of being found liable in default. This Writ will be 'endorsed' with a brief statement of claim by the plaintiff, and one copy filed in either the Central Office of the High Court in London, or one of the local District Registries. The other copy is served on the defendant, and he 'enters an appearance' by returning the appropriate form to the Court Office, and serving a copy on the plaintiff's solicitor.

This is normally an indication that the action is being defended, and the parties begin elaborating on the 'pleadings' (i.e. the plaintiff's statement of claim and the defendant's defence and possible counter claim, together with the plaintiff's further reply and so on, until the parties can find nothing further to add). Once the pleadings are 'closed', the plaintiff requests directions from the court, which will assess what further information is required before trial may be fixed.

Trial will normally be in open court, with a shorthand transcript being taken of the entire proceedings. Once again, it is for the plaintiff to prove his case on a balance of probabilities. Only rarely will there be a jury; normally, judgement will be by a single Queen's Bench Division judge. As with County Court proceedings, a successful party would normally expect to have his costs awarded against the other party.

Either party may appeal to the Court of Appeal (Civil Division); this normally exists as of right, but there are certain circumstances in which leave is required from the High Court. Appeals must normally be lodged within six weeks of judgement. Very rarely, an appeal 'leapfrogs' direct to the House of Lords from the High Court where an important point of law is involved.

The magistrates courts, County Courts and High Court are the only civil courts of 'first instance' (i.e. with the power to hear a case for the first time). The remaining courts in the civil hierarchy, the Court of Appeal (Civil Division) and the House of Lords, are simply 'appellate' courts (charged with the duty of hearing appeals), although it will be recalled that some appellate functions are carried out by the High Court.

The Court of Appeal (Civil Division)

The Court of Appeal (Civil Division) is the successor to the old Court of Appeal and exists to hear appeals from judgements in the High Court and County Courts; it also hears appeals from bodies such as the Employment Appeal Tribunal, the Restrictive Practices Court and the Pensions Appeals Tribunal. The court is headed by the Master of the Rolls and staffed by sixteen Lords Justices of Appeal.

An appeal will normally take place before three appeal judges, and take the form of a full rehearing of legal argument from both sides, based on transcripts of the witnesses' evidence. It will, on rare occasions, hear fresh evidence, and at the end of the rehearing, the court has full power to make any order which could have been made by the trial court. It may also refer a question to the European Court for a preliminary ruling on a question of Community Law.

Most appeals to the Court of Appeal (Civil Division) are on a point of law, and the court normally restricts itself to that point. However, it does have the power to 'find' facts for itself, and to substitute findings of fact for those found by the lower court. Exceptionally, it may order a new trial.

Appeal may be made from a ruling of the Court of Appeal to the House of Lords.

The House of Lords

The House of Lords is of course a political body, but for many hundreds of years it was also the most senior court in both civil and criminal matters. It was reconstituted as such in the reorganization of the courts in 1875, and today its 'Appellate' Committee, consisting of eleven Law Lords headed by the Lord Chancellor, is the final court of appeal in our civil hierarchy of courts.

It hears civil appeals primarily from the Court of Appeal (Civil Division) (plus its equivalents in civil matters in Scotland and Northern Ireland), but cases involving an important point of law of general public importance may leapfrog into the House of Lords direct from the High Court. The same test normally determines whether or not an appeal may be heard from the Court of Appeal and leave must be granted by either court.

There is a quorum of three Law Lords, who hear argument from counsel before retiring and preparing written judgements. Although it has the power, it will be reluctant to disturb a finding of fact from the lower court. As mentioned elsewhere, a ruling of the House of Lords is the most powerful 'precedent' possible, and may only be overruled by a statute, a contradictory later decision by the House of Lords itself, or a ruling of the European Court of Justice.

Before leaving the subject of courts of law, some further mention must be made of the role and function of this last court.

The European Court of Justice

Since 1 January 1973, the House of Lords has not been the supreme court of the United Kingdom in civil matters because, at least in matters which refer to the Community, it is subservient to that Community's own Court of Justice, which consists of eleven judges, and three Advocates-General to 'present' cases to the judges. They are appointed from the member states for six-year terms of office, and headed by a President elected by them for a three-year term.

Apart from its jurisdiction over pure Community matters, the Court also has, under Article 177 of the Treaty of Rome (which is part of UK law), jurisdiction to give rulings concerning the validity of the Treaty itself, the validity of Community institution actions and the interpretation of Community legislation. When it does give such a ruling, it is binding even on the House of Lords, but no UK court is bound to ask for such a ruling unless it is a court from which no appeal lies (i.e. the House of Lords). Experience so far has shown a marked reluctance on the part of English judges to request a ruling from the European Court.

Tribunals

In addition to the network of courts described above, the UK is fortunate in possessing a fairly comprehensive collection of tribunals, which provide a more specialized, less formal and frequently less expensive means of settling a dispute than the more traditional courts of law. The tribunal has become more and more important in the post-war years, as life in general, and the business world in particular, has become more specialized and technical.

General political control of the tribunals is imposed by the Tribunals and Inquiries Act, 1971, by virtue of which many tribunals must be chaired by a legally qualified person appointed by the Lord Chancellor. There is also a Council on Tribunals which exercises general supervisory jurisdiction over the working of the tribunal system, and recommends changes where these are felt to be necessary. Some tribunals are also subject to legal control by the High Court, in the sense that a right of appeal exists from their findings to that court; virtually all tribunals are subject to the High Court in the sense that the Queen's Bench Division of that court may issue 'prerogative orders' to a tribunal which it is felt has overstepped its authority.

There are basically three types of tribunal with which the business manager is most likely to become involved during his professional life.

Domestic tribunals

These are tribunals set up by professional associations such as the Law Society and the General Medical Council in order to resolve matters (frequently of a disciplinary nature) concerning their own members. These members agree to submit themselves to the jurisdiction of the appropriate tribunal (e.g. the Solicitors' Disciplinary Tribunal and the Disciplinary Committee of the General Medical Council) when they first become members, and the tribunals have the power to take away their livelihoods by 'striking them off' in suitably serious cases. Because of the gravity of matters handled by this type of tribunal, there is usually a right of appeal to the normal courts (usually the High Court) under the statute which sets up the tribunal in the first place.

Tribunals of inquiry

A tribunal of inquiry is set up by the Queen or a government minister to investigate a particularly serious incident or matter (e.g. Aberfan and the Profumo scandal). It is appointed for this specific purpose and will eventually report its findings and then be dissolved. During its period of appointment it may well have the same powers as the High Court to summon witnesses, demand documents, examine witnesses on oath, and remit for contempt of court. Tribunals of inquiry are normally conducted in public, with interested parties being represented by counsel.

Industrial tribunals

Industrial tribunals are rapidly becoming the most important feature of modern employment law, and a sizeable proportion of all legal disputes between employer and employee are required by statute to be heard by a tribunal rather than by a traditional court. As a result, tribunals have almost exclusive jurisdiction over the hearing of claims involving contracts of employment, redundancy, equal pay, trade union rights, maternity rights of employees and unfair dismissal. This has all happened since 1964.

Each industrial tribunal is chaired by a full time salaried lawyer, who sits with two fellow tribunal members, one drawn from a panel nominated by employers' representatives, and the other from a union panel. Its function is to provide a swift, informal and specialized arena for the ventilation of legal grievances arising at work; the normal rules of evidence may be dispensed with in the search for the truth in a particular case, and the parties may present their own cases without fear of being faced with lawyers from the other side who will seek to 'blind them with science'.

In certain cases, tribunals may award compensation of well over £10,000 to ex-employees who have suffered an injustice at the hands of an employer. A tribunal may also order reinstatement or re-engagement in suitable cases, and obviously wields considerable power. Because of this, it is only sensible that it should be subject to a higher authority, and appeals may be taken from the decision of an industrial tribunal before the Employment Appeal Tribunal, the successor in all but name to the ill-fated National Industrial Relations Court. It is staffed by judges of High Court status and above, plus 'lay' advisors as in the case of tribunals themselves.

More will be said about industrial tribunals in later chapters on the law of employment.

Arbitration

The parties to a dispute do not always take the matter before a court of law, or even before a tribunal. In many cases they settle it themselves, and this may be regarded as the ideal outcome of any difference of opinion. Sometimes, while not being sufficiently close to an agreement to feel that they can come to a private arrangement, the parties are determined that they will not expend time and money, and incur a delay of possibly many months, by bringing the matter before a court. They therefore agree to submit their disagreement for a ruling by a third party. This is a process known as 'arbitration', and is of considerable importance in the commercial world.

A submission to arbitration is known in law as a 'reference', and it may come about in a variety of ways. The parties may have agreed from the outset of their relationship that any disputes would go to arbitration, or alternatively, they may agree to this only when it is obvious that they cannot agree. However it comes about, the agreement to refer operates as a separate contract between the parties, and either party may sue if the other breaches it, for example by raising the matter in the normal civil courts before the reference is completed.

The arbiter may be almost anyone whom the parties choose; he is frequently a lawyer, but often also a specialist in the particular subject matter of the dispute (e.g. a work of art or a specialist building contract). Once appointed, an arbiter has the power to examine witnesses, inspect documents, and reach a 'determination' on the issue. He may then issue an 'award', which in fact is his judgement on the issues upon which reference was made. This award may be enforced by the successful party as if it were a court decree, so that any financial compensation specified in the award can be recovered by the person entitled to it. Any of these arbitrator's powers may be amended or added to by the terms of the arbitration agreement.

The court will normally only set aside an arbitrator's award where it is shown that some exceptional reasons for doing so exist, such as proven bias on the part of the arbitrator or fraud by one of the parties. Under the Arbitration Act, 1979, any question of law arising during the course of a reference to arbitration which could substantially affect the rights of either party may be referred to the High Court, either on the agreement of the parties or with the leave of the court. The court may ask the arbitrator for further or more detailed reasons for his rulings, and may vary, confirm or set aside all or part of the award, or remit it to the arbitrator for reconsideration.

There are many advantages in the system of arbitration, some more obvious than others. For one thing, it will normally be cheaper than litigation, although not always. Secondly, it is, or should be, less formal and it will certainly be quicker. But perhaps the greatest advantage is that the arbitrator can be, and usually is, an expert whose knowledge of the particular subject area under consideration gives him a considerable advantage over any judge, however erudite. This latter advantage is frequently lost because the parties, following a traditional enough policy, appoint a judge as arbitrator!

Arbitration agreements are particularly prevalent in the insurance, building and shipping industries.

Scots law

Much of what follows in this book will be of equal interest to the business executive who is either based in Scotland, or has business contacts there. This early opportunity is therefore taken of noting the major distinctions between the English and the Scots legal systems.

The sources of law are basically the same for Scotland as for England and Wales, and much of the legislation which is passed by Parliament is intended to cover both jurisdictions equally. This is particularly true of what one might call 'economic law', and statutes dealing with matters such as taxation, sale of goods, consumer protection and competition apply equally to Scotland as to England and Wales.

The Common Law (i.e. that law which has emerged by means of case judgements) of Scotland will obviously vary from its English counterpart in places, if only because the courts themselves are different. However, it is remarkable how close the two legal frameworks (i.e. the English and the Scots) have remained in important areas such as contract and employment law. The major differences are noted 'in context' in the chapters which follow, but here we should look briefly at the different courts which exist in Scotland.

In *criminal* cases, there are only three courts, namely the District Courts, the Sheriff Courts and the High Court. The District Courts deal with the most minor criminal offences, such as breach of the peace and drunkenness, and the maximum penalties are £200 by way of a fine, or 60 days in prison. The District Courts are staffed by magistrates who on the whole are unsalaried laymen, although in Glasgow some are full time stipendiary magistrates with legal training.

The bulk of Scots criminal cases are heard in the Sheriff Court, where the proceedings may be either 'summary' (i.e. trial by sheriff only, maximum Common Law penalty £1,000 or 3 months' imprisonment), or 'solemn' (trial by sheriff and jury, £1,000 or two years). The most serious crimes of all (normally only murder, rape and serious assault) are reserved for trial by judge and jury in the High Court (limitless sentence). All crimes in Scotland are reported to, and prosecuted by, a local civil servant known as the Procurator Fiscal, who works under the direction of the Lord Advocate and the Crown Agent, whose 'Advocates Depute' prosecute cases in the High Court.

So far as *civil* cases are concerned, the 'Pursuer' (the person bringing the action) has a choice of two courts in which to bring his action against the 'Defender', depending upon the size of the claim. The Sheriff Court deals with all the minor and medium-sized claims, leaving the Court of Session (Outer House) to deal with the largest claims of all.

So far as actions for damages are concerned (and these make up the majority of commercial actions), they must be brought in the Sheriff Court if they are 'summary causes' (i.e. for £500 or less). If they are over this limit then they may be raised instead in the Court of Session (Outer House) at the option of the Pursuer. The case will be heard in the Sheriff Court by a sheriff and in the Court of Session by a judge; civil jury trials are very rare, but not unusual in actions involving accident claims against employers.

Appeals in civil cases lie to the Court of Session (Inner House) and then to the House of Lords, which is the final court of appeal for Scots civil cases as well as English. It is this commonality which has, more than anything, led to the fusion of Common Law principles between the two legal systems.

2 Different types of business

The private individual who is thinking of starting up a new business has a basic choice between three types of organization, each governed by a different set of laws. These are sole trading, partnership and incorporation, and each of these will from time to time make use of the services of agents, authorized to conduct business on behalf of a 'principal'. Each of these is examined in this chapter.

In this age of multinational corporations, it is easy to ignore the one-man firm and, unless one is concerned with a profession, even the partnership. But they are both still vital to our economy, and many of the large corporations of the 1980s began in the 1880s as small family concerns. The amount of space allocated to each form of business enterprise in this chapter reflects the legal complexity of each of them, and should not be taken as indicating their relative economic importance.

The sole trader

As the phrase suggests, sole trading is, from a legal point of view, merely the sum of the business activities of one entrepreneur, although 'sole traders' often engage other members of the family as full time employees. The local greengrocer, the village post office and the nearby filling station are all usually traditional 'one-man businesses', and there are virtually no special legal rules governing them. Whether the private individual is making a contract for purchase of a car, the booking of a holiday, the supply of a regular weekly grocery order or twenty gallons of petrol, he makes his contract in the same way – as a private individual.

However important he may be to the economist or the politician, the sole trader poses no interesting questions for the lawyer; he is just a natural person making contracts of a business nature in the manner outlined in Chapter 3. Until, that is, he begins to trade under a business name: then he becomes the concern of the lawyer.

Under the Registration of Business Names Act, 1916, no business organization other than a company (which registers its name under the Companies Acts) may carry on a business under a name *other* than the true surname of the proprietor(s) unless its business name is registered for that purpose by the Registrar of Business Names. This rule applies equally to partnerships; thus, whether the Apex Laundry Company is really the business name of sole proprietor John Smith, or the partnership of Smith, Jones and Brown, the true identity of the owners must be registered.

The details which must be registered include the business name, the principal place of business, the general nature of the business, and the Christian name, surname, nationality and usual residence of all the proprietors. Any changes must be notified as and when they occur. The Registrar may refuse to register any name which he regards as unsuitable, but issues written 'Notes for Guidance' on request.

The main sanction against failure to register is that the business will be unable to enforce any contract entered into while its name remains unregistered, unless the court is satisfied that the failure was unintentional, or that it would be unjust not to allow the contract to be enforced.

Not only must the true identity of the proprietor(s) be registered along with the business name; it must also appear on all business stationery, trade catalogues and other literature circulated by the business. The certificate of registration must be displayed on the main business premises.

Partnerships

Among professional men such as doctors, lawyers, accountants, brokers, architects and vets, the partnership is the most popular form of business association even today. The partnership is very old in legal terms, but was regulated by the Partnership Act of 1890, which still contains the main guidelines on what may be called 'partnership law'. Future references in this section to the 'Act' mean the 1890 Act.

Identifying a partnership

Section 1 of the Act states simply that 'Partnership is the relation which subsists between persons carrying on a business in common with a view of profit.' While this might sound reasonably straightforward, there are in fact certain situations (e.g. share fishing) in which it is not immediately obvious whether or not the relationship between two persons is that of partner and partner. Since the alternative relationship in most cases is that of employer and employee, and since, as will be seen in Chapter 8, this relationship is one with serious legal implications, it is of some importance to be able to identify a partnership precisely.

Section 2 of the Act offers limited assistance, by indicating certain situations in which a partnership will not automatically be presumed, as for example where property is jointly owned, or two people share the gross or net returns on a business enterprise, or a person is paid a regular share of the business profits of an enterprise. Each of these situations may well provide strong evidence that there is a partnership, but it is not conclusive.

Hopefully, the partners themselves will place the matter beyond doubt by drawing up a contract (known in England as 'Articles of Partnership' and in Scotland as a 'Contract of Co-partnery') to the effect that they are to be partners. This document will regulate the relationship of the partners in all relevant areas (share of the profits, participation in the management of the business, etc.), and may well be in a standard form or style appropriate to the particular profession or business.

The mere fact that there is no such written agreement does not mean that there is no partnership; the existence of a partnership may be inferred by the courts from appropriate circumstances, and it is in order to assist this process that s. 2 is drafted as it is. Any person with full legal capacity may be a partner with the exception of an enemy alien. A minor (i.e. someone under eighteen) may be a partner, but may repudiate the agreement within a reasonable time after becoming eighteen. As a general rule, no partnership may exceed twenty partners in size, but this rule does not apply to solicitors, accountants or stockbrokers, who may create firms of any size, or any other groups (e.g. estate agents) specially exempted by the Department of Trade and Industry. Banking partnerships are limited to ten partners, except with Department of Trade permission to exceed this limit.

The status of a partnership

In England and Wales, the formation of a partnership does not create a new legal entity distinct from the partners themselves (as it does in Scotland). The 'firm' is still in effect all or any of the partners, and in order to sue the 'firm', a creditor must sue the partners, either collectively or individually, although for convenience they are allowed to make use of the firm name. This point is examined in more detail below.

This also constitutes the main distinction between a partnership and a company, the formation of which does create a separate legal entity (see later section on companies). The other major distinction is that whereas the legal liability of the members of the company for its debts is limited to the unpaid price of their own shares, the members of the partnership enjoy no such protection, and are liable *in full* for the firm's debts.

All that was written about registration of business names in the context of sole traders is equally applicable to partnerships.

Partnerships and their relationships with third parties

One of the most important principles of partnership law is contained in s. 5 of the Act, which states that each of the partners is an agent (see below) for the firm, and for all the other partners, and may bind them all under any contract connected with any business of the kind normally carried on by the firm. If the contract is for a matter outside the normal scope of the firm's business, the partner must be specially authorized before he may bind anyone else to it; again, no one else will be bound if the third party with whom the partner was dealing knew that he was not authorized. Just what is authorized 'in the normal course of the firm's business' will depend to a large extent on the nature of the business, but all partnerships are taken to hire staff, sell their own goods and chattels and purchase items for use in the business, so that a partner will always bind the others in a contract for one of these purposes.

Partners are jointly liable for the firm's debts, in the sense that, as between themselves, they can insist that the debt be shared equally between them. But a creditor may, if he wishes, sue just one of the partners for the entire debt; each is therefore personally liable, although he may demand a contribution by the others of their share of the debt. A creditor with judgement against the firm may execute it against any partner to the extent of his entire personal estate.

The authority of a partner to bind the firm and the other partners, and his liability for the firm's debts, may both continue after the partnership has ceased to exist. Thus, even after the firm has been completely dissolved, a partner has authority left to take such actions as are necessary to wind up the affairs of the firm and settle any outstanding transactions. Similarly, when a partner retires from the firm, the old firm is technically dissolved and a new one begins, but unless the retiral of the outgoing partner is adequately communicated to creditors, they are entitled to assume that he remains a partner, and he will still be liable for new debts. Even when the retiral is adequately notified, the outgoing partner remains liable for debts incurred during his period with the firm, unless the creditors have agreed to absolve him. Unless a special agreement is made an incoming partner is not liable for debts incurred before he entered the firm.

Under s. 14 of the Act, any person who describes himself as a partner or who allows himself to be 'held out' as being one will be liable for any debt incurred on the strength of that representation. This is why, as explained above, outgoing partners should ensure that their departure is adequately publicized, or they may be taken to still be 'holding themselves out' as partners, particularly if their name still appears on the notepaper while old stocks are used up. A notice in the *London* or *Edinburgh Gazette* is recognized as the correct way of obtaining the necessary publicity, together with a circular or local advertisement for existing customers, etc.

The Act also makes the firm liable for any negligence or misapplication of funds by a partner in the ordinary course of the firm's business.

Rights and duties of the partners among themselves

The actual rights and duties of the parties among themselves will, of course, depend on the terms of the partnership agreement they have drawn up, but in the absence of any such agreement, or any particular term in the agreement, the following are presumed by the Act.

1 All partners have the right to participate in the management of the firm.
2 Any partner can prevent any new partner being taken into the firm.
3 No partner may be expelled by the others unless there is an express agreement to this effect in the partnership contract.
4 Each partner will be indemnified by the firm against

expenses incurred and payments made in the course of the ordinary business of the firm.

5 Each partner may share equally in the profits or losses of the firm, and may be paid interest on any capital loaned by him to the firm over and above the amount of capital he agreed to subscribe.

6 Each partner may examine the books of the firm, which must be kept at the principal place of business.

7 Each partner must deal in partnership affairs with the utmost good faith. In particular, he must account to the firm for any benefits he may receive from any partnership transaction, and he must not compete with the firm.

Dissolution of partnership

A partnership may be dissolved either by the parties themselves, or by some legal process. The following are the major ways in which a partnership is dissolved.

1 By the expiration of the time limit or period of notice specified in the partnership agreement.

2 At the will of any of the partners if no time limit has been specified.

3 By the bankruptcy or death of a partner.

4 On the order of the court, upon the application of a partner where any partner is insane, or where one of the other partners has become mentally or physically incapable of carrying out his obligations to the firm, has been guilty of misconduct calculated to prejudice the business, wilful or persistent breach of the agreement, or some other conduct which makes it not reasonably practicable for the others to continue in partnership with him. The court may also dissolve the partnership where it can only be carried on at a loss, or where it is just and equitable to do so.

Limited partnerships

A limited partnership, formed under the Limited Partnerships Act, 1907, is one which consists of at least one full or 'general' partner, who is liable for all the debts and obligations of the firm, and any number of 'limited' partners, who contribute a sum of capital upon entering the partnership, but are not liable for any more than that, regardless of the firm's debts. Such a partner may not remove his capital, at least not while he remains a partner, and he may not take part in the management of the firm, nor may he bind it as an agent.

Limited partnerships have never been popular or numerous because of the greater advantages to be gained from forming a company.

Registered companies

In Chapter 3, under the general heading of 'The capacity of the parties' to a contract, the section on corporations deals with the contractual capacity of corporations, of which the registered company is merely one, if by far the most important one. This section looks in more detail at the registered company as a form of business entity.

Formation of a registered company

A registered company is 'registered' under the Companies Acts, 1948 to 1980, with the Registrar of Companies. A company may be either 'public' (i.e. one with a minimum authorized share capital of £50,000 in which the general public may become shareholders), or 'private' (i.e. any other type of company). Neither type of company may apply for registration without a minimum of two members. Application is accompanied by the submission of four other documents:

1 *The Memorandum of Association.* Signed by the founder members, it contains the formal intimation of the name and location of the company, its nominal capital, the liability of the members (see below), and the 'objects' for which the company is being formed (see the section on corporations in Chapter 3 for further details on the significance of 'objects').

2 *The Articles of Association.* The regulations which are to govern the relationship between the members themselves and the company. If a company chooses to utilize the standard Articles laid down in Table A of the 1948 Act, it need not submit separate Articles.

3 *Statutory Declaration.* This states that the requirements of the Companies Act, 1948 have been complied with.

4 *Statement of Directors and Secretaries, and address of registered office.*

Having considered the terms of these documents, the Registrar may issue a Certificate of Incorporation, which allows private companies to commence trading immediately. Public companies must obtain a further 'certificate', which will only be granted after statutory share capital requirements have been satisfied.

Types of registered company

Registered companies are classified according to the liability of the members for the debts of the company, which in all but the rarest cases will be limited in some way. Leaving aside these 'unlimited liability' companies, which occur mainly among Stock Exchange organizations, there are basically two types of limited company.

The first is the company 'limited by shares'. In this type of company, the liability of the members to contribute to the company's assets is limited to the full nominal value of the shares which they have agreed to take up. Thus, if a company becomes insolvent while a shareholder has paid only 50p of the nominal

£1 value of each of his shares, he will be liable for the 50p outstanding on each of his shares.

Alternatively, the liability of the members may be limited by 'guarantee'; that is, each member, in the Memorandum of Association, guarantees to contribute a certain amount to the company's assets in the event of a winding-up. A company limited by shares may be either 'public' or 'private' (see above). A company limited by guarantee is 'private'.

Status of registered companies

When a new company is registered, a new legal life is created. A registered company is a distinct entity from the individual shareholders who comprise it, and may both sue and be sued in its own name. It may hold land, grant mortgages, in fact do everything which a human being may lawfully do, subject to the obvious physical limitations.

The best illustration of this principle in action is the leading case of *Salomon* v. *Salomon* (1897), in which S, a boot repairer, formed a company with himself as leading shareholder and his wife and children as additional shareholders. He then loaned money to the company on the basis of debentures secured on the assets of the company. When the company went into liquidation, he was allowed priority over trade creditors for preferential repayment on the debentures, since S, as a person, was a distinct entity from the company, even though he was the only person responsible for the company's sorry financial state.

The exercise of power within a registered company

The members of the company (i.e. those who have subscribed to the shares) *are* the company, in the sense that between them they have created the company. No one may become a member unless and until his name is recorded as such on the Register of Members kept by the Company Secretary. The shares of a company are freely transferable, and anyone's name may appear on the Register following a share transaction. Lack of space prohibits any detailed reference to the various types of shares, debentures etc., which may be issued by a company, but it should be noted that the rights of all members will normally be laid down in the Articles of Association, and that different rights may attach to different classes of share. The total amount of the company's nominal or authorized capital will be fixed in its Memorandum, but may be amended following a meeting of members (see below).

The members are all-powerful, and have the full and final say in the management of the company. This is normally exercised at the Annual General Meeting (AGM), and the fact that the whole body of the members may not then come together again until the next AGM illustrates the very practical need for the body of members as a whole to delegate their functions to those who can spend more time in the day-to-day management of the company. These people are the 'directors'.

Every public company must by law have at least two directors, and every private company at least one. The Articles of Association will contain rules for their election, and the Companies Acts require the company to keep a register of its directors. The Articles will also indicate how much power the directors shall wield within the company, whether they are entitled to a salary (by no means an automatic right of any director), and whether or not they must hold a minimum number of 'qualifying' shares before or after their election. Any service contract of a director must be open to inspection by the members.

Having been elected by the members, the directors may or may not (depending upon the Articles) be required to retire and seek re-election after a certain period. A director may also resign, or be removed by an ordinary resolution at a General Meeting; he may also be disqualified from holding a directorship by bankruptcy, or any other ground specified in the Articles, or by statute. Over the age of seventy, a director of a public company must seek re-election.

Once elected, a director owes a considerable duty to the

company, for whom he acts as agent in all business matters. In particular, the director owes a 'fiduciary' duty of honesty and good faith to the company, and must avoid any conflict with his private interests. He may be held liable to the company for any acts of negligence which cause loss to the company. The actual powers delegated to the directors by the members will be specified in the Articles or implied by law (e.g. the right to employ staff).

Even if the directors overstep their authority, the company may still be bound by any contract which has been made with outside bodies, provided that the purpose of the contract was *intra vires* the objects of the company (for an explanation of this term, see Chapter 3). On the whole, whether or not the company will be bound depends upon how much knowledge the third party had as to the internal affairs of the company.

There are provisions in the Companies Acts to ensure that minority interests are not overridden unfairly by the majority; at the same time, of course, the majority view must be allowed to prevail. The result is a compromise whereby the minority (i.e. those whose views have on a particular matter been overruled by the majority) are entitled to certain guarantees under the law.

The first is that the rights of an individual shareholder under the Articles may never be taken away or ignored. The second is the existence of several 'minority protection clauses' in the Acts themselves (the right to petition the court where certain rights are being infringed, or where a specified portion of the members are against a particular proposal). Thirdly, even an individual shareholder can challenge an act which is unlawful, even if it has been approved of by the majority (see *Ashbury Railway Carriage Company* v. *Riche*, on page 79 in Chapter 3). This type of challenge is normally before the courts, who have the power to request Department of Trade Inspectors to examine the company's affairs.

Meetings

The means by which shareholders call upon the directors to account for their actions is of course the company meeting. By law, every company must hold at least one General Meeting (called the Annual General Meeting) every calendar year and not more than fifteen months may elapse between meetings. These meetings tend to be predictable and formalized, but certain vitally important business is conducted at them, such as the declaration of a dividend, the presentation of the annual accounts, suitably audited, together with the directors' reports, the election of directors where required by the Articles, and the appointment of auditors.

The AGM is only one (albeit an important one) example of a general meeting of members. It is the only one which the directors are automatically forced by law to hold, and to prevent them simply ignoring the members, the Acts also provide the members with the right to demand Extraordinary Meetings in accordance with the rules laid down in the Articles. Whatever the Articles say, however, one tenth of the paid-up voting shareholders may demand that a date for a General Meeting be fixed within twenty-one days, failing which they may call the meeting themselves at the company's expense.

The Articles will specify the periods of notice to be given in respect of such general meetings, failing which Table A (see above) specifies twenty-one clear days for the AGM, and any meeting involving special business, and fourteen days for any other meeting.

The decisions of meetings take the form of 'resolutions', and there are basically three types. The 'Ordinary Resolution' is simply a vote in favour by a simple majority of those present and voting, and requires no prior formality or special notice. All business may be conducted by this method unless the Acts or the Articles require a Special or Extraordinary Resolution.

A Special Resolution is one which has been passed by not less than 75 per cent of the members voting, either in person or by proxy, at a general meeting of which twenty-one days' notice has been duly given, specifying the intention to propose the resolution as a Special Resolution. Such a resolution is required by law before the company may, for example, alter its Articles or change its name.

An Extraordinary Resolution is the same as a Special Resolution, except that only fourteen days' notice is required. Typical uses of this type of resolution would be a decision to wind up the company, or a variation of 'class rights' (see above).

All voting is normally by a show of hands, unless the Articles allow for proxy voting. Again, the Articles will usually entitle any specified group of members present to demand a poll. Proxies may be used in a poll vote.

Dissolution of registered companies

A registered company may only be dissolved by what is called a 'winding-up'. This may be either voluntary or compulsory.

Voluntary winding-up

The Act allows a company to apply its own Articles, and wind itself up, or if the Articles do not make such provision, to vote for winding-up.

A company may simply cease at the end of any fixed period set for it under the Articles, or an event may occur which is specified in the Articles as bringing the company to an end; all that the members are required to do is to pass an Ordinary Resolution to the effect that the company will be wound up. Even if there is no such event, the members may vote by Special Resolution to wind up the company. The same effect may be achieved by Extraordinary Resolution when by reason of its liabilities, the company cannot continue in business. If the directors are prepared to give to the Registrar of Companies a 'Declaration of Solvency' to the effect that the company will be able to meet its debts in full within twelve months, the members will be left to control the winding-up themselves. If not, then the members and creditors will between them appoint a liquidator, to do the job on behalf of both sides.

Occasionally a voluntary winding-up may be under the supervision of the court.

Compulsory winding-up

There is a definite list of situations in which a company may be wound-up by the court, namely:

1   It has not commenced business within a year of incorporation, or has suspended business for a year.
2   It has less than the statutory minimum number of members.
3   It is unable to meet its debts.
4   It fails to submit the Annual Report or hold the Annual Meeting.
5   It is, in the opinion of the court, just and equitable to wind up the company.

The petition for compulsory winding-up will normally come either from a shareholder (who must normally have held the shares for six months) or a creditor, although it may come from the Department of Trade. If it grants the petition, the court will appoint a liquidator, who will set about winding-up the company, and securing as much as possible for the creditors. It is at this stage that those whose shares are not fully paid up will be called upon to make up the final payment.

Agency

'Agency' is a term used by lawyers to describe the situation in which an 'agent' (A) makes a contract on behalf of someone *else* (known as the 'principal') (P) with a third party (T). Once the contract is finalized, A drops out of the picture, from the legal point of view, and a valid contract remains between P and T. It is basically as simple as that, although certain problem areas have been identified over the years, and are indicated below.

The picture is obscured somewhat by the fact that the term 'agent' is used in industry and commerce to describe a whole host of situations which a lawyer would not necessarily regard as agencies. While, for example, there is little doubt that the theatrical agent does represent a principal (i.e. the artist) and the travel agent does make contracts on behalf of the traveller, it is doubtful whether the motor 'agent' is really an agent for the manufacturer. On the other hand, there are occasions upon which one man is the agent of another without the term being used at all; for example, an auctioneer is an agent for the seller, while a broker may act for either the buyer or the seller of securities or commodities.

An agent may be an employee (e.g. a sales assistant who brings the employer into contractual relations with his customers), or an independent contractor (e.g. a solicitor). An agent may be a partner (see above) and he may also be a company director. He may be a 'general' agent (i.e. with authority to act in all matters of a particular type in a particular business, for example a solicitor) or a 'special' agent (i.e. with authority limited to a particular transaction, as in the case of an estate agent). He may use a variety of names, such as 'broker' and 'factor', but whether or not he is what the law calls an 'agent' will depend upon legal tests, and not necessarily simply the name he uses.

The formation of agency

The purpose behind forming an agency is for A to make contracts on behalf of P; it is therefore the contractual capacity of P which will determine whether or not there is a valid contract. The agent may therefore be a minor provided that the principal is an adult, should the contract be one which only an adult may validly make.

The following are the major ways in which a 'contract of agency' may be created, i.e. whereby A becomes the agent of P, and authorized to negotiate contracts on his behalf with third parties.

(1) Express agreement

In a routine commercial situation, an agency will probably be created on a standard form contractual document, but such formality is not required by law. An 'express' agency may even be created by word of mouth, provided that the words can be proved later should the need arise. Even if the agent is to be given the power to make written contracts on P's behalf, it is not necessary for him to be appointed under a written contract. If, however, future contracts are to be under seal (i.e. what is being created is a 'power of attorney'), then the agent must be appointed under seal.

(2) Implied agreement

In some cases, despite the absence of any apparent express agreement, the actions of the parties, or their relationship with each other, are explicable only on the basis that an agency exists, and one will therefore be implied by the court. Thus, it has been held that an insurance agent employed by the insurance company may also be the agent of the proposer filling in the form (*Bigger* v. *Rock Life Insurance Company*, 1902), that shop stewards are agents of their unions (*Heatons* v. *TGWU*, 1972), and that a managing director is the agent of the Board when he hires architects to assist in a planning application (*Freeman and Lockyer* v. *Buckhurst Park Properties*, 1964).

Also, when a client hires a professional man (e.g. solicitor, architect, accountant), he automatically invests him with the authority normally implied from such a relationship.

(3) Estoppel

In some cases, a principal is prevented by law ('estopped') from denying that a particular person is his agent, where he has 'held him out' as being such. This principle applies both to the situation in which A had no actual authority at all, and the situation in which he has exceeded the authority which he was in fact given. Thus, in *Watteau* v. *Fenwick* (1893), it was held that although the manager of a public house had been specifically told not to order cigars on credit, the owner was 'estopped' from denying to the supplier that he had such authority by virtue of his managerial status. The only way to prevent this kind of agency being created is to refrain from 'holding out' such people as having such authority, or to specifically notify third parties that they have *no* such authority. It is the same principle which imposes liability for continuing debts upon a partner who retires but fails to notify creditors that he has done so (see above).

(4) Ratification

Even though, at the time when A purports to make a contract on behalf of P, he has no authority to do so, P may 'ratify' or adopt the contract later, provided that the agent at the time of the original contract clearly identified the principal, that the principal existed at the time (e.g. it was not a company still in the process of formation), that the contract is one which the principal may lawfully make, and the principal has full knowledge of all the facts when he ratifies.

The effect of a valid ratification is retrospective, in that the contract, from the start, becomes one not between A and T, but between P and T. But it must be made within a reasonable time, and must not be for an insurance contract other than marine insurance; also, ratification will not be allowed where it would cause excessive hardship to the third party.

(5) Necessity

On very rare occasions, A may act as the agent of P without any actual authority, where he has been placed in a position of 'urgent necessity', and it is impossible to communicate with P. While this principle was very useful to ships' captains in the days before radio, it is of extremely limited application with modern communications.

The rights and duties of agent and principal

The agent owes the following duties to his principal:

(1) To carry out his instructions

The agent must do precisely what he has been appointed to do, no less and no more (i.e. he must not exceed his actual authority), unless he is expressly or by implication given a discretion, and he employs it reasonably. The agent must also perform his duties personally, and may not normally delegate them to anyone else, unless he has express or implied authority to do so. Thus, in *John McCann and Co.* v. *Pow* (1975), it was held that an estate agent instructed to sell a certain property had no authority to delegate the task to sub-agents.

(2) To display ordinary skill and diligence

Even an agent who is receiving no reward for his services will be liable to the principal for negligent *performance* of his duties; however, he will not be liable for taking no action at all. A paid agent, on the other hand, will be liable in both situations.

(3) To act in good faith towards the principal

A must act at all times in P's best interest, and must secure him the best possible contract terms, etc. He must pass on to P the benefit of any discount, bonus, etc., and must never let his own personal interest conflict with that of P; if it does, he must notify P at once. If he is guilty of taking bribes, he may be sued, he loses his commission, he may be dismissed, he must hand over the bribe, and both he and the giver of the bribe may be prosecuted under the Prevention of Corruption Act, 1906. An agent may not make unauthorized use of confidential information given to him by P.

(4) To account to the principal

This duty covers all money and property received by A either from P, for use in the agency, or for P in the course of business. A should always keep his assets and accounts separate from P's.

In return, the principal owes the following duties to his agent:

(1) To remunerate the agent

If and when A has performed his tasks, P is under a legal duty to pay him the fee or commission agreed upon. It can be a moot point exactly when A can be said to have finished his task, and not even an apparently clearly worded agreement is guaranteed to eliminate disputes, as recent cases involving estate agents have demonstrated. If no time for payment is specified by the contract, the court will fix one, or calculate a *quantum meruit* payment (see Chapter 3).

(2) To indemnify the agent

P must indemnify A against all expenses and liabilities incurred in the course of conducting the agency in the manner agreed. The agent must have been acting within his authority in order to claim this indemnity, and his actions must have been lawful, and taken in good faith.

(3) Lien

The agent has a right of 'lien' over (i.e. the right to detain) property belonging to his principal as security for unpaid services by A to P. Sometimes (e.g. in the case of carriage of goods) the lien is 'special' in that it relates only to the goods in respect of which the debt was incurred, while in other cases it is a 'general' lien. Thus, for example, a solicitor has a right of lien over the title deeds of any client of his who owes him outstanding fees in respect of any matter (e.g. a divorce action). A right of lien may only be exercised over goods which A already has in his possession, and the right of lien is lost if the goods leave his possession. The right of lien does not of itself carry the right of sale.

The position of the third party

The point has already been made that in the straightforward agency situation, A, having brought P and T together, bows out and leaves them to get on with their contract, having collected his fee or salary from P. It follows from this that T will not normally be in any contractual relationship with A, and will therefore have no legal rights against anyone but P.

Where the agent was acting *within* his authority from P, and made the contract expressly in P's name, then T will only be able to take action under the contract against A where the latter gave a personal undertaking, where there is a trade custom imposing liability on agents, or where the alleged 'principal' did not exist. Where the principal is unnamed, although A makes it clear that he is acting for someone else, then it is at least arguable that T should be able to choose ('elect') which of the two parties he holds liable under the contract. The point is unsettled under English law. Certainly, where A pretends all along that he is the principal (i.e. he fails to disclose to T the existence of P), then T has the right to hold A personally liable under the contract, or to proceed against P under the contract brought about by A. Having once elected to proceed against one of the parties, in full knowledge of the true facts, T cannot later revert to the other party.

If A *exceeds* his authority in his negotiations with T, and P is not prepared to *ratify* the contract he has made, then T will have no full contract with either A or P (assuming that the contract was stated to be with P). He may, however, sue A for 'breach of warranty of authority'. If P did not even exist at the time of the contract, then A is personally liable to T under the main contract.

Termination of agency

There are basically only two ways in which the contract of agency may come to an end, i.e. in which A may cease to be the agent of P.

(1) By the actions of the parties

Obviously, the parties may simply agree that the agency shall come to an end, and that will be the end of the matter, but it is also possible that the actions of only *one* of the parties will serve to terminate the relationship. Thus, P may revoke A's agency, and the effect of this is that A no longer has P's authority to act for him, may not earn future commissions, etc.

It may well be that by acting in this way, P exposes himself to an action for damages by A, but this does not alter the fact that A may no longer represent P. The one thing which P may *not* do is to revoke his own liability in respect of contracts which A has already negotiated.

If A is an employee of P, then he will be entitled to notice to terminate the contract just like any other employee (see Chapter 8). Even if he is not, he will normally be entitled to some form of notice under the agency contract, failing which Common Law requires that a 'reasonable' period of notice be given, by either side.

This is because the agent, too, may bring the contract to an end by simply giving notice to his principal that he wishes to do so; he too may be liable for damages if he does so without the correct amount of notice, and he must complete the contracts which he has commenced.

(2) By the operation of law
The occurrence of certain events will also have the effect of bringing the agency contract to an end. Obvious examples are frustrating events (as in *Morgan* v. *Manser* (1947), in which the agent was conscripted into the forces), and events such as the death of either party, the bankruptcy of the principal, and the insanity of the agent.

Where P dies, A's authority is revoked by his death, whether A knows of that death or not. The insanity of the principal is normally regarded as a revocation of the authority of the agent, and therefore of similar effect to the insanity of the agent, but in this case, A's apparent authority continues until T becomes aware of P's insanity, and T may therefore still be liable under the contract up to that point.

3 Making a contract

Introduction

A contract may be defined simply as 'a legally binding agreement between two parties', and contracts are essential to the commercial life of any nation. It is therefore important that the law ensures that contracts are well regulated, certain in form and effect, and regarded by the business community with a high degree of confidence.

The law of contract is still very largely Common Law, i.e. unaffected by Acts of Parliament, although this state of affairs is fairly regularly threatened by rumours that the Common Law is to be codified. The law of contract is largely the expression of a *laissez-faire* philosophy, and most of its basic principles were laid down during the 'boom' years of the mid-nineteenth century, when men were making commercial agreements every day of their bustling, energetic lives.

The prevalent mood was one of 'freedom', that each entrepreneur should be allowed to pursue his business instincts to the full. A bargain, once struck, was sacred, and should not be broken, or the thin fabric of the new society might perish. Men were expected to stand by their contracts, however ill advised, and the courts would not intervene to rescue them from their folly. The role of the courts was felt to be that of upholding contracts, not setting them aside, and there was a binding contract once the parties were *ad idem* ('of the same mind') on the subject matter, the date and the price.

This underlying philosophy has not changed, although it is applied more realistically. Even at the high point of *laissez-faire*, it was still acknowledged that certain types of persons such as the infant, the insane and the feeble, required special rules for their own protection. Similarly, not even the sanctity of the business agreement could override stern Victorian moral propriety, and certain types of 'contract' (e.g. those for sexual immorality) were denied legal status, and therefore enforceability. Again, not even a Victorian judge would uphold a commercial 'agreement' as legally binding unless the parties had at least supplied some evidence of an agreement; concern for the formalities was at times almost obsessional.

The greatest change this century has been the recognition by Parliament that all parties to a contract are not equal in their bargaining strengths, which was always the underlying assumption in the old days. In an age of 'consumerism', the irony is that the average consumer has very little opportunity to argue with the international conglomerate or the supermarket chain as to the precise terms upon which he or she will do business. In a substantial contract (e.g. for a new car or a deep freeze from a discount centre) it is a matter of 'sign the standard form or go elsewhere'. Parliament has reacted to this by requiring that the standard form be stripped of its worst excesses, and statutes such as the Consumer Credit Act, 1974, the Unfair Contract Terms Act, 1977, and the Sale of Goods (Implied Terms) Act, 1973, have endeavoured to reverse the trend and restore the balance between the parties. Where one of the parties is an employee, and the contract is one of employment, successive statutes have converted it into what at first glance looks like a charter of rights (see Chapter 8).

By far the great majority of contracts made in Britain are what are called 'simple' contracts (that is, they are not made under seal in a deed). Before they will be enforceable by the parties, they must be shown to be commercial bargains in the sense that both parties are contributing something (called 'consideration') towards them. It must also be shown that the parties intended that their agreement should be subject to legal sanctions, and that, where this is required by law, they have observed the due formalities. Each party must have the legal capacity to make a contract, and must have genuinely consented to what was agreed, uninfluenced by an disability on his part (e.g. insanity), or any fraud, misrepresentation or undue influence by the other party. The contract must be for a lawful purpose, and must not be contrary to public policy.

Above all, the parties must in the first place have reached a clear agreement; without evidence of agreement, there is not even the basic framework for a contract.

The agreement

Before there may be 'a legally binding agreement between two parties', there must first of all be sufficient evidence of an agreement between them. The usual sign that there has been an agreement is the presence of *offer* and *acceptance*.

The offer and acceptance test requires the court to examine the behaviour of the parties, and identify the point at which an offer by one party was clearly and unequivocally accepted by the other. This, according to the test, is the point at which a contract is formed, and after which the parties may not go back on their agreement, except by mutual consent. The test covers every type of contract, from the simple word-of-mouth arrangement under which I buy my morning newspaper, to the multi-million pound deal arranged after months of correspondence, hundreds of cables and several meetings in different parts of Europe.

It is because of the difficulty of applying such simplistic tests to the most complex international negotiations that the courts over the years have occasionally abandoned the 'offer and acceptance' analysis, and simply looked for evidence of agreement from the general circumstances, or the subsequent actions of the parties. It is, after all, the existence of the agreement which matters, not the method by which it is arrived at; nevertheless, 'offer and acceptance' is still the most important, and most prevalent, test of agreement, and must therefore be examined in more detail.

Offer

An offer may best be described as an unequivocal statement by one of the parties (the 'Offeror'), containing all the terms and conditions upon which he is prepared to enter into a contract with the other (the 'Offeree'). It is a promise to be bound on certain conditions and all that is required is for the Offeree simply to reply 'I accept', and there is a binding contract. This is because the offer was sufficiently detailed to leave no doubt as to the terms upon which the arrangement would proceed if agreed upon.

Generally, an offer will be either written or oral, but in suitable cases it may be *implied* from the circumstances or the actions of the parties. If I enter a newspaper shop, silently pick up a newspaper, price 12p, show it to the proprietor and drop 12p into his waiting hand without comment, there is a binding contract, fully completed, without a word having been spoken. My offer consisted simply of indicating the desired item of purchase and the money.

Again, an offer may be made to any number of people, all at the same time (as in the case of a newspaper advertisement); it may even be made to the whole world. Thus, in the famous case of *Carlill* v. *Carbolic Smokeball Company* (1892), a company claimed, in a leading newspaper, that the use of their medical preparation would protect the user from influenza; they promised £100 to anyone contracting it after using the product, and lodged £1,000 in a bank 'to show their sincerity'. Mrs C caught influenza after using the product, and was eventually successful in claiming the £100, despite a plea by the company that there had been no offer made to any particular person. This case also established that an advertising 'stunt' may in some cases be taken seriously, and that in certain cases there is no need for the Offeree to communicate acceptance of an offer if he or she simply carries out the action requested (e.g. finds the lost dog or fills in and returns the competition form).

The greatest problem in practice is that of distinguishing between offers and statements which fall short of offers, in that they are not sufficiently comprehensive or definite to form the basis of the contract by the simple application of the word 'I accept' or something similar. A great number and variety of statements can exist which thus fall short of being offers, and which in fact can only be followed by offers, and cannot be accepted straight away so as to form the basis of a contract. Among these will be statements of price, requests for further information and declarations of interest. What these lesser statements all have in common is that they are expressing a person's interest in exploring the possibility of eventual agreement – for convenience, lawyers label them all as 'invitations to treat'.

Thus, under the Sale of Goods Act, 1979, s. 57(2), the fall of the auctioneer's hammer is the 'acceptance' which completes the contract of sale by auction. The making of the successful bid is the 'offer', which means that the call by the auctioneer of 'What am I bid ?' or suchlike is merely an invitation to treat, at least if the auction is not 'without reserve'.

Similarly, it has been accepted for over a hundred years that the mere issue of a price label or a catalogue is not an offer, with the result that the purchaser cannot 'accept' an item shown in a catalogue. Any 'offer' in such a case will be made by the customer when he or she sends away, or otherwise applies for, an item and it will still be for the Offeree to decide whether or not to accept that offer. Thus, in *Grainger* v. *Gough* (1896), it was held that the distribution by a wine merchant of his price list could not constitute an offer to be accepted by each and every customer, otherwise 'the merchant might find himself involved in any number of contractual obligations to supply wine of a particular description which he would be quite unable to carry out'.

The same analysis has been applied to the retail trade, and it is now established beyond all reasonable argument that in normal circumstances, the display of goods by a shopkeeper, whether on his shelves or in his window, is merely an invitation to treat. The customer offers to buy the goods at the price stated, and it is for the shopkeeper to accept or reject that offer. Whatever offence he might commit under the Trade Descriptions Act, 1968 (see Chapter 5, p. 162), by refusing to sell goods on display with a price marked on them, he is not contractually bound to do so. This emerged in *Pharmaceutical Society of Great Britain* v. *Boots Cash Chemists (Southern) Ltd* (1952) in which Boots escaped prosecution for 'selling' poisons in a supermarket without the presence of a pharmacist, by showing that the 'sale' took place in the presence of a pharmacist at the cash desk, when the cashier took the customer's money, that the customer made the 'offer' at the cash desk, and that the display of goods was therefore merely an invitation to treat.

Among the other statements which have, over the years, been classed as mere 'invitations to treat', and not therefore capable of acceptance so as to form the basis of a contract, are requests for interested parties to submit tenders for a contract, a statement by a local authority of the likely purchase price of one of its council houses to the sitting tenant, and an announcement by an auctioneer that certain goods would be auctioned on a certain day.

An offer may meet with a variety of fates after it has been made. First of all, of course, it may be rejected, in which case that is the end of the matter. Another possibility is that it is made subject to some time limit, which expires without any acceptance having been made; again, that will bring matters to an end. If no time limit is fixed, the offer will lapse after a 'reasonable time', which will obviously be a question of fact in each case.

Where the Offeror undertakes to keep the offer open for a specified period of time, he may still revoke it, unless he has entered into a separate contract with the Offeree to keep it open. Similarly, where the Offeror has not made any promise to keep the offer open, he may revoke the offer at any time before acceptance is 'completed'. No revocation will be valid until effectively communicated to the other party, and the Offeree may accept at any time before he receives credible information to the effect that revocation has occurred, which need not be from the Offeror himself. The revocation of the offer, to be valid, must reach the Offeree before he accepts the original offer; thus, in *Byrne* v. *Van Tienhoven* (1880), an offer made on 1 October was not validly revoked by a letter sent on 8 October but not received until 20 October, because acceptance had been made on 11 October.

An offer may also lapse, or be automatically revoked, when it is *conditional*, and the condition has not been fulfilled; thus, in *Financings Ltd* v. *Stimson* (1962), S filled in an application form for hire purchase on a car, which was stated to be of no legal effect until F Ltd had also signed to indicate their acceptance of the proposal. Before they did so, the car was damaged after being stolen from the showroom, and it was held that F Ltd could now no longer accept, the offer having been subject to the implied condition that the car remain unchanged until the moment of acceptance.

An offer also normally lapses once the Offeree learns of the death of the Offeror, but this is not the case when it is accepted before the Offeree learns of the death, and the identity of the other party is not vital to the contract anyway. The common sense view is also that the death of the Offeree terminates the offer.

Acceptance

A contract cannot come into existence until a valid offer is accepted by the other party (the Offeree); this acceptance may be express, implied, or inferred from the parties' subsequent conduct. The person who 'accepts' the offer (e.g. by performing the act requested in it) must have been aware of it before he may be said to have 'accepted' it, but if he was then his motives for acceptance are irrelevant, as in *Williams* v. *Cawardine* (1833), in which it was held that a woman might claim a reward for information leading to an arrest of which she was aware at the time, although her sole motivation had been one of conscience.

Before any statement by an Offeree will be taken as being an acceptance, it must be a clear and unconditional agreement to the terms of the original offer. If it contains further conditions, or seeks to change certain terms in the offer, it will be a 'counter-offer' instead of an acceptance, and it will then be for the Offeror to accept the new offer before there will be a binding contract. A counter-offer is in effect a rejection of the original offer, as may be seen in the leading case of *Hyde* v. *Wrench* (1840), in which W's offer to sell an estate to H for £1,000 met with a reply from H offering to buy for £950, which was refused by W. H then purported to 'accept' the original offer of £1,000, but it was held that this offer had been cancelled by his counter-offer of £950, and was no longer available for acceptance.

It should be noted, however, that if the Offeree merely requests further information, or asks for clarification of a point in the offer, this will not constitute a counter-offer, and will not kill the original offer. But where an acceptance is made 'conditional' (e.g. upon a surveyor's report), then there will at that stage be no final contract, and either party may back out.

A classic example of this process is the agreement which is often drawn up between the potential buyer and seller of a house, under which the sale is 'subject to contract'. What the parties are doing is postponing the point at which they become legally bound by the transaction (e.g. until the mortgage position has been clarified, or until the solicitors have drawn up the conveyance). The agreement 'subject to contract' is a worthless document from which either party can withdraw whenever he wishes.

Similarly, if the parties have failed to express themselves with sufficient clarity, and some vital part of the contract remains obscure, the courts may well have to conclude that there is no contract, unless they are able to clarify the point by reference to previous dealings between the parties, or a trade custom, or make good the deficiency themselves (e.g. fix a 'reasonable' price under the Sale of Goods Act, 1979).

The process of offer, counter-offer and acceptance can become quite a battle where two large organizations seek to impose upon each other their own standard terms of business as laid down in standard contract forms. Such a 'battle of forms' occurred in *Butler* v. *Ex-Cell-O* (1979) in which B offered to sell a machine tool to E, only on the 'terms quoted', which included a price variation clause. These were to 'prevail over any conditions' imposed by E when making an order. E in fact placed an order on their own standard form, which required a fixed price, and required B to reply by tear-off portion acknowledging that they had received the order on the terms and conditions stipulated by E. B did this, but sent a covering letter stating that the order had been taken 'in accordance with our revised quotation'. It was held that E's placing of an order had not been an acceptance of B's original offer, but a counter-offer which B had accepted by returning the acknowledgement slip. There was therefore a fixed price contract.

In practice, many of the problems surrounding acceptance concern, not the terms of the acceptance, but its communication. The Offeror may stipulate the manner in which he wishes acceptance to be communicated (e.g. orally, by post or by telegram), although at Common Law, and now under the Unsolicited Goods and Services Act, 1971 (see Chapter 5), he may not stipulate silence as a means of communication (e.g. 'If I don't hear from you in seven days, I'll assume you want the car'). The Offeror may, however, dispense with the need for the communication of acceptance, as where he offers a reward to anyone returning his dog; all that the Offeree need do is to return the dog, and he does not need to notify the Offeror that he is setting out to look for it. See also the *Carbolic Smokeball* case, p. 57.

Where the Offeror stipulates a mode of acceptance, then normally this, and this alone, will suffice to communicate acceptance, except perhaps where a swifter method is used, or the Offeror accepts another method. Where there is *no* specified mode of communication of acceptance, the Offeree is free to choose his own, although it is generally assumed that an oral offer normally calls for an oral acceptance, a written offer a written acceptance, and so on.

In the case of an oral acceptance, it will not be validly communicated unless and until it is actually *received* by the Offeror; 'oral' communications are taken to include the use of the telephone and the teleprinter. Thus, in *Entores Ltd* v. *Miles Far East Corporation* (1955), the question arose as to whether a contract was governed by English or Dutch law, following an exchange of telex messages between Amsterdam and London. It was held that since the message of acceptance from Amsterdam was not valid until received in London, the contract was formed in London, and therefore subject to English law.

The most complex problems usually surround *postal* acceptance (which includes telegrams), and in particular the now well-established rule that postal acceptances are validly communicated once they are posted, whether they actually reach their destination or not. An example of the effect of such a rule has already been given, in the case of *Byrne* v. *Van Tienhoven* (see p. 59); in that case, the acceptance which was deemed to have been validly made on the 11th, was simply posted on that day. As such, it was, in the eyes of the law, validly communicated before the revocation of offer made on the 8th, which was not valid until received on the 20th.

The parties themselves may exclude the effect of this Common Law rule, as in *Holwell Securities* v. *Hughes* (1974), in which an option to purchase a set of premises was said to be exercisable 'by notice in writing', and the court held that this meant a letter actually received by the Offeror. Also, under the Uniform Laws on International Sales Act, 1967, which the parties to any contract are free to adopt, and which may well be used as the guide in any international contract, the mere posting of an acceptance will not suffice; it must arrive before it will be valid.

There is no direct authority under English law on the question of whether or not an acceptance may be revoked, although Scottish authority suggests that it may, at least provided that it reaches the Offeror no later than the original acceptance, or where it was a qualified acceptance and the conditions have not yet been fulfilled.

Constructing a contract

As indicated above, it is the agreement between the parties which lies at the root of a contract, and forms its base. Although the courts find it convenient, and usually profitable, to apply the analysis of offer and acceptance to a set of facts in the search for agreement, they may nevertheless be quite satisfied that the parties have reached agreement even though offer and acceptance cannot be readily identified. In such cases, they will rule that a contract exists.

A recent example was *Bigg* v. *Boyd Gibbins Ltd* (1971), in which the Offeror wrote 'for a quick sale, I would accept £26,000', to which the Offeree replied 'I accept your offer'. The Offeror then indicated that he was instructing his solicitor to sell, and that 'my wife and I are both pleased that you are purchasing the property'. Although it was uncertain whether or not offer and acceptance in the true sense had occurred, the court could not 'escape the view that the parties would regard themselves at the end of the correspondence, quite correctly, as having struck a bargain for the sale and purchase of the property'. It was held that there was a binding contract.

Likewise, in *Clarke* v. *Dunraven* (1897), it was held that each entrant for a yacht race, by agreeing with the organizers as a term of entry that he would compensate any other yacht owner for damage caused by him, was making a contract with all the other yacht owners, even though they were not in direct contact.

The intent

The mere fact that two parties have made an agreement will not, of itself, guarantee that the courts will conclude that they have made a contract, which may be legally enforced. For example, I may agree to play for a friend's local football team on a particular day; we have reached an agreement, but no-one would seriously suggest that my friend could sue me for failing to appear on the day. On the other hand, if I am a fulltime professional player under contract to a League club, the management would quite rightly expect to be able to sue me should I decide to take a Saturday afternoon off without permission. What is it that distinguishes the two cases? Simply the intention of the parties.

In formal language, a lawyer would say that before the courts will dignify an agreement with the title 'contract', they must be satisfied that the parties 'intended to create legal relations'. Something said by the parties, or the very circumstances in which the agreement is made, will normally decide the issue.

In most cases, the parties do not expressly declare whether or not it is their intention that their agreement shall be deemed a 'contract', and therefore legally binding. It is then for the courts to infer their intentions from the surrounding circumstances, and, not surprisingly, the rule of thumb has developed that where the parties are in a *commercial* relationship to each other, or are negotiating in a *business* setting, their agreement is intended to have a legal effect (i.e. it is a contract), but that when the situation is *domestic*, it is not.

Thus, the theory goes, if I make an 'informal' agreement with my wife, concerning how much she may spend on clothes, she will have no legal right to sue me to enforce that agreement, whereas if I undertake to guarantee her credit account at the department store, the owners of the store may enforce the guarantee. In practice, it is never as simple as that, and there have been decisions on both sides of the line which have gone against the general trend.

Thus, in *Merritt* v. *Merritt* (1970), the Court of Appeal held as enforceable an agreement between husband and wife concerning the repayments of the mortgage on the family home after the husband had gone to live with another woman, while in *Ford Motor Company Ltd* v. *AUEF* (1969), it was held that a formal agreement between management and nineteen separate trade unions concerning future relations between them was not legally binding. This point was subsequently overruled by statute, but now, by virtue of the Trade Union and Labour Relations Act, 1974, s. 18, a collective agreement between employer and union is not legally enforceable unless it is in writing and expressly declared to be so enforceable.

Notwithstanding these 'rogue' cases, it is still a reasonably valid general rule that a mere domestic agreement will not be enforceable as a contract, whereas an agreement reached in a commercial environment will. There are inevitably 'grey areas', and none more so than the dilemma facing the court in *Simpkins* v. *Pays* (1955), in which an elderly lady, her grand-daughter and the lodger won £750 in a Sunday newspaper competition which they regularly filled in between them. Despite the 'domestic' nature of the relationship, the court felt that there was enough evidence of a 'syndicate' for the arrangement to be legally enforceable, and that a contract therefore existed under which the prize money was to be split three ways.

Sometimes the parties themselves seek to place the matter beyond doubt by making an express statement on the status of their agreement. They may, for example, expressly declare that it is intended to be legally binding (as they must for a collective agreement as explained above), or they may provide for *penalties* (see below) or *arbitration* (see above) should things go wrong. On the other side of the coin, they may state that their agreement is 'to be of no legal effect', or 'binding in honour only'.

In the latter situation, the courts will normally have no jurisdiction, however bizarre the consequences. This emerges very forcibly from the amazing case of *Jones* v. *Vernons Pools Ltd* (1938), in which a punter was denied the money which he appeared to have won on the pools because the company chose to invoke the 'binding in honour only' clause, and the court had no authority to order them to pay over the money.

However, in a commercial situation such as this, there is a very strong presumption that the parties do intend to create legal relations, which can only be rebutted by a very clear statement such as the one in the above case. Likewise, where the courts are being asked to uphold as a contract what appears to be a mere domestic agreement, the party seeking to enforce it will require cogent evidence of the commercial intentions of the parties.

The bargain

It is a fundamental principle of the English law of contract (but not its Scots counterpart) that before there may be a binding 'simple' contract (i.e. one made other than under seal in a deed), both parties must have agreed to provide something of value to the other. Put another way, each must have 'bought' the agreement of the other in some way, and the 'price' which each is to pay must be capable of measurement in terms of value. This 'price' is known to lawyers as 'consideration', and it may take many forms.

In its most obvious form, it consists of money or goods. If I enter a shop and buy a bar of chocolate, the 'consideration' which I am providing is the money, whereas the consideration 'moving from' the shopkeeper is the chocolate. We have each provided consideration, and there is a binding contract (assuming that all other requisite tests are satisfied).

Alternatively, consideration may take the form of a *promise* to hand over money or goods. If I book an hotel room in advance, there is a binding contract long before I actually drive the car into the car park; the consideration moving from me is the promise to pay the price asked, and the consideration from the management is the promise to make the room available. Valid consideration can also take the form of a promise in exchange for money (e.g. payment in advance for a train ticket), or goods in exchange for a promise (e.g. hiring office equipment). Consideration may even take the form of refraining from taking action; thus, if I have the right to sue you, but agree to part with that right for £5,000 (in popular parlance, we 'settle out of court'), we are both bound by that agreement.

In order for consideration to be valid it must be measurable in terms of *material* gain or loss; a mere *moral* obligation is not sufficient. But once there exists something which is measurable or identifiable in a material sense, however small in value it may be, this will constitute valid consideration. To use the lawyer's phrase, the consideration must be *sufficient* (to constitute consideration), but it need not be *adequate* (in commercial terms). Using this test, for example, the law would regard as binding my agreement to sell my new car for £1, but not my agreement to part with the car in return for prayers said for me every Sunday.

What, then, will constitute sufficient consideration to support a contract, bearing in mind that it must come from both sides ? Clearly the payment of money, the delivery of goods or the performance of an act (or simply the promise of any of these) will be sufficient provided that the party offering it is not already legally *bound* to provide it anyway. For example, in *Glasbrook Brothers* v. *Glamorgan County Council* (1925), it was held that the police authority, while they could not charge a fee to a colliery owner for guarding a picketed colliery by *mobile* patrol (since this was their duty anyway), could charge for mounting a permanent guard at the request of the management, since this went beyond their normal public duty ro protect property.

An important consequence of this general rule is that, normally, a debtor may not discharge a debt by paying less than is due since he is in effect claiming the existence of a contract under which the creditor agrees to forgo part of his rights (valid consideration) in return for the debtor paying less than he was legally obliged to pay already (not valid consideration). In order to be able to rely on this sort of arrangement, the debtor must be able to show that, in return for the elimination of part of the debt by the creditor, he, the debtor, gave him something to which he was not already entitled (e.g. payment in advance, payment in a foreign currency, or even payment by another *party*). In addition, a court will sometimes enforce this kind of agreement in order to avoid a fraud on the debtor, or in the exercise of its 'equitable' jurisdiction to see justice done between the parties, where the creditor has agreed to 'waive' (i.e. forgo) his right to full payment, and the court feels that it would be 'inequitable' to allow him now to claim his full rights.

But generally speaking, consideration may not normally consist of the performance, or the promise of performance, of some action which one is already legally obliged to perform. Nor may it take the form of a service already performed, without prior agreement as to payment, unless the action was requested by the other party, and the circumstances were such that one would normally expect payment to be made. Thus, if a stranded motorist is offered a lift by another motorist, and only offers to pay him for his trouble after he has been taken to his destination, there is no valid consideration, and therefore no binding contract, whereas if he flags down a passing taxi and asks to be taken to a certain address, there is an implication that payment will be made sufficient to render the passenger liable to pay at the end of the journey.

In short, consideration must normally take the form of a *future action* (e.g. payment of money, or performance of an act), the promise of a future action, or a forbearance from future action (e.g. the right to sue for damages). It must be supplied by both parties to the agreement before the agreement may become a legally binding contract, since a person who does not provide consideration cannot normally be a party to the contract, and without two parties, there will not be a contract at all.

Recording the agreement

So far, we have seen that before there can be a legally binding contract, there must be an agreement consisting of an offer by one party which is accepted by the other, on terms which involve each of the parties providing 'consideration', and in circumstances which leave little room for doubt that the parties intend their agreement to be legally binding.

As a general rule, we may say that the parties are free to make their contract in any way they wish (e.g. orally, in writing, by telex, and so on), and that the law will not insist that they 'put it in writing', or sign in arterial blood, or act out any other of the myths sometimes associated with the law. However, to that general rule there are exceptions, which, so far as English law is concerned, may be summarized as follows:

Contracts which must be under seal

It has already been noted that a contract under seal does not require to be supported by 'consideration' from both parties, since the solemnity surrounding the use of a seal leaves no doubt that the parties intend to create a legally binding obligation. A contract under seal is also often called a 'deed', and it becomes a deed by being signed at the foot, sealed by the application of a disc of red paper, also at the foot, and being 'delivered' to the other party. Hence the immortal phrase 'signed, sealed and delivered', which reflects the fact that the deed is the most formal type of contract known to English law.

To confuse matters somewhat, 'delivery' is not required where the party creating the deed is a 'corporation' (e.g. a registered company or a local authority), and it may in most cases take the form of 'constructive' delivery, i.e. it is regarded as delivered even though it has not left the granter's possession.

There are only certain types of contract which still require to be in deed form, although for additional security, many commercial specialists in the legal profession insist that their client companies take executed deeds for even routine contracts. Deeds are today only essential in the case of

(a) gratuitous promises – i.e. obligations undertaken by one party without corresponding 'consideration' from the other;
(b) the transfer of ownership of a legal estate in land, including a lease of more than three years;
(c) the transfer of a British ship, or shares in a British ship.

Contracts which must be in writing

Although not many contracts need go the whole way and be recorded in deed form, certain contracts are required by law to be in writing, in the sense that if they are not, they will be void. The most important of these are 'bills of exchange' (a term including cheques and promissory notes), contracts of marine insurance, agreements to transfer shares in a limited company, and 'consumer credit agreements', which are dealt with in greater detail in Chapter 5.

Contracts which must be evidenced by writing

This slightly peculiar phrase means that certain contracts, while theoretically valid and binding in whatever form they may have been made will only be *enforceable* (i.e. of any commercial use) if supported by written evidence, both of their very existence and of their terms. Among the types of contract covered by this rule are assignments of copyright, 'contracts of guarantee' and contracts for the sale or other disposition of land (NB not the actual transfer of the land itself, which as explained above must be in *deed* form).

A 'contract of guarantee' is a 'promise to answer for the debt, default or miscarriage of another person', and must be distinguished from an 'indemnity' (e.g. an insurance policy) under which the contracting party makes himself liable to reimburse the other party for any loss suffered in certain defined circumstances. Both contracts of guarantee and contracts for the sale, etc., of land require, for their proof, a 'memorandum' in writing which must include the signature of the party against whom it is being enforced, or his agent, together with all the material terms of the contract (i.e. the parties, the subject matter, the price in the case of a sale, etc., of land, and any other vital terms). It may be made at any time after the contract itself is agreed, and need not take any particular form. A simple letter will suffice, or even a scrap of paper.

Although the normal effect of the absence of a memorandum where one is required is to render the contract unenforceable, the courts will not take this action in the case of the sale, etc., of land where they feel that to do so would be 'inequitable' because there has been 'part performance' by one of the parties. Thus, in *Wakeham* v. *McKenzie* (1968), the court granted a house to a woman who had been persuaded to give up her own house and look after an old man in his last years on the promise that he would leave it to her in his will. She had done so, paying for her own board during his lifetime, and his will made no mention of leaving the house to her. It was held that the oral contract had been sufficiently 'part performed' for it to be enforceable.

Variation of the terms of a written contract

There is a general rule in the law of contract (known to lawyers as 'the parol evidence rule') to the effect that one may not seek to vary, contradict or supplement the clear terms of a *written* contract with mere oral evidence of what was allegedly the parties' real intention. In other words, the parties are normally bound by whatever they have recorded in writing.

As usual, there are exceptions to the rule. For example, it is possible to produce oral evidence to show that what was recorded in writing was arrived at by fraud, misrepresentation or illegality on the part of the other party, or where it is necessary for the courts to *imply* certain terms into the contract to make commercial sense of it, or where it is necessary to resolve an ambiguity, or where the parties made a simple mechanical mistake in recording their real agreement (e.g. one extra nought in the purchase price!).

Perhaps the most important exception to the general rule arises where it is shown that the contract between the parties is only intended to be partly in writing, and partly oral. Thus, in *Curtis* v. *Chemical Cleaning Co. Ltd* (1951), the owner of a wedding dress which was returned from a dry cleaner's shop covered in oil stains was able to circumvent the effect of an exemption clause which she had signed which covered 'damage howsoever arising' by proving that when she took the dress in for cleaning and inquired about the clause, the assistant stated that it merely covered damage to beads and sequins. The court held that in this particular case, this would be taken as being the limit of the exemption clause, which was thus altered by the statement of the assistant.

Under Scots law it is also the general rule that a contract may take any form (i.e. written, oral or even inferred from the actions of the parties). To this rule there are two major exceptions, namely those contracts (e.g. contracts concerned with land and buildings, contracts of employment for longer than a year and contracts of insurance) which must be in written form, and those contracts (e.g. loans over £8.33 in amount, and trusts) which may take any form, but may only be proved either by written evidence or by the admission of the party under oath.

The capacity of the parties

Even at the height of the *laissez-faire* theory of contract, it was conceded that certain parties, because of an inherent weakness or disability, could not be expected to manage their own affairs adequately, and therefore required the protection of the law against exploitation. The development of the limited company as a business unit also created special problems, since it is not a human entity and cannot function like one. For all these parties, special rules were developed, which lawyers group loosely together under the heading of 'capacity'.

Infants

Under English Law an 'infant' (or 'minor') is a person under eighteen, although until 1 January 1970, this age was twenty-one. The law which limits the contractual capacity of a person under eighteen is a mixture of Common Law and statute, and the detailed rules depend upon the type of contract under contemplation. We shall also require to distinguish between contracts which are 'binding' on an infant (i.e. enforceable both by and against him), contracts which are 'voidable' (in the sense that they become binding on him unless he repudiates them reasonably soon after attaining the age of eighteen), and contracts which are 'void' (i.e. of no legal effect whatsoever if entered into by an infant).

Contracts binding upon an infant

There are two main types of contract which a person may enter into, however young he may be, and which the law will enforce against him. These are (1) contracts for 'necessaries' sold and delivered to him, and (2) beneficial contracts of service.

1 'Necessaries' are goods and services actually required by
   the infant to maintain him according to his 'station in life'.
   They clearly include food, drink, clothing and living
   accommodation, and probably also services such as shoe
   repairs, hairdressing and dry-cleaning. The type and quality
   of goods and services which may be included in the category
   of 'necessaries' will apparently increase in accordance with
   the wealth and status of the infant's background, so that
   the sons of the rich will be bound by more contracts for
   necessaries than their poorer counterparts.

   In the case of goods, the Sale of Goods Act, 1979, s. 3,
   requires that the infant pay a 'reasonable' price (NB Not
   necessarily the *contract* price) for necessaries in the form
   of goods actually sold and delivered to him; in other words,
   he is liable to pay nothing until he actually acquires the
   goods (the mere promise of payment not being sufficient,
   unlike the normal rule of 'consideration' for adults). The
   Common Law applies the same rule to the supply of
   'services'.

   But in all cases, the necessaries must be actually needed
   by the infant, and commensurate with his style of living.
   Thus, in the famous case of *Nash* v. *Inman* (1908), it was
   held that a Cambridge undergraduate, while he might order
   fancy waistcoats from a Savile Row tailor, was not liable to
   pay for eleven of them in one order, since he could hardly
   be said to have needed that number.

2 'Beneficial contracts of service' include contracts of employment, training, apprenticeship or education, and
   reflect the law's desire to allow a young person to make a
   career for himself. He is entitled to enter into such a
   contract provided

   (a) that the price is reasonable;
   (b) that on balance it will ultimately be for his benefit;
   (c) that its terms are not unduly onerous towards him.

The types of contract which have been upheld as binding
under this heading include a contract under which a young
professional boxer came under the British Boxing Board of
Control rules, a contract under which a young billiards

professional undertook a tour, and a contract under which the infant son of a famous comedian contracted to write a book on his stormy life with his father. But the court drew the line in *De Francesco* v. *Barnum* (1890), and refused to uphold the contract of apprenticeship of a young girl dancer who among other things was required to engage in no other performances than those arranged for her by her employer, nor to marry without her employer's permission, while at the same time receiving no remuneration except when engaged in actual performances.

While the phrase 'employment' has already been extended to contracts under which an infant pursues a profession (e.g. author, snooker player, boxer), it will not cover the infant who simply sets up in a normal business enterprise. Infant entrepreneurs are not, under this heading, bound by any business contracts which they may make.

Contracts voidable by the infant

Certain categories of contract are regarded as basically safe for an infant to enter into, provided that he has a period in which to reflect upon his actions. This period runs from the date of his entry into the contract to a reasonable period after his eighteenth birthday; if he has not expressly repudiated the contract during that period, it becomes fully binding upon him. The main practical examples of such contracts are leases, contracts to take shares in a company and partnership contracts.

During the period before the infant repudiates the contract (if ever) he is liable for payments, etc., arising under it; thus, the infant tenant must pay the rent when it falls due, and the infant shareholder must pay any 'calls' on his shares. From the moment when he does repudiate the contract, however, he is not liable for any future payments. But he may not then recover any money already paid over by him, unless there has been a total failure of 'consideration' from the other party (i.e. the infant has received absolutely nothing for his money).

In order to exercise his right to repudiate, the infant must do so expressly within a 'reasonable' time after becoming eighteen. What is 'reasonable' will vary from case to case, but in *Edwards* v. *Carter* (1893), it was held that four and a half years was far too long after attaining eighteen for an infant to repudiate a trust deed granted by him disposing of property he was to acquire under a will.

Void contracts

Under the Infants' Relief Act, 1874, Parliament set out to render three classes of contract 'absolutely' void in so far as they were made with an infant. They are (a) loans of money; (b) contracts for non-necessary goods; (c) any contract under which an infant admits the existence of a prior debt. In fact, despite the Act, there are certain circumstances in which such contracts may still be of legal effect.

For one thing, although such contracts are void *against* the infant (i.e. they cannot be enforced *against* him), it seems that they may be enforced *by* him. Secondly, the infant may only get back any goods or money which he may have paid over in pursuance of the contract if there has been a total failure of consideration from the other side; if the infant has received *something* then he will not be able to retrieve his money or goods; thus in *Valentini* v. *Canali* (1889), the infant who paid £65 of the £102 he contracted to pay for non-necessary furniture was not allowed to recover the money because he had enjoyed the use of the furniture during that period.

Also, where an infant attempts to make fraudulent use of the law, by, for example, buying non-necessary goods, re-selling them and refusing to pay for them, the law will normally allow the defrauded party to recover the 'ill-gotten gains' from the infant. Also, in such a case, the fraudulent infant apparently passes good title to the innocent buyer of the goods from him. If the infant still possesses the goods, he will be ordered to hand them back.

Another case in which such contracts are not completely 'void' arises where a person lending money to an infant takes the precaution of seeking an 'indemnity' from an adult. In such a case, although the contract of loan will be a nullity, the indemnity will not. (NB that this will not work with a mere 'guarantee', which depends upon the validity of the main contract for its very existence.)

Finally, when money lent to an infant is spent on 'necessaries', the lender has the same rights as an unpaid supplier of such necessaries to recover that portion of the money which relates to the necessaries.

Apart, however, from these loopholes, the effect of the 1874 Act is that the contracts specified under it are void as against the infant. The Betting and Loans Act, 1892, extended the principle by stating that an infant might not even 'ratify' a loan after he became of age, so as to make him liable in respect of it. The 1874 Act contains a similar provision relating to all other debts (e.g. for non-necessary goods or services).

Scots law divides persons under eighteen into two categories: those who are called pupils (i.e. boys under fourteen and girls under twelve), and those who are called 'minors' (those between twelve or fourteen and eighteen).

As a general rule, pupils have no contractual capacity at all, and any purported contract would be void. Even so, a pupil will be liable to pay for 'necessaries' (see above), while any money lent to a pupil and spent for his benefit will be recoverable. Normally, however, a pupil may only make binding contracts through the agency of his 'tutor' (i.e. normally his father or mother), and even these may be set aside up to the time that the young person becomes twenty-two, if he has suffered considerable loss as the result of a contract which was not proper and reasonable at the time when it was made.

The contractual capacity of a minor depends upon whether or not he has a 'curator' (i.e. the same person who will qualify as his tutor). If he has then any contract which he makes will only be valid if the curator consents to it, unless it is one for 'necessaries' (see above), a contract of employment (see above), or a contract in the normal course of a trade or business conducted by the minor. But even where the curator does consent, the minor may still set aside the contract at any time up to his twenty-second birthday on the grounds indicated above. A minor without a curator is in the same position as one who has a curator who consents to the contract.

Drunkards and persons of unsound mind

A person who is drunk or of unsound mind when he makes a contract may well have been at a disadvantage when he did so, and the law is prepared to display a certain degree of sympathy for him in certain cases. The law is so similar in both cases that they may be conveniently classed together.

A 'person of unsound mind', for the purposes of the law of contract, is one who at the time of making the contract was so mentally unsound as to not understand what he was doing. It is for the party alleging this state of affairs to prove it, and also to prove that this condition was known to the other party, or ought to have been known to him. If both factors are proved, then the contract is in fact voidable; the person of unsound mind may always ratify it when and if he recovers his sanity, if he still feels that he has a good bargain. But even if a person is so incapable, normally, of understanding what he is doing, and this fact is known to the other party, the insane person may still make a valid contract during a 'lucid interval'.

Notwithstanding the general rule, an insane person may also make binding contracts for 'necessaries', and the rules are the same as for infants (see p. 74).

Once a mentally ill person has his affairs placed in the hands of a nominee of the courts under the Mental Health Act, 1959, he no longer has any contractual capacity of his own, and cannot therefore make valid contracts of his own volition.

The general opinion of lawyers is that drunken persons are to be treated for the purposes of contractual capacity in exactly the same way as persons of unsound mind, and are equally bound by contracts for necessaries.

Corporations

A 'corporation' is a separate legal entity, distinct in law from its members. A good example is a local authority, or a company registered under the Companies Acts. The legal significance of corporations is that they constitute a separate legal entity, and can sue and be sued, and may make contracts, in their *corporate* name. Thus, the ABC Glazing Company may be sued for breach of contract without the need to sue all or any of its individual shareholders. It may also sue or make contracts on its own behalf, in just the same way as a natural person, acting through some authorized agent such as a director.

No corporation may be formed without the permission of the Crown, given either in an individual case, or by means of some machinery already laid down under an Act of Parliament (e.g. the Companies' Act, 1948). A corporation will also only be able to exercise such powers as are granted to it when it is formed; in other words, its contractual capacity may be limited. Since by far the most important form of corporation in the business world is the *company*, the rest of this section concentrates on companies.

Companies created by Act of Parliament
In such cases, the Act of Parliament which creates the company will also usually define the limits of its contractual capacity.

Chartered companies
Companies formed by Royal Charter have unlimited contractual capacity, just as if they were adult, sane humans.

Companies formed under the Companies Acts
Such companies, before they will be granted registration, are required to submit various documents to the Registrar of Companies, one of which is a Memorandum of Association, which must contain an 'Objects Clause', specifying the purposes for which the company has been formed. Thereafter, any purported contract for a purpose outside these objects will be deemed *ultra vires*, and void, even if approved of by the entire membership and board of directors.

This was held to be the position in the leading case of *Ashbury Railway Carriage Company* v. *Riche* (1875), in which a company formed to manufacture railway carriages entered into a contract to actually construct a railway. Realizing that this was almost certainly *ultra vires*, the company's directors obtained the unanimous approval of the shareholders for the contract. It was held that the contract was still *ultra vires*; the only way to validate it would have been to alter the objects clause (by notifying the Registrar), and then renegotiate the contract.

The usual response to the problem is for company lawyers to draft Objects Clauses so widely that nothing can ever come outside them, often with the open encouragement of the courts. Since our entry into Europe, the matter has become somewhat more academic, since under the European Community Act, 1972, s. 9(1), a person dealing with a company in good faith may enforce the contract against the company even if it is *ultra vires*, provided that it was a contract 'decided on' by the directors. In other words, the innocent outsider is protected, but the *ultra vires* rule still survives in so far as it applies against the company, or where the outsider only dealt with the company at junior management level, and the contract was never considered by the directors themselves.

Misrepresentation

Misrepresentation may be defined as a false statement of fact by A which, although it never becomes a term of the contract (and thus actionable in the event of a breach), is at least partly responsible for inducing B into entering into the contract. The effect of a misrepresentation is to make the contract 'voidable', i.e. B may, if he wishes, take steps to have the contract set aside upon discovery of the truth. But until he does so, any third party who has innocently purchased an interest in the subject matter of the contract will acquire a valid title. B may or may not be entitled to the additional remedy of damages, depending upon the nature of the misrepresentation by A.

If one were to cling rigidly to the Victorian *laissez-faire* concept of 'the bargain', then the injured party would receive no compensation at all for a 'mere misrepresentation', since it never became part of the bargain between the parties. Fortunately, wiser counsels have prevailed, and it is now well recognized that a statement made during the pre-contractual negotiations (e.g. 'this car has only done 10,000 miles', or 'the drains are in perfect working order') can be just as powerful an inducement as anything in the contract itself, and should be actionable if false. As will be seen later, this approach also led to the Trade Descriptions Act, 1968, which imposes criminal sanctions against false inducements. Unfortunately, as will be seen, this concern for the underdog has not extended to the point at which a misrepresentation automatically results in the same remedies as a breach of contract might do.

The elements of misrepresentation

Before the courts will even recognize that a misrepresentation has occurred, the following factors must be proved.

(1) There must be a statement

One would imagine that this requirement would cause little difficulty – either A has made a statement or he has not. But considerable sophistication has, over the years, crept into the definition of a 'statement', and the position is no longer as simple as it might seem.

For example, it will be an actionable 'misrepresentation' for the seller to disguise the appearance of something, or to cover up a defect, or to create a false visual impression of what the buyer will receive, as many a holiday brochure designer has learned to his cost. Similarly, a person's conduct may constitute misrepresentation, as where a person purports to be a pensioner so as to obtain concessionary travel terms. In such cases, no actual statement may be made, but the misrepresentation is just as effective, and will be treated accordingly by the courts.

Also, although as a general rule, mere silence will not constitute a misrepresentation (and it is for the other party to satisfy himself concerning the matters not dealt with, in accordance with the general maxim *caveat emptor* – 'let the buyer beware'), there are certain circumstances in which silence will be actionable. For example, where a statement is a half-truth in the sense that it is true so far as it goes, but creates a false impression by what it leaves unsaid, it will constitute a misrepresentation. A clear example of this was in *Dimmock* v. *Hallett* (1866), in which a party selling certain farms informed a prospective purchaser that they were all let to tenants; while this was perfectly true, it left out the vital fact that all the tenants had given notice to quit, and it was held to be a misrepresentation.

Silence will also constitute a misrepresentation where, although true when made, the statement is rendered untrue or misleading by subsequent events *before the contract is completed*, and the maker of the original statement fails to notify the other party of the change. In *With* v. *O'Flanagan* (1936), for example, a doctor selling his practice told the potential purchaser that it was worth £2,000 a year, which it then was. The contract was not signed for another four months, during which time the value of the practice fell to £250 per year due to the seller's ill-health. It was held that the seller's failure to notify the buyer of the change in circumstance amounted to a misrepresentation.

There must be a full statement of all known material facts whenever the contract is one of 'utmost good faith' (*uberrimae fidei*). This normally arises where one of the parties, and he alone, is in possession of all the factors which are likely to influence the terms of the contract, and he must disclose them all to the other party. The clearest examples in practice are contracts of insurance, company prospectuses and 'family arrangements' between relatives. Thus, a 'proposer' filling in a proposal form for insurance must state all those material facts which are likely to influence the size of the premium, or else the resulting policy may well be void.

The duty to state all known facts also exists where the contract is between parties who are in a 'fiduciary relationship' to each other. This arises where one of the parties owes a duty of trust to the other, and the clearest examples are those of parent and child, doctor and patient, solicitor and client, and principal and agent. Such contracts are governed by the same rules as contracts *uberrimae fidei*.

(2) It must be a statement of fact

As a general rule, only a statement of *present fact* will constitute a misrepresentation. Clearly, a statement of law cannot be a misrepresentation, since everyone is presumed to know the law anyway, and therefore could not be misled by such a statement. But certain other types of statement often lay claim to being representations.

To what extent, for example, will it be a misrepresentation for A to falsely state to B his intentions for the future? It apparently will be a misrepresentation if that intention is not genuinely held at the time of the statement, for 'the state of a man's mind is as much a fact as the state of his digestion'. This quotation comes from the leading case of *Edgington* v. *Fitzmaurice* (1885), in which it was held to be a misrepresentation for a company to state in a prospectus inviting loans from the public that the money would be used for expansion, when in fact it was intended to use it to pay off existing debts.

Again, a statement of *opinion* will never be a misrepresentation unless it can be shown that it was not validly held at the time (however wrongly) or that the speaker was entirely ignorant on the matter. But a statement of opinion is not easy to distinguish from a statement of fact, and in *Smith* v. *Land and House Property Corporation* (1884), it was held that to describe someone as 'a most desirable tenant' was not simply a statement of opinion, but one of fact when it was made in the knowledge that a substantial amount of rent was owing.

Finally, it should be remembered that statements of fact must be distinguished from mere extravagant 'sales talk'. In the light of decisions such as *Carlill* v. *The Carbolic Smoke Ball Company* (see p. 57) and statutes such as the Trade Descriptions Act, 1968, it is uncertain how far one may these days retreat behind the defence of 'a mere sales gimmick', but clearly, there are some advertisements which are so wildly exaggerated that no one in his right mind would believe them. It is only when the advertiser begins to make use of what may reasonably be interpreted as 'solid facts' that he is in danger of misrepresentation.

(3) The statement must induce the contract

No one may legitimately complain about a misrepresentation unless it has *influenced* him, and led, at least in part, to his entering into the contract. So, for example, if B was not even *aware* of a statement made by A, he can hardly claim to have been misled by it; thus, in *Horsfall* v. *Thomas* (1862), the purchaser of a gun which flew apart after only a few rounds could not claim that he had been deceived by a clever piece of camouflage over the defective part, since he had not even examined the gun.

Again, if B is aware of the statement, but does not believe it, or is not impressed by it even if it *is* true, then there can be no misrepresentation. This can happen, for example, where B makes his own assessment or calls in an independent expert, as in *Attwood* v. *Small* (1838), in which the seller's stated opinion of the earning capacity of a mine was corroborated by the independent expert called in by the purchaser, and it was held that this cancelled out any influence which the seller's statement might have had.

It is also the case that if B is aware of the misrepresentation, but also aware of the truth, then he cannot rely on the misrepresentation as an excuse for setting aside the contract. But the courts will not extend this principle to cover what B should have known, and it is not enough simply for A to offer him an opportunity to make his own checks. Thus, in *Redgrave* v. *Hurd* (1881), it was held that a solicitor could set aside a partnership contract which he had made with another solicitor on the basis of false financial statements given by him, despite the fact that the purchaser had been afforded an opportunity of examining the books, and could have learned the truth from them had he made the effort.

The types of misrepresentation and their consequences

There are three types of misrepresentation recognized by the law, and they are categorized according to the 'state of mind' of the person making the statement. It is necessary to distinguish between them because the remedies available to the injured party vary according to the type of misrepresentation.

(1) Fraudulent misrepresentation

This is a misrepresentation made by a party who either knows that what he is saying is untrue, or is so reckless that he does not care whether it is true or not (i.e. he has taken no reasonable steps to verify the truth of his statement). It appears, however, that if the party honestly believes that what he is saying is true, however unreasonable that belief may be, then it cannot be a fraudulent misrepresentation; this emerged from the leading case of *Derry* v. *Peek* (1889), in which a company, in a prospectus to attract new shareholders, stated that it had permission to run steam trams; it was honestly believed by the directors that the necessary consent by the Board of Trade was a mere formality, but in fact it was refused. It was held that the honest belief, however unreasonable, prevented the statement from being fraudulent. NB However, that under the Companies' Act, 1948, s. 43, any director making such a statement without reasonable grounds for believing it, even if innocently, may be liable to compensate those deceived by it.

A person who has been the victim of a fraudulent misrepresentation may, of course, if he wishes, continue with the contract as if nothing had happened. Alternatively (and more commonly) he may seek to 'rescind' (i.e. set aside) the contract, with or without damages. Both remedies are provided by the Common Law.

The right to rescind the contract may be lost if the injured party once 'affirms' the contract, i.e. does or says something which indicates that, despite knowing the truth, he still wishes to go ahead with it. The safest way to rescind a contract is therefore for the aggrieved party to communicate direct with the other party, making it clear that he no longer regards himself as bound.

Rescission will also be refused by the courts where it is no longer possible to restore the parties to their original positions (i.e. to make *restitutio in integrum*, as lawyers call it). A clear example of this was the case of *Lagunas Nitrate Company* v.

Lagunas Syndicate (1899), where the court refused to rescind a mining contract after a considerable amount of the mineral had been extracted. Similarly, if an innocent third party has acquired, for payment, some rights in the subject matter of the contract, the courts will not rescind the contract so as to prejudice his position.

Whether or not the injured party elects to rescind the contract on the grounds of fraudulent misrepresentation, he has the separate right to sue for damages, not for breach of contract, but for the 'tort' (i.e. civil wrong) of 'deceit'. He will not receive any damages unless he can show that he has suffered some financial loss, but the damages awarded will normally cover the whole of such loss.

(2) Innocent misrepresentation

An 'innocent' misrepresentation is one in which the maker of the statement not only honestly believed that what he was stating was the truth, but also had reasonable grounds for that belief (i.e. he did not act negligently). The victim of such a misrepresentation may, if he wishes, elect to continue with the contract; if, however, he seeks a remedy for the wrong done to him, then he runs into complications.

Before 1967, the only remedy available to him was in fact rescission. Since rescission is an *equitable* remedy (i.e. one granted by the courts in the interests of justice rather than according to the strict letter of the law), it is *discretionary*, and the court need not grant it if it does not wish. It is in any case subject to all the limitations mentioned above in the context of fraudulent misrepresentation, plus the additional limitation that the claim must be brought within 'reasonable time'.

If rescission were refused by the court, the injured party therefore had no other remedy to fall back on, since the Common Law would not award damages in respect of an innocent misrepresentation. This state of affairs was remedied under the Misrepresentation Act, 1967 (which does not apply to Scotland), s. 2(2) of which allows the court, in any case in which rescission is claimed, to award damages in lieu of rescission, if it is of the opinion that it would be 'equitable' to do so. But the claimant must still have the right to rescind before damages will be granted; if, for example, *restitutio in integrum* is impossible, he will still get nothing.

(3) Negligent misrepresentation

This type of misrepresentation falls between the previous two; it is a mis-statement by A which is honestly believed by him to be true (and is therefore not fraudulent), but in respect of which no reasonable grounds for belief existed (i.e. it was not purely innocent). Again, the aggrieved party may, if he wishes, simply affirm the contract and ignore the misrepresentation; alternatively he may seek a remedy.

The position with regard to rescission is exactly the same as for an innocent misrepresentation; indeed, before 1967, the law made no distinction between negligent and non-negligent misrepresentation. The main reason for distinguishing between the two is in fact the substantial one that under s. 2(1) of the Misrepresentation Act, 1967 (which does not apply to Scotland), the victim of a negligent misrepresentation may, as a matter of right, claim damages, provided that he can show that he has suffered some loss. It is for the maker of the statement to show that he had reasonable grounds for believing the truth of it, that it was therefore made 'innocently', and that the injured party has no automatic right to damages (although they may be awarded in lieu of rescission, as explained above). Damages awarded in respect of a *negligent* misrepresentation may be *in addition to* rescission as well as in lieu of.

Quite apart from the 1967 Act, the victim of a negligent misstatement has, since 1963 at least, had the right to sue the maker of such a statement for simple negligence, without any reference to any contract between them. Thus, in *Esso Petroleum* v. *Mardon* (1976), the operator of a filling station leased from a petrol company obtained damages in respect of a negligent statement made at the time of the negotiation of the lease by a senior executive of the petrol company as to the potential sales figures. The damages were awarded without any reference to any contract or to the 1967 Act.

Finally, it should be noted that s. 3 of the 1967 Act prohibits any exemption clause in a contract which seeks to exempt a party from liability for *fraudulent* misrepresentation; in any *other* case, such an exemption clause must be 'reasonable' before it will be enforceable. The test for 'reasonableness' is the same as that laid down for exemption clauses generally under the Unfair Contract Terms Act, 1977, for which see Chapter 4, below.

Mistake

As a general rule, the law will not protect those who have made a bad bargain; the mere fact that a contract turns out to be less favourable to one of the parties than he had anticipated will give him no legal grounds for terminating it. But there are circumstances in which the parties have made such serious errors in their dealings with each other that they have not even succeeded in reaching an enforceable agreement, although they believe they have. Since the law requires that before there may be a valid agreement there must be *consensus ad idem*, such mistakes, where they are of *fact* (and not, for example, of law), will render the contract *void* (i.e. of no legal effect). One of the consequences of this process is that not even innocent third parties, who have acquired an interest in the subject matter of the contract in all good faith, will be able to enforce their rights. The entire original contract is a nullity, unlike the contract tainted with mere misrepresentation, which is merely *voidable*, at the option of the aggrieved party, and under which innocent third parties may meanwhile acquire enforceable rights.

The following general types of mistake will normally be 'operative', i.e. they will normally have the effect of making the contract void.

Mistakes common to both parties

In some cases, although the parties have undeniably reached an agreement, they have done so on the basis of some underlying and fundamental assumption which turns out to have been incorrect. Since the parties have at least reached an agreement, the attitude of the courts often is that there is a valid and enforceable contract. But the law also sometimes recognizes that it would be unfair to enforce such contracts in some situations in which the agreement would be impossible to implement.

One example arises under a contract to sell 'specific' (i.e. identified) goods which unknown to the seller have perished before the contract is finalized; the effect of s. 6 of the Sale of Goods Acts, 1979, is that such a contract is void. Again, in the admittedly rare cases in which a party has contracted to buy something which, unknown to both parties, already belongs to him, the courts will normally conclude that the contract is void.

In addition, where, in negotiating a contract, the parties have assumed that some 'state of affairs' exists when it does not, this may well have the effect of rendering the contract void. One example was the case in which an attempt was made to assure the life of a man who, unknown to the parties, had already died, while in *Galloway* v. *Galloway* (1914), the court refused to give any legal effect to a separation agreement between a man and a woman who believed themselves to be husband and wife when they were not.

Finally, where the parties have reached a perfectly valid agreement, but some error has occurred in the recording of that agreement (e.g. an extra nought has appeared in the purchase price), the courts will allow the parties to 'rectify' the formal agreement so as to reflect their real intentions.

Mistaken identity

Where A makes a contract with a person he believes to be B, but in fact turns out to be C, then if A can show that the identity of the other party was of fundamental importance to him, that B was aware of A's belief, and that he, A, took reasonable steps to verify the identity of the other party, the courts may well set aside the contract as being void.

In the great majority of such cases (and a surprising number have come before the courts over the years) the 'other party', B, knows perfectly well that A is mistaken, and is in fact a 'con-man' posing as someone else. The contract could therefore be set aside on the basis of misrepresentation, but this only has the effect of rendering the contract voidable, whereas in most cases, by the time the error has been discovered, an innocent third party has possession of the goods.

The courts are more prepared to find that the identity of the other party was of fundamental importance to the aggrieved party where the parties are negotiating with each other over a distance, and not face to face. Thus, in the early leading case of *Cundy* v. *Lindsay* (1878), the courts held as void a contract made between L and a rogue called Blenkarn of 37 Wood Street, who ordered goods from L under the name of an established firm called Blenkiron of 200 Wood Street. The goods were delivered to 'Blenkiron and Co., 37 Wood Street', and it was held that, in the circumstances, L had intended to deal only with Blenkiron and Co. and therefore there was no valid contract under which Blenkarn could have taken a valid title to the goods; the innocent purchaser to whom he had resold them was therefore obliged to hand them back to L.

But where the parties are face to face, the normal attitude of the courts is that the innocent party must have intended to deal with the person standing before him, whoever he might be. Indeed, in many of the cases, the identity of the other party only became relevant after the contract had been concluded, and credit or cheque facilities were being discussed. In such cases, the contract, while possibly voidable for misrepresentation, is certainly not void for mistake.

A good example of this process was *Lewis* v. *Averay* (1971), in which L offered his car for sale to a man who claimed to be Richard Greene, the actor. His cheque was accepted only after he had produced a gate pass in the name of Richard Greene to the Pinewood Film studios; he then took the car and sold it to A, an innocent purchaser. The cheque bounced and 'Richard Greene' turned out to be a 'con artist'. The Court of Appeal ruled that L had intended to sell the car to the man himself, whoever he might be, and that the contract was therefore merely voidable for misrepresentation, and not void for mistake. A therefore had a valid title to the car.

Mistake as to subject matter

In some cases, the parties do not even succeed in reaching an agreement as to the subject matter of the contract; for example, A is attempting to sell a Ford Cortina while B is attempting to buy a Ford Capri. It may be, of course, that one of the parties is totally unjustified in holding the belief which he has as to the subject matter, and if the courts feel that this is the case, then they will simply uphold the contract on the terms intended by the other party. In order words, by applying an 'objective test' to the situation (i.e. they ask the question 'what would a reasonable man have thought ?'), the courts choose between the two versions of the agreement and uphold the more reasonable of the two as an enforceable contract.

But there are occasions when not even that method yields an answer; where the parties have got themselves hopelessly tangled, the courts have no option but to rule the contract void. The classic example was *Raffles* v. *Wichelhaus* (1864), in which the contract was for an assignment of cotton 'ex Peerless from Bombay'. There were two ships called Peerless sailing from Bombay with cotton, and while the buyer was referring to the October vessel, the seller meant the vessel sailing in December. The court held that there was no valid contract.

Mistake as to the nature of the contract

As a general rule, a person signing a document is bound by it, and cannot later turn round and claim that he was unaware of what he was signing; hence the importance of 'reading the small print'. It is therefore a rare event for a party to a signed written contract to be allowed to withdraw from it on the grounds that he was mistaken.

This will, however, be permitted by the courts where he is

able to claim the defence of *non est factum* – 'it is not my deed'. This means, in effect, that A has been induced by B into signing a document which is completely different in character and effect from the one he intended to sign; he has, in short, been 'conned'. A clear example would be of a man tricked into signing a guarantee of a bank overdraft in the belief that he was in fact giving someone a reference.

Whatever may have been the position historically, the law was restated in its modern context by the House of Lords in the case of *Saunders* v. *Anglia Building Society* (1971), in which Mrs G, an elderly lady who had mislaid her spectacles, was induced by her nephew to sign what she believed to be a deed of gift of her house to him, but was in fact an assignment of the house to his business associate. She had not attempted to read the document, being minus her spectacles, but had merely accepted her nephew's assurance that it was a deed of gift to him, on condition that she might live in the house for the rest of her life. The business associate immediately mortgaged the house but fell into arrears with the payments; it was then that Mrs G sought a declaration from the court that the house was still hers, since the assignment had been made mistakenly, and by virtue of the plea of *non est factum* she was not bound by it.

The House of Lords held that she *was* bound by it, and ruled that before anyone may claim *non est factum*, they must be able to show (a) that the document was radically different in type from the one intended; in Mrs G's case it was not; (b) that he or she has not been careless; (c) that he or she would not have signed had the true facts been known.

Duress and undue influence

A contract obtained under 'duress' is one which has been obtained by either actual personal violence, or threats of such violence. At Common Law, such a contract is certainly voidable and probably void, since it is not based on the free assent of the parties. The threat of violence need not be to the other party himself, and it is sufficient to constitute duress if it is made towards his wife and family or other relatives, and if the violence consists of unlawful imprisonment, or the threat of it.

At present, it is uncertain whether or not duress can be extended to cover threats to one's goods; the traditional view is that it may not, but there is a growing school of opinion to the effect that 'economic threats' should constitute duress.

'Undue influence' is the term used to describe the situation in which one of the parties to a contract uses his position of influence to pressurize or coerce the other into making the contract. This may make the contract voidable if the courts, in the exercise of their 'equitable' jurisdiction, feel that the contract should, in the circumstances, be set aside.

Where the party under suspicion stands in a 'fiduciary' (i.e. trusted) relationship to the other, undue influence will be *presumed* until the contract is shown to be 'above board'. Relationships which will attract this presumption include parent–child, solicitor–client, priest–parishioner, doctor–patient and principal–agent, and it may only be rebutted by evidence that a fair price was paid, that all the facts were disclosed, that the weaker party received full independent advice, or that any 'gift' was spontaneous.

In all other cases, it is for the party alleging undue influence to prove facts to show that there was; even then, the right to rescind the contract may be lost through inordinate delay or behaviour on the part of the 'innocent party' which leaves much to be desired, in addition to the other grounds upon which rescission may be lost (see under Misrepresentation, p. 85).

Examples of cases in which undue influence has been found to exist include false messages from a dead son transmitted by a medium (*Lyon* v. *Holme* (1878)), threats by a bank to prosecute a son for forgeries he had actually committed (*Williams* v. *Bayley* (1866)) and persuasion by the manager of a pop group that the members of the group should sign away their musical copyrights to a management company (*Clifford Davis Management* v. *WEA Records* (1975)).

Void and illegal contracts

A contract may be expertly negotiated, clearly expressed, between parties of undoubted capacity and impeccable motives, in precisely the right form and yet still be a complete waste of paper because it is for a purpose which Parliament or the courts have deemed unworthy of support. It may be rendered void by statute, regarded as illegal, or simply denied enforceability because it contravenes some vital principle of public policy.

The subject area is vast, and only those topics of most direct relevance to the business manager have been selected; even then, only an outline sketch can be supplied in a book of this length. The material to be covered can best be divided into four main groups.

Contracts illegal at Common Law

Quite apart from those contracts rendered illegal by statute, the courts themselves, as the guardians of the Common Law, exercise the right to refuse to enforce certain types of contract on the grounds that they are illegal, although only some of them would coincide with the layman's definition of an illegal act or purpose. The following are some of the surviving modern examples of this process.

(1) Contracts to commit crimes or civil wrongs
It goes without saying that no court will enforce a contract whose purpose is the commission of a crime (e.g. an agreement by two burglars to rob a house and divide the proceeds equally), but the principle extends to cover civil wrongs such as defamation of character, nuisance and trespass.

(2) Contracts prejudicial to public safety
In practice, contracts rendered 'illegal' under this heading are confined to those which either benefit an alien enemy country with which Britain is at war, or else threaten to disrupt

Britain's good relations with a friendly country. The outbreak of war has the effect of terminating any existing contract with an enemy alien so far as future obligations are concerned, although rights already accrued may be enforced when peace is restored.

(3) Contracts leading to corruption in public life

'Corruption scandals' are now depressingly familiar, and the courts express their distaste for this type of immorality by refusing to enforce any contract which might lead to corruption in public office. Early examples included the sale or purchase of public offices, the procurement of titles and the selling off of sinecures. The rule is confined to 'public office' in the strict sense of the term, but more commercial corruption is rendered illegal by the Prevention of Corruption Acts of 1906 and 1916, for which see Chapter 2.

(4) Contracts to defraud the Revenue

Such contracts are probably criminal offences anyway, but to make doubly sure that no one is encouraged to make such agreements, the courts single out 'tax evasion' (NB Not 'tax avoidance') contracts as being a separate category to which they will give no legal effect whatsoever. The rule applies not only to the Inland Revenue, but also other revenue-collecting agencies both national and local (e.g. local authority rates).

The consequences of an illegal contract vary according to the type of illegality and the 'intentions' of the parties. If the contract was illegal 'on the face of it' (i.e. it was for an illegal purpose), then it is illegal *ab initio* (from the very start) and neither party may enforce any of it. No other contract which is based on this illegal contract may be enforced either. So far as the parties are concerned, the illegal contract is void, although as a general rule, if money or goods have passed to an innocent third party, then he may keep them.

It follows from this that if one of the parties has parted with money or goods to the other in pursuance of the illegal contract, he may not recover them unless he is not *in pari delicto* with (equally as guilty as) the other party. Thus, in *Davidson* v. *Pillay* (1979), it was held that the ex-manageress of a dry-cleaning business could still recover redundancy payment from her former employer even though the contract had been illegal in the sense that she had been paid weekly by means of cash from the till, because there was no evidence to show that the employee was aware that no tax or national insurance deductions were being made. Again, in *Shelly* v. *Paddock* (1979), a woman who had been swindled into parting with money for a non-existent Spanish villa was able to secure its return even though, unknown to her, the contract had been in breach of the Exchange Control Regulations. Similarly, if one of the parties genuinely repents, and the contract has not been substantially performed, the repenting party may be allowed to recover what he has paid over or contributed already. The same is true where the innocent party is one whom the law was designed to protect.

Where the contract is not itself illegal (i.e. it is not for an illegal purpose), but becomes illegal because of the manner in which it is performed, or because it is exploited for some unlawful purpose, then the rule is that the guilty party may not enforce it, but the rights of the innocent party are not affected. Thus, the wholesale supplier of intoxicating liquor may still recover his money even if his customer is convicted of selling that drink without a licence.

Contracts illegal under statute

As the result of Acts of Parliament, many potential contracts are rendered illegal in the sense that, were they to be performed, they would contravene the Act. This proposition requires little consideration in cases in which the statute imposes such illegality expressly, since it was Parliament's clear intention that such contracts should not be performed. Thus, for example, by virtue of the Resale Prices Act, 1976, s. 1, it is unlawful to make an agreement between suppliers to blacklist retailers who fail to charge a minimum retail price, while under the various Truck Acts, it is illegal to pay workers in kind.

The problems begin when a statute appears to make a certain kind of contract illegal by implication; the difficulty is that of deciding whether the real intention of Parliament was to make the contract illegal, or whether it was really intended to have some other effect (e.g. to force a person to take out a licence, or to ensure that he supplies the other party with all the information he needs before entering into a contract). In the latter case, the contract will *not* be illegal, whereas in the former case it will.

Thus, a stockbroker who fails to issue a stamped contract note concerning a transaction as per the Stamp Act, 1891, may still recover his commission from his principal, since the primary concern of the Act is not to make such contracts illegal, but to ensure that the Revenue gets its 'cut' on each transaction (*Learoyd* v. *Bracken* (1894)). In *Cope* v. *Rowlands* (1836), on the other hand, it was held that a commission could not be claimed by an unlicensed broker because the main purpose behind the statute requiring brokers to be licensed was to protect the public, and therefore any contract with an unlicensed one was illegal.

Certainly, the mere fact that a statute has been broken in the course of performance of a contract does not render that contract unlawful, as may be seen from *Archbolds (Freightage) Limited* v. *Spanglett Ltd* (1961), in which S agreed to transport a consignment of whisky, but did so in a vehicle which did not have the requisite 'A' class licence. The load was stolen *en route*, but A were allowed to sue S under the contract because the contract itself was perfectly lawful and 'to hold the contract illegal would injure the innocent, benefit the guilty and put a premium on deceit'.

The consequences of illegality of contract as the result of a statute are precisely the same as those explained above in the context of contracts made illegal by Common Law.

Contracts void under statute

In some cases, instead of rendering a particular type of contract *illegal* (i.e. contrary to law), a statute simply declares it to be 'void' (i.e. of no legal effect). The distinction may be considered a fine one, even an unnecessary one, particularly since, from a businessman's point of view, the effect is the same – the contract may not be enforced. But any subsidiary contract dependent upon a void contract will still be valid, unlike those tainted by illegality.

There are many examples of this type of statute, but only four of any real relevance to modern business.

(1) Restrictive trading agreements

Under the Restrictive Trade Practices Act, 1976, all agreements by which producers, suppliers or exporters of goods seek, by means of 'collective agreements', to restrict the manufacture, supply or distribution of goods are declared void unless they are registered for the purpose with the Director-General of Fair Trading. They will then be considered by the Restrictive Practices Court.

Further information on these important provisions appears in Chapter 6.

(2) Resale Price Maintenance

Under the Resale Prices Act, 1976, collective resale price maintenance agreements are presumed to be void unless the Restrictive Practices Court is satisfied that the agreement is in the public interest. Again, further details may be found in Chapter 6.

(3) Articles 85 and 86 of the Treaty of Rome

Under these provisions, which are binding in the UK, all agreements which have the effect of preventing or restricting competition within the Community are declared void. Even if the agreement complies with UK law (e.g. the two 1976 Acts referred to above), it will still be void under Articles 85 and 86 in so far as it relates to any other country within the Community. Further details appear in Chapter 6.

(4) Registration of Business Names Act, 1916

Any firm in the UK which is trading or otherwise doing business under a name which is not the real name of the individuals or corporation who comprise it, must register that name under the above Act. Failure to do so can result in any contract made by that firm being declared void by the courts. This matter has been dealt with in more detail in Chapter 2.

Contracts void at Common Law

In addition to their power to declare contracts illegal under the Common Law, the courts also have the power to declare them void as being contrary to public policy. In practice, there are only two which are relevant to the business world (although the second of them is extremely important and highly topical), and they are as follows.

(1) Contracts to oust the jurisdiction of the courts

No contract can be enforced in so far as it purports to deny either of the parties the right of access to the courts in the event of a dispute. In the case of 'binding in honour only' clauses, of course, there is no contract anyway, since the parties are expressly declaring that they do not intend to be legally bound, so neither party will require access to the courts. Nor is an arbitration clause void unless it seeks to prevent the parties having access to the courts after the arbitration.

(2) Contracts in restraint of trade

A contract 'in restraint of trade' is one which unreasonably restricts a person from exercising a trade or profession, or simply earning a living. It is in keeping with the *laissez-faire* roots of the law of contract that such contracts should be frowned upon, although in more recent years economic reality has obliged the courts to look more sympathetically upon them.

In order for such contracts to be valid and enforceable, it must be shown that they are reasonable, both so far as the parties themselves are concerned (i.e. they are not unreasonably wide) and so far as the *public interest* is concerned. Certain types of restrictive agreement have already gained universal acceptance by the courts, and no one may now claim, for example, that the 'tied house' brewery system is void, or that 'sole agencies' in the motor trade should be set aside.

There are, however, four kinds of restraint of trade contract which are always treated with suspicion, and they are:

(a) Restraints on employees It is not unusual, particularly when employing someone with a recognized skill, or in a position of trust, for an employer to include a clause in the contract of employment prohibiting the employee from working in a similar capacity for another employer for a certain length of time and within a particular geographical area. The courts will normally only uphold such agreements where the employer has some genuine trade secret or customer goodwill to protect, but even then, the restraint must be reasonable both in time and area.

Thus, while it may be valid to restrain a solicitor's managing clerk from practising his profession for the rest of his life where it is only for a seven-mile radius of a market town (*Fitch* v. *Dewes*, 1921), it will *not* be permissible to prevent a salesman from selling, anywhere in the UK, any beer brewed in a particular town (*Allsopp* v. *Wheatcroft*, 1872). The greater the area of restraint, the shorter should be the time period, and vice versa. In particular, the employee should not be unreasonably prevented from earning a living in his chosen profession, and the community should not be denied his services and skills.

The same argument was used (and slightly extended) in the 1978 case of *Greig* v. *Insole*, in which it was held that the ICC and Test and County Cricket Board's attempt to 'black' from county and test cricket all those taking part in the Kerry Packer World Series was unreasonable, *ultra vires*, and void, because it unreasonably prevented the players from earning at least a partial living.

The classic justification for a restraint clause in employment was perhaps that illustrated in *Home Counties Dairies* v. *Skilton* (1970), in which the court upheld a restraint clause preventing a milk roundsman, for a period of one year after leaving his employers, from serving milk to any customer served by him in his last six months with his former employer.

(b) Restraints on vendors of businesses It is quite commonplace, when A is selling a going concern to B, for B to insist on the inclusion in the contract of a clause preventing A from setting up a rival business immediately thereafter, using old customers and goodwill built up by the business which has been sold. The law is a little more lenient in this situation than in the case of an employee restraint, but the enforcing party must be able to show that it is no wider than reasonably necessary to protect the business he has purchased.

In *Nordenfelt* v. *Nordenfelt* (1895), the court upheld such a restraint clause even though it covered the whole world for a twenty-five year period, because the product was specialist armament, and the only likely customers were national governments. But the courts are careful not to be seen giving support to unfair restriction of competition, and in *British Concrete Company* v. *Schelff* (1921) refused to uphold a restraint clause concerning the manufacture of one form of road reinforcement when the business sold had been for the manufacture of another type.

(c) Restraints within Trade Associations Although these are now nearly all covered by the Restrictive Trade Practices Act, 1976, there are occasions upon which such agreements are deemed lawful under the Act; in such cases, they must also be shown to be 'reasonable' at Common Law, or they will be declared void as being in restraint of trade.

Thus, in *English Hopgrowers* v. *Dering* (1928), the court upheld as reasonable an agreement between hop manufacturers under which each would deliver his entire year's crop to the Association, since this would help to alleviate market fluctuations. This arrangement would today almost certainly be caught by the 1976 Act.

(d) Solus agreements A 'solus agreement' is an arrangement whereby a party agrees to limit the items in which he trades, often to simply one. The classic example in modern times has been the petrol filling station which, in return for special discounts, capital grants, loans, etc., is restricted to serving only one proprietary brand of petrol. Again, it must be shown to be a reasonable agreement.

The leading case is *Esso Petroleum Ltd* v. *Harpers Garage* (1968), in which a garage proprietor made two agreements which tied him to buying and serving Esso petrol in return for financial assistance. The contracts were for four years and twenty-one years respectively, and the House of Lords held that while in general there was nothing unreasonable in the concept of a restraint clause, particularly when the parties are negotiating as experienced businessmen, twenty-one years was an unreasonably long period, although four years was acceptable.

A contract in restraint of trade will be void, but only in so far as it is in restraint of trade. Thus, any money or property transferred under the contract may still be recovered, and the unlawful parts of the contract may be severed from the lawful parts, which may then continue in force if they still make sense. For example, the sale of a business may still proceed even though a restraint clause cannot be enforced; and no one would suggest that an employee who has worked under a contract of employment containing an unacceptable restraint clause cannot claim wages for the work he has done.

However, the remaining parts of the contract must form a coherent and workable whole; in severing the offending parts, the courts will not redraft the contract so as to make it workable. An example of the 'blue pencil rule' (as it is called) in action was *Goldsall* v. *Goldman* (1915), in which an unacceptable restraint clause covering the sale of real or imitation jewellery in any part of UK, France or the USA was restricted so as to apply to imitation jewellery in the UK.

The parties to a contract

The so-called 'Doctrine of Privity of Contract' is simply a rule under which no one who was not a party to the original contract may seek to enforce it or to benefit from it; nor, of course, may he be made liable under it. It is reasonable enough to suggest that a contract made between A and B should not be enforceable by or against C, D or anyone else, and is simply a continuation of the 'consideration' principle that a person who has not supplied something of value should not be a party to a contract.

The same principle applies in Scots law (where of course the principle of consideration is not crucial to the existence of a contract) under the defence of *jus tertii*, which is in effect a claim that the party suing is not a party to the contract, and therefore has no right to sue.

The rule operates in two ways, in that (a) it prevents 'strangers to the contract' from taking any benefit under it, and (b) it prevents such strangers incurring any liability under it.

A stranger may not enjoy the benefit of a contract

What this means, strictly speaking, is that the stranger cannot enforce the benefit himself; but if, for example, A and B make a contract under which money will be paid to C, both A and B may enforce it for C's benefit so that in that sense, C may benefit under the contract.

The operation of the general rule may be illustrated by the 1968 case of *Beswick* v. *Beswick*, in which a coal merchant (P) sold his business to his nephew (J) in return for £6.50 per week for himself during his lifetime, and £5 to his widow after his death. When P died, J refused to make payment to the widow. It was held by the House of Lords that while the widow, in her personal capacity could not enforce the contract since she had not been a party to it, she could enforce it as executrix of her late husband's estate (i.e. acting in place of her husband).

A stranger may not incur liability under a contract

One would hardly expect a contract between A and B to validly impose some legal burden on C, and this is the attitude normally taken by the courts. Thus, in the leading case of *Scruttons* v. *Midland Silicones* (1962), A agreed to transport a drum of chemicals belonging to B under a contract which limited A's liability for damage to $500. A then made another contract with C to unload the drum in London, during the course of which the drum was damaged. When B sued C, C tried to rely on the $500 limit in the contract between A and B, but it was held that he could not extend the 'burden' upon B (i.e. the limit on the right to sue A) in this fashion, nor could he, C, benefit from an exemption clause in a contract to which he was not a party.

This general rule, which emerged finally in 1861, appealed to the logical minds of Victorian judges, but has proved inconvenient in business practice. There are now many exceptions to it, and only a few of the more important ones may be mentioned, namely:

1 *Agency*. A 'Principal' may sue to enforce the benefit of a contract made on his behalf by his agent. This topic has been dealt with more fully in Chapter 2.
2 *Assignment*. Many types of rights under contract may now be assigned by the original party entitled to them; each such assignment is governed by its own rules, and further detail is beyond the scope of this book. Common examples are shares in a company, life insurance policies, copyrights and patents. Debts may also usually be assigned.
3 *Negotiable instruments*. This somewhat archaic expression includes cheques, bills of exchange and promissory notes, and whoever becomes the holder of such an instrument in return for value is entitled to the value of it in cash, assuming that he acquired it in good faith. It is thus negotiable from party to party.
4 *Bankers' confirmed credits*. This complex system of financ-

ing international trade involves liability for payment under a contract between A and B being assumed by a third party, a bank.

5 *Life, fire and motor insurance policies*. By statute, third parties (e.g. widows) are entitled to sue for the money due under such policies.

6 *Resale price maintenance*. By statute, a supplier of goods may sue to enforce an approved resale price agreement against a third party retailer. The point is taken up in more detail in Chapter 6.

7 *Restrictive covenants*. These agreements, which limit the use to which land or buildings are put, may be enforced by interested parties who were not parties to the original covenant. See Chapter 7 for more detail.

The terms of the contract

Express and implied terms

Every contract contains 'express terms' (or 'clauses' as they are frequently called in the case of written contracts). These are the terms which the parties have actually stipulated for themselves when making the contract, whether orally or in writing. They may give rise to difficulties of interpretation, but at least there is usually little doubt that the parties intended them to be part of the contract. The point has already been made (see under 'Recording the Agreement', p. 69) that normally, the clear terms of a written contract may not be varied by oral evidence, but that sometimes the court recognizes that only *part* of the contract was intended to be in writing. The reader is referred at this point to the section on 'standard form contracts' under the heading 'Acceptance' earlier in this chapter (see page 61).

In addition to what the parties have expressly agreed for themselves, the courts may on occasions be obliged to imply certain terms into the contract, for a variety of reasons. The most obvious of these reasons is that a statute requires them to do so, and clear examples of this process are the implied terms of the Sale of Goods Act, 1979 (see Chapter 4) and the implied 'equality clause' in all contracts of employment of women (see Chapter 9).

It may also occasionally be necessary for the courts to import a particular trade custom into a contract, when satisfied that both parties were aware of it, and must have intended it to apply. This is less likely to happen in modern times, most customs having been absorbed into statute (e.g. the Sale of Goods Act, 1979). What is more likely is that the court finds itself obliged to imply a term into a contract simply to make it workable, or, to use the appropriate legal phrase, 'to give business efficacy' to it. This will only involve those terms which the parties must have taken for granted, as in *The Moorcock* (1889), in which a contract under which A was to berth his ship at B's jetty was taken to have in it an implied undertaking by B that the river-bed was fit for a ship to 'bottom' on.

Conditions and warranties

Having established what the terms of the contract actually are, it may on occasions (e.g. when a term has been breached) be of crucial importance to decide whether a particular term was a 'condition' or a 'warranty' (it must be one or the other). A 'condition' is a term of the contract which is so important that it goes to the very root of the contract, and the breach of it entitles the injured party, if he so wishes, to *repudiate* (i.e. wash his hands of) the entire contract. A 'warranty', on the other hand, is a lesser term, which entitles the injured party, upon breach, merely to damages. The distinction is of no practical importance under Scots law.

Sometimes, a statute dictates whether or not a term shall be a condition (NB The implied conditions and warranties of the Sale of Goods Act, 1979, in Chapter 4), but normally, it is left to the court to classify the term which has been breached. Even where the parties themselves have given it a label, this will not be conclusive if the court feels that it is inappropriate.

In more recent years, the courts have tended to work backwards, assessing the effect of the breach, and labelling the appropriate terms accordingly (i.e. it is a condition where its breach has 'gone to the very root of' the contract).

One frequently quoted example of the distinction in action concerns two similar cases in 1876. In *Bettini* v. *Gye*, an opera singer hired for a series of concerts undertook to attend six days of rehearsals beforehand, but only arrived in the country three days before the series was due to commence. It was held that this was only a breach of warranty, and the main contract should have continued. In *Poussard* v. *Spiers*, on the other hand, the failure of an actress to appear for an operetta until a week after the first night was treated as a breach of condition, and it was held that the management had been correct in regarding the contract as being at an end, and hiring another actress.

Exclusion clauses

Probably no other single factor has helped to create more confusion over the law of contract (and done so little for the collective image of lawyers!) than the exclusion clause. It is the reason why one is, quite rightly, exhorted to 'read the small print'.

Basically, an exemption clause is a term of the contract under which A limits, restricts or evenly totally eliminates his liability for breach. Taken to its wildest extremes, it would allow A to contract to sell a car to B, but to include a term in the contract which absolved him from any failure to deliver a car!

The courts (and latterly Parliament) have interceded to ensure that matters do not reach that ridiculous stage, but the subject is still riddled with uncertainty and injustice. Perhaps the best way of tackling this complex subject is to ask, of any given exemption or exclusion clause, (a) is it part of the contract in the first place?; (b) is it to have the effect desired by its author?

Judges frequently seek to protect the underdog from the effects of exclusion clauses by ruling that they have not been validly incorporated into the contract. In the case of a written contract this is not normally possible, and anyone signing an exemption clause, or a contract containing one, without reading it, could in a sense be said to have only himself to blame. This was the attitude taken by the courts in the leading case of *L'Estrange* v. *Graucob Ltd* (1934), in which L signed an agreement with G for the purchase of a fruit machine, but when it proved defective was unable to sue for damages because of an exclusion clause in the contract which she had signed which eliminated 'any express or implied condition, statement or warranty, statutory or otherwise'. It may be, of course, that the terms of the written contract are varied by some statement made at the time, as in the case of *Curtis* v. *Chemical Cleaning Company*, see p. 72.

Where the alleged exclusion clause is not contained in a written contract, then the party seeking to rely upon it must show that it was incorporated into the contract by some other means (e.g. orally, or by means of a notice brought to the other party's attention). Once the contract has been agreed, it is too late to add in further terms, and therefore too late to attempt to impose exclusion clauses; thus, in *Olley* v. *Marlborough Court Ltd* (1949), it was held that the management of an hotel could not rely upon an exclusion clause displayed on an hotel bedroom wall, because the contract with the guest was made at the reception desk.

The most common way in which one party attempts to impose an exclusion clause upon the other is by either displaying a notice simply informing him of the clause (e.g. in an hotel car park, the familiar sign 'The management regrets that it is unable . . .') or by handing him a ticket or similar piece of paper referring him to terms and conditions governing the contract, which may be examined by him upon request, and which invariably contain exclusion clauses.

The courts will not recognize this as a valid method of incorporating an exclusion clause into the contract where the piece of paper which the other party was handed did not appear to be a contractual document; if, for example, it looks like a mere receipt for payment, or a ticket of authorization, and not a document of a contractual nature, then the reference in it to exclusion clauses will not be effective. Thus, in 1940, the court held that a ticket given by a deck chair attendant could not validly inform the hirer of the deck chair of exclusion clauses (*Chapelton* v. *Barry UDC*), while in *Thornton* v. *Shoe Lane Parking* (1971), the same was held to be true of a ticket dispensed by the machine at the barrier of a multi-storey car park.

But if the existence of exclusion terms or clauses *is* validly communicated to the other party before the contract is finalized, he is bound by them whether he takes the trouble to read them or not. In some cases, he may have to go to considerable trouble to even locate a copy of them, but this has not stopped the courts from ruling in the past that the passenger receiving a railway ticket which refers to exclusion clauses is bound by them, even though one might have to write to British Railways in order to acquire a set of Regulations.

It may be also that the courts will imply an exclusion clause into a contract where the parties have done business with each other previously, under a contract containing an exclusion clause, and the other party was made aware of the clause at the time. It is then assumed by the courts that the other party was 'put on warning' of such a clause in the new contract, and that it is incorporated into the new contract by reference to the previous dealings. This is more likely to happen in a case involving two business concerns than with a private consumer, and even then the courts are reluctant to deprive a party of a legal remedy by such a method.

Even where the exclusion clause has been validly incorporated into the contract, there are several ways in which its effect can be lessened, or even neutralized completely. For example, many statutes now attempt to eliminate those exclusion clauses which Parliament feels are harmful to the consumer; examples dealt with elsewhere in this book include the Misrepresentation Act, 1967 (see above), which prohibits exclusion of liability for fraudulent misrepresentation, the Unfair Contract Terms Act, 1977 (see Chapter 4) which prohibits exclusion of liability for death or personal injury, and limits the exclusion of liability for other loss or damage, the Supply of Goods (Implied Terms) Act, 1973 (see Chapter 4) which limits exclusion clauses concerning the implied terms of the Sale of Goods Act, 1979, and the Consumer Credit Act, 1974 (see Chapter 5) under which the owner of goods cannot exclude the duties which he owes to the hirer under a hire-purchase agreement.

Quite apart from limitations imposed by Parliament, the courts have, over the years, shown themselves very eager to suppress exclusion clauses whenever they can find an excuse. The first line of attack will be to ascertain whether or not the type of breach which has occurred is one against which the guilty party is protected by the exclusion clause. Thus, for example, the garage proprietor who excludes liability for negligent damage to the car under repair will not be able to use the clause as a shield against legal action in respect of deliberate malicious damage by a mechanic. By virtue of what is called the *contra proferentum* rule, any ambiguity in wording will be interpreted strictly against the party seeking to rely on the exclusion clause.

However, there will be plenty of situations in which the exclusion clause has been too well drafted to succumb to this line of attack, and then the courts must find some other ground for refusing to uphold it. They may do so if it is contrary to public policy, or immoral, or illegal, and they may do so when the extent of the clause was misrepresented to the innocent party (see *Curtis* v. *Chemical Cleaning Co.*, p. 72). They may also refuse to allow C to obtain the benefit of an exclusion clause between A and B as in *Scruttons* v. *Midland Silicones*, above.

If none of these lines is available, the court may make use of what is called the 'repugnancy rule', and refuse to allow A to rely on an exclusion clause which is repugnant to (i.e. inconsistent with) the rest of the contract. Thus, if A is obliged to deliver a car, an exclusion clause which allows him to substitute a motor-cycle will, under this rule, be unenforceable. This rule, taken to its extreme, has broadened into what lawyers now call the 'fundamental breach doctrine'.

Under this so-called doctrine, the courts claim the right to refuse to implement any exclusion clause which protects a party from the consequences of performing his part of the contract in a manner fundamentally different from that agreed. But the validity of this approach was questioned in the recent case of *Photo Productions* v. *Securicor* (1980), in which a night security guard supplied by S under contract to P deliberately damaged the factory by fire. S relied on the strict wording of an exclusion clause, which could have covered deliberate damage by one of their own employees, and the House of Lords upheld the clause. In the light of rulings such as this from the highest court in the land, it is difficult to see how one may claim that despite exemption clauses one must still fulfil the basic contract.

Discharge of contract

A contract is 'discharged' when it comes to an end. This may arise in one of the following ways.

Performance

A contract is discharged whenever both parties have performed their obligations to the full; if either or both of the parties have not done this, then there has been a breach of contract, and the other party may sue. This apparently simple principle is deceptively so.

For a start, there are circumstances (such as instalment contracts), in which A becomes obliged to pay B even though B has only partly performed his part of the bargain; likewise, A normally only has to pay a proportionate amount of the price at that stage. Secondly, A may have 'accepted' partial performance by B in circumstances in which he had a free choice, in which case he will be required to pay on a *quantum meruit* ('how much is it worth?') basis.

Again, the court may rule that B has performed substantially what he undertook to perform, and that no reasonable man could expect any more, even though the strict letter and last syllable of the contract have not been fulfilled. In such cases, B will received the full contract price, less the amount required to complete the contract fully. Also, B will be entitled to a *quantum meruit* payment where he has been prevented from completing the contract by some action on A's part.

These exceptions apart, the courts are frequently asked to decide whether or not one or both of the parties have performed their obligations, and a variety of factors will be taken into consideration.

So far as the performance of an act is concerned, we have already seen that a *quantum meruit* payment may in some circumstances be awarded for performance of less than was due. Before full payment may be claimed, the act must have been fully performed. As will be seen in Chapter 4, this rule is applied particularly strictly in the case of the Sale of Goods. But once goods of the specified quality and in the specified quantity are 'tendered' (i.e. offered for delivery) by A, he is free of further liability if B unreasonably refuses to accept them.

So far as *payment of money* is concerned, this must normally be payment of the full amount due, and it must normally be made by the party due to make payment, or his agent. Payment by cheque is conditional on the cheque being honoured, and if payment is made by post without such method being stipulated by the creditor, the risk of loss lies with the sender.

Instead of actual payment, the courts will recognize the validity of 'tender' of payment; where for some reason the creditor has refused payment, the debtor is absolved from further liability if he has tendered it in accordance with the rules of tender. These rules are that it must be made on time, and that it must be made in 'legal tender' (i.e. Bank of England notes of any amount, 50p pieces up to £10, silver or cupronickel up to £5 and decimal bronze coins up to 20p).

The *time of performance* can be crucial, depending on the circumstances. As a general rule, failure to perform or pay on time will only be a breach of 'warranty' (see above) and will not bring the contract to an end. But in some cases, the parties may make it a condition of the contract that performance by one or both of the parties shall be made by a certain time. The usual way in which this is done is to stipulate that time shall be 'of the essence' of the contract; if, in such cases, one of the parties fails to perform or pay by that date, the contract will be at an end because there has been a 'material breach' (i.e. a breach of a condition). Where time is not 'of the essence', performance or payment must be within a reasonable time of the date fixed, or the completion of the contract.

Agreement

It is, of course, always open to the parties to agree that the contract shall come to an end before it has been fully completed. If it has not even been started, then the law refers to it as an 'executory' contract, and it may be terminated by the simple agreement of the parties. This agreement is in itself a binding contract since each party is giving something of value (i.e. giving up the right to demand performance from the other party), and it cancels out the original contract.

The potential problems begin when the contract has been only part-performed, particularly if this performance has been by one party only. This is known as a 'partly executed' contract, and before it may be discharged, the other party (i.e. the one who has done nothing) must either receive a discharge *under seal* from the performing party or provide 'satisfaction' (i.e. some form of consideration to compensate the performing party). This must be something new, to which the other party was not entitled, and this, together with the agreement to discharge, is known as 'accord and satisfaction'.

An alternative way of discharging a partly performed contract is by 'novation' (i.e. a completely new contract to replace the existing one). Alternatively, the contract itself may contain terms and conditions which bring it to an end upon the occurrence of a certain event. The classic example used to be the period of notice required to terminate a contract of employment, but this is now subject to the laws of unfair dismissal, which apply even if the strict letter of a contract of employment has been complied with. Perhaps the clearest example today is that of a hirer to terminate a hire-purchase contract at will (see Chapter 5).

An agreement to discharge a contract may normally take any form, regardless of the form (e.g. oral or written) of the original contract.

Frustration

A 'frustrating' event is one which occurs between the contract being agreed and it being completed, which is the fault of neither party, but which renders the contract incapable of performance in its originally intended form. The effect is to discharge both parties from any further obligations under the contract, without any liability being incurred towards the other party. The classic example, and indeed the case which first established the doctrine, was *Taylor* v. *Caldwell* (1863), in which it was held that a contract for the hire of a concert hall was 'frustrated' by a fire which burned it to the ground a few days before the hire was to take effect.

The destruction of what may be termed the 'subject matter' of the contract is a clear example of frustration, and similarly, the ill-health of a vital employee or contractor has been held to have the same effect; thus in *Condor* v. *The Barron Knights* (1966), it was held that the contract of a drummer with a busy pop group was frustrated when for medical reasons he was only able to perform on four nights of the week.

If a contract depends for its existence upon the occurrence of some external event (e.g. a coach hired to take supporters to a sports fixture), then that contract may be frustrated when the event fails to occur, provided that the other party was aware of the purpose which underlay the contract, and the external event was the sole basis of the contract. This explains why in *Krell* v. *Henry* (1903), the hire of a room overlooking the scene of a coronation procession was held to be frustrated by the cancellation of the coronation itself, whereas in *Herne*

Bay Steamboat Co. v. *Hutton* (1903), the cancellation of the same coronation review of the fleet at anchor did not frustrate the hire of a steamship where only part of the hire involved the naval review, and the remainder involved a trip around the bay.

A contract will also be frustrated if it becomes illegal (NB If it was illegal to start with, it is void, as explained above), or it is prohibited by government intervention. This will include action by a foreign government which renders it impossible to continue (see the case of *BP Exploration Company* v. *Hunt*, p. 116). A contract can also become frustrated if its commercial purpose is defeated (e.g. the departure of a chartered vessel is delayed for several weeks).

There are a number of conditions to be satisfied before the courts will hold that a contract has indeed been frustrated, not the least of which is that the event must be such as to fundamentally change the nature of the contract. It will not be sufficient simply to show that events have made the contract more onerous to one of the parties; In *Davis Contractors* v. *Fareham UDC* (1956), for example, the courts refused to regard as frustrated a contract for the erection of seventy-eight council houses over an eight-month period simply because an unforeseen labour shortage made the contract uneconomic.

Nor will it constitute frustration where the event in question is self-induced. Thus, in *Taylor* v. *Caldwell*, see p. 114, had the theatre burned down through the negligence of the management, they would have been liable for damages for breach of contract in the normal way, while the actor or singer who pleads ill-health as a frustrating event in a theatrical contract will meet with little sympathy if the illness has been brought on by riotous living. Nor, finally, will frustration apply when the parties themselves have made provision in the contract for just the sort of eventuality which occurs.

The practical consequences of frustration are dealt with under the Law Reform (Frustrated Contracts) Act, 1943, which provides that following the frustration of a contract, all sums of money paid or payable under the contract are either recoverable or not payable, that either party may recover his expenses from the other to cover events up to the frustrating event, and that any party benefiting from the partial performance of the other must pay him such sums of money as the court shall deem reasonable.

A fairly spectacular recent example of this last provision was the 1979 case of *BP Exploration Company* v. *Hunt*, in which BP entered into an exploration deal with H in the Libyan desert, spent millions of pounds in furtherance of the agreement, and were evicted from the site by the Libyan government before they had received even one third of the oil to which they were entitled. The court had little difficulty in ruling that the contract had been frustrated, but added that in all these cases, the award given to the plaintiff for services rendered may never exceed the actual benefit accruing to the other party as a result. This benefit is to be measured at the date of the frustration, with no account taken of the 'time value of money'. And the expenses to which the benefiting party has been put may be deducted as well! Even so, BP were awarded over £5½ million, with interest, which will normally run from the date of the frustrating event.

Breach

The point has already been made (see 'The Terms of the Contract' p. 105), that where one party, A, is in breach of a condition of a contract, the other party, B, may if he wishes regard the contract as being at an end. In other words, the breach of a condition discharges the contract at the option of the injured party. The injured party is also absolved from any obligation of performance on his part, if he chooses to treat the breach as discharging the contract. The greatest difficulty is often experienced in determining whether or not the particular breach is sufficiently serious for it to constitute a breach of condition.

The breach by A will normally take the form of a failure to perform the particular undertaking by the appointed day; alternatively, it may take the form of his simply making it impossible for the contract to be performed (e.g. selling goods to C which he had undertaken to hire out to B). It is also possible that the breach takes the form of an 'anticipatory breach', in which A indicates well in advance of the day due for performance that he has no intention of performing his obligations under the contract.

In such cases, the injured party, B, has a choice. He may, if he wishes, treat the contract as breached there and then, before the performance date, and sue for the damages then due, or may wait for the final date for performance, and sue for the extra damages which may well have accrued. This is what happened in *White and Carter (Councils) Ltd* v. *McGregor* (1961), in which a garage proprietor cancelled, on the same day that he had ordered, a series of advertisements on litter bins for a three-year period. The contractor displayed the advertising for the full three-year period in full knowledge of the declared breach, and was allowed to recover the full charge for three years of advertising when the defendant failed to pay.

This can backfire, as was discovered by the plaintiff in *Avery* v. *Bowden* (1855), in which the owners of a ship chose to wait after a hirer had announced in advance that he could not get a cargo, and would not require the ship. Within the hiring period the port was closed by the outbreak of the Crimean war, a frustrating event which absolved the hirer from finding a cargo.

Remedies for breach of contract

Time limit on actions

Under the Limitation Act, 1939, no action based upon a breach of contract may normally be brought after six years have expired since the date upon which the cause of action arose; the time limit is twelve years for contracts under seal. In cases involving personal injuries, the time is reduced to three years.

Where the plaintiff is of unsound mind, or is a minor, the

six- and twelve-year periods do not begin to run unless and until the disability ceases, although once the period has started to run, no intervening disability will stop it. If the cause of action involves fraud, or has been concealed by fraud, or is based upon a mistake, the period will not run until the plaintiff ought reasonably to have discovered the truth.

Even though the 'limitation period', as it is called, may have expired (i.e. it is said to be 'time barred'), the cause of action, where it involves a debt, may be revived by either an acknowledgement in writing, signed by the debtor to the creditor, or by a part-payment clearly referable to the original obligation (e.g. 'payment on account').

Damages

Every breach of contract entitles the injured party to damages, to compensate him for his loss. It follows that if there is no loss, there will be no damages other than 'nominal' damages to reflect the fact that a contract has been broken. The purpose of damages is not to penalize or punish the defaulting party, although occasionally his conduct may be so outrageous that the court expresses its disgust by awarding 'exemplary' damages. Damages are awardable in respect of mental distress (e.g. a spoiled holiday), and the general aim of the courts is to put the injured party back where he started, in so far as this is possible by financial means.

But before he may claim *any* damages, the plaintiff must be able to show that the loss which he suffered was the direct consequence of the breach by the defendant, and was not too 'remote' from it. This usually amounts to a question of how *foreseeable* a particular form of loss was, given the facts known to the defendant at the time, and in *Victoria Laundry* v. *Newman Industries* (1949), it was held that the seller who was late in delivering a new boiler to a laundry, while he was liable to compensate the owner for loss of profits arising from the use of the new boiler, was not liable for the loss on a special form of dyeing contract which unknown to him would have yielded exceptional profits.

Once the type of loss is foreseeable by the defendant, he will be liable for the full extent of it, even if it turns out to be much greater than expected. At the same time, the plaintiff is expected to take reasonable steps to 'mitigate' (i.e. minimize) his loss.

Since damages are not intended to be a punishment to the defendant, the courts will not enforce so-called 'penalty clauses' in contracts, which provide that a defaulting party shall pay a sum of money to the plaintiff should he default; in such cases, the plaintiff is not bound by the sum specified in the contract, but may sue for the actual loss. The courts will, however, enforce a 'liquidated damages' clause, which may be defined as the 'genuine pre-estimate of the probable loss which would be suffered following a breach', and which will prevail whatever the actual loss may have been. It is often very difficult to distinguish between the two.

In the case of the sale of goods, the normal method used to determine the actual *quantum* (amount) of damages is to take the difference between the contract price and the ruling market price at the date of the breach. If there is no ready market for the goods, an independent valuation will be commissioned, while in the case of services performed or part-performed, the plaintiff may recover a *quantum meruit* payment.

Specific performance

Sometimes, instead of receiving damages for a breach, the aggrieved party is more interested in getting the contract actually performed, and in the exercise of its equitable discretion, the court will order the defendant to actually perform the contract by means of a decree for 'specific performance' (known in Scotland as 'specific implement').

A typical example would be the sale of a valuable and unique collector's item, or the completion of the sale of a house; in both cases, the buyer wants the contract fulfilled rather than mere compensation, which could not be adequately measured anyway. But specific performance will not be awarded in the case of a contract for personal services (e.g. a contract of employment), where it would be necessary for the court to constantly supervise the working of the contract, where it would cause undue hardship for the defendant, or where the contract would not be enforceable if applied to the plaintiff (e.g. because he is a minor). Needless to say, nor will it be awarded where damages would be adequate as a remedy.

Injunction

An injunction (in Scotland, an 'interdict') is a court order prohibiting the party to whom it is addressed from doing something, e.g. breaking a contract. Like specific performance, it is a discretionary remedy which is normally only awarded where damages would be inadequate as a remedy. Disobedience to either order is a contempt of court.

We have already noted one context in which injunctions are used in connection with contracts, namely to prevent the breach of a 'restrictive covenant'. But an injunction may not be used as an indirect method of enforcing a contract (e.g. of employment) which could not be enforced by specific performance, as in *Page One Records Ltd* v. *Britton* (1967), in which the manager of the pop group the Troggs failed in his attempt to obtain an injunction prohibiting the group from employing anyone else as their manager, since this was in effect a request for enforcement of the original contract.

4 Selling the product

The law relating to sales of goods is a classic illustration of the historical development of business law outlined in Chapter 1. By 1893, there was a mass of 'case law' which had been created by the courts to deal with the frequent problems which arose over contracts for the sale of commodities, and not just the exotic ones such as spices, sugar and cotton, but the more mundane soap, leather and iron. The late nineteenth century hosted a movement towards the codification of mercantile law, and the Sale of Goods Act, 1893, one of the most comprehensive and workable pieces of legislation in the history of English Law, served the business community well for eighty years.

Its main drawback was that it assumed equality of bargaining power, and was really designed for use by merchants and shopkeepers. In particular, the 'implied' terms which were aimed at the protection of the purchaser could be avoided by the simple expedient of the exclusion clause contained in the standard-form contract. This would not do in the post-war world of 'consumerism', and the Supply of Goods (Implied Terms) Act, 1973, set out to prevent sellers from excluding the effect of the implied terms of the 1893 Act, while the Unfair Contract Terms Act of 1977 hit out generally at 'unreasonable' exclusion clauses in contracts with 'consumers'.

Things were getting untidy again, and so, with effect from 1 January 1980, the law was recodified under the Sale of Goods Act, 1979 ('the Act'). It is a tribute to the Victorian draftsman that so much of his original phrasing remains.

Sale of goods defined

The phrase 'sale of goods' covers, with total impartiality, transactions as diverse in formality and commercial importance as the sale of a morning newspaper from a news-stand and the placing of an order by a national government for twenty jet fighters. If they are covered by English (or Scots) law, then they are covered by the Act as if they were identical transactions.

Section 2(1) of the Act defines a contract of sale of goods as 'a contract by which the seller transfers or agrees to transfer the property in goods to the buyer for a money consideration, called the price'. There are clearly several points here which require clarification.

First of all, 'property' in this context is used to denote, not the goods themselves, but the 'title' or 'ownership' of them. What is being transferred in a sale of goods is therefore the *ownership* of the goods themselves. The *timing* of this transfer can also be important, for a variety of reasons which will emerge later in the chapter, and s. 2(4) reserves the term 'sale' for those transactions in which the ownership of the goods is being transferred immediately (as, for example, when one buys a newspaper from a news-stand). Where the ownership is not to be transferred until later (for example where a customer pays in advance for goods to be delivered in a week's time), the transaction is referred to in s. 2(5) as an 'agreement to sell'. Both types of agreement are somewhat confusingly 'sales' in the eyes of the law, as can be seen from the definition of 'sale' given above.

The definition of 'goods' is a complex one, but it includes all those items which a laymen would regard as 'goods', and naturally enough excludes items such as land and buildings. Items such as trees and minerals, which may be 'severed' from the land, may be the subject of a contract of sale. Money and cheques are not 'goods', unless they are being acquired as *objects* (e.g. of historical interest).

There cannot be a sale of goods unless there is a 'price' which is expressed in terms of money. This serves to distinguish sales of goods from free gifts, from mortgages, from hire and from 'barter' (i.e. the exchange of goods for goods). The fact that a contract involves a part-exchange arrangement will not, however, prevent it being a 'sale', as was shown in *Dawson* v. *Dutfield* (1936), in which it was held that it was still a 'sale' when the £475 price of two lorries was to be paid by means of £225 in cash, and £250 in the form of 'trade-in' lorries.

The price may be fixed in the contract, or may be left to be fixed in a manner agreed under the contract, may be determined by the course of dealing between the parties, or may be a 'reasonable price' imposed by the court. If, however, the parties agree that a third party shall value the items, and he fails to do so, the contract is void and the court may not intervene, except to fix a 'reasonable price' for those goods which have been delivered to and accepted by the buyer. And whereas 'deposits' are forfeited in the event of a breakdown in the contract, 'part payments' are returnable.

Two other matters should be noted before proceeding further. The first is that contracts of sale may take any form, even oral, or by implication from the actions of the parties (e.g. the silent exchange of money for a newspaper). Secondly, the question of the 'capacity' of a particular party to make a contract (see Chapter 3) is the same as for other contracts, except that, as already noted, s. 3 of the Act requires minors, drunks and persons of unsound mind to pay a 'reasonable price' for 'necessaries' sold and delivered to them even though they are otherwise incapable of making binding contracts.

The transfer of the property

The declared purpose of a contract for the sale of goods is the transfer of the property in goods, and it is therefore logical that we should examine this process in detail first.

The point has already been made that the moment of transfer of the property in the goods marks the transition from a mere 'agreement to sell' to a full 'sale'. Since what is being transferred is in fact the ownership of the goods, it would be logical and convenient if property simply passed along with physical possession. In other words, that the physical transfer of the goods should be the moment of 'the transfer of the property'.

Not even the old Common Law would recognize this as being the case, and the passing of the 1893 Act was taken as an opportunity of putting the point beyond doubt – ownership and possession do not necessarily pass together. Sections 16-19 of the Act in fact contain certain rules for determining when the property in goods has passed, but before we may consider these, there is one further distinction to be made, namely that between specific and unascertained goods.

'Specific' goods are defined as 'goods identified and agreed upon at the time a contract of sale is made'; in short, the item has been individually selected, and it is 'that car', or 'that book', or 'that hi-fi'. When a customer hands a shopkeeper a particular tin of beans, he has made the goods 'specific'. 'Unascertained' goods, on the other hand, are goods which have not yet become specific; for example, the customer has simply ordered 'two pounds of potatoes', or 'a copy of that record' without specifying which two pounds or which copy.

Making use of this important distinction, we may now appreciate the rules concerning the passing of property. First of all, s. 16 of the Act states quite firmly that the property in goods may never pass unless and until those goods are specific. Section 17 goes on to state, first of all, that when the goods are specific, then the property in them may pass at such time as the parties intend that it shall pass – in other words, that the parties may make their own arrangements if they wish, or their intentions may be inferred from their actions.

Section 17 then, somewhat illogically, lays down guidelines for 'ascertaining the intentions of the parties as to the time at which the property in the goods is to pass to the buyer', which will of course only be resorted to where the parties have not expressly stated when the property shall pass. These appear in the form of 'Rules' as follows (s. 18).

Rule 1. If the sale is unconditional, and the goods are ready to be delivered, then the property passes to the buyer as soon as the contract is made. This will be the case whether payment has been made or not, and whether or not there is physical delivery to the buyer. Thus, in *Dennart* v. *Skinner* (1948), it was held that in an auction, a van which was 'knocked down' to the purchaser became his as soon as the auctioneer's hammer fell.

This rule can have serious consequences, as will be seen below, when the question of the passing of the *risk of destruction* is considered.

Rule 2. Where some action is required from the seller to make the goods 'deliverable', the property will not pass until this has been done, and the buyer informed.

Rule 3. Where the goods are in a deliverable state, and are specific, but still require to be weighed, measured or otherwise tested by the seller for the purpose of pricing, then the property does not pass until this has been done, and the buyer notified.

Rule 4. Where goods are sent to the buyer 'on approval' or on a 'sale or return' basis, or some similar arrangement, then the property passes to the buyer when he signifies his acceptance of it in some way, or retains it beyond the time period agreed, or beyond a 'reasonable' time where no such period has been agreed.

Under this rule, the property will pass if the buyer does something which makes it unlikely or impossible that he will be able to return the goods (e.g. he resells them). In *Poole* v. *Smith's Car Sales (Balham) Ltd* (1962), P left his car with S on sale or return terms in August. After repeated requests, he got it back in November in a damaged state after it had been used by one of S's staff for private purposes. It was held that the 'reasonable time' had run out and that the property had passed to S under s. 18, Rule 4.

These four rules, then, deal with the *implied* passing of the property in specific goods in the absence of any stipulation to the contrary by the parties. Section 18 has a fifth rule, which in effect determines when the property passes in specific goods which have been 'carved out' of a larger consignment.

The rule is that the property passes whenever goods of the description requested by the buyer, in a deliverable state, are allocated to the buyer unconditionally either by the seller with the consent of the buyer, or the buyer with the consent of the seller. This may happen, for example, when the goods are handed to an independent carrier for delivery, or where materials are absorbed into a long and lengthy contract (e.g. the building of a house or a ship).

Even where there is a contract for the sale of specific goods, it is open to the seller to reserve the right of disposal until certain conditions are fulfilled (e.g. the buyer has paid for them); the effect of s. 19 of the Act is that the property does not pass until these conditions are fulfilled. The sellers in *Aluminium Industrie Vaassen BV* v. *Romalpa Aluminium Ltd* (1976), went one better and imposed a clause in a contract of sale under which the property in the goods was only to pass when the buyers paid for it, but that the 'risk' was to pass to the buyers as soon as the property was physically transferred. This is perfectly permissible since, in terms of s. 17 of the Act, the property in the goods may pass whenever the parties intend it to pass; in this case, the seller was able to repossess unpaid-for goods from under the nose of a receiver appointed to wind up the company.

The question of the transfer of the property in goods is far from academic, because as a general rule the 'risk of loss' passes with the property. This arrangement may, of course, be varied by agreement (as in the *Romalpa* case above), and it applies regardless of whose possession the goods may actually be in at the time. The other exceptions to the general rule are where the delivery has been delayed (in which case the risk lies with the party at fault), and where one of the parties is acting as 'bailee' or 'custodier' of the goods (in which case he is under a duty to take reasonable care of them).

The title to goods

Section 12(1) of the Act states that in a contract of *sale*, there is an implied condition that the seller has a right to sell the goods, and that in an *agreement to sell*, there is an implied condition that he will have a right to sell the goods at the time when the property is to pass. Since this is a condition, its breach entitles the buyer to regard the contract as at an end if he so wishes.

At the same time, s. 12(2) of the Act creates an implied *warranty* under which the seller is guaranteeing to the buyer that the goods are free (and will remain free at the time when the property is to pass), from any charge or encumbrance not disclosed or known to the buyer before the contract is made, and also that the buyer will enjoy quiet possession of the goods except to the extent of any charge or encumbrance disclosed or known to him. Since it is only a warranty, the breach of s. 12(2) will entitle the buyer only to damages, and not to the right to rescind the entire contract. See Chapter 3 for a fuller account of the distinction between conditions and warranties.

In short, when the buyer buys goods, he is entitled, in the absence of any express term in the contract notifying him of a limitation in the title he is receiving, to assume that he is buying a free and unchallengeable title to the goods, and that he will be able to use them without hindrance or challenge. Under s. 12(3), where the seller is only purporting to transfer a *limited* title in the first place, then the rest of s. 12 applies subject to that limitation, provided that all charges and encumbrances known to the seller have been communicated to the buyer.

By virtue of the Unfair Contract Terms Act, it is impossible for a seller to exempt himself from the provisions of s. 12 of the Act, whether or not the buyer is a 'consumer', and whether or not the exemption is contained in a written contractual term. The law simply will not allow sellers to sell items which they do not fully own, and pocket the money with impunity.

The most obvious situation covered by s. 12 is, of course, that in which the seller transfers goods which he does not have the authority to transfer, either because he does not own them himself, or because he does not have the authority of the owner. He may do so innocently, or he may be a 'con man', but either way, if he purports to sell goods to which he does not have a valid title, he contravenes s. 12(1) and the buyer may rescind the contract. This is true even if he has made some use of the goods, and in *Rowland* v. *Divall* (1923), the buyer was able to recover the full purchase price, even though he had used the car in question – which turned out to have been stolen – for three months, and so in effect he received a free use of it for that period.

Section 12(2) covers the situation in which, although there is nothing wrong with the buyer's title to the goods (i.e. they are indisputably his), there is some impediment to his 'quiet possession' or full use of them. Since he has at least got the legal title to them, there has not been a total failure of 'consideration' (see Chapter 3), and the buyer will only receive damages in recompense. A good modern illustration of s. 12(2) in action is *Microbeads* v. *Vinhurst Road Markings* (1975), in which M bought from V certain road marking machines; several months later, a rival manufacturer secured a patent over that type of machine which he was able to enforce against anyone not licensed by him, i.e. M. This was a clear threat to M's 'quiet possession' of the goods, and they were granted damages for breach of warranty per s. 12(2).

Section 12 is all very well where the buyer is able to identify and locate the seller, and get damages from him, but in many cases, the seller is a seasoned rogue who is never seen again. There is a general rule in the law of sale of goods which is referred to by its Latin tag as the *nemo dat* rule (*nemo dat quod non habet* – 'no one can give away what he has not got') which states quite simply that only an owner can validly transfer the title to goods. In many cases, the courts are being asked to choose between the rival claims to goods of (a) the owner who was defrauded into parting with them, and (b), the innocent purchaser, who was induced to pay for them. The rogue has disappeared, and *someone* has to lose.

The general rule to be applied will be the *nemo dat* rule, and the title will remain with A, the original owner; B will simply have to hand the goods back and put it all down to experience. This general rule is now encapsulated in s. 21(1) of the Act, which states that 'where goods are sold by a person who is not their owner, and who does not sell them under the authority or with the consent of the owner, the buyer acquires no better title to the goods than the seller had, unless the owner of the goods is by his conduct precluded from denying the seller's authority to sell'.

The owner will be 'by his conduct precluded from denying the seller's authority to sell' in the following situations.

Agency

This topic was dealt with in Chapter 2, and it will be apparent from what was written there that if A authorizes B to sell his goods for him, he cannot later deny the validity of the sale to C, the purchaser. Reference back to Chapter 2 will remind the reader that agency may arise by 'estoppel', i.e. A may be precluded by his own words or actions from denying that B is his agent for a particular transaction. Thus, in *Eastern Distributors* v. *Goldring* (1957), M, the owner of a van who wished to raise a loan on it, devised a scheme with a car dealer whereby they would pretend that the dealer owned the van, and he would 'sell' it to an HP company (C) who would then hand it back to M on HP terms. It was subsequently held that C were the lawful owners of the van, since M, by his actions, was estopped from denying that the dealer had his authority to sell the van to C.

Factors

The mere fact that B is in possession of goods which belong to A does not, of itself, give him the right to pass a valid title to them; he must normally have A's express authority to do so, or A must be 'estopped' from denying B's authority, as was seen above. However, there are special rules in the case of 'factors' (a particular form of mercantile agent such as an auctioneer, broker or dealer), laid down under the Factors' Act, 1889, s. 2(1) as follows:

Where a mercantile agent is, with the consent of the owner, in possession of goods or of the documents of title to goods, any sale, pledge or other disposition of the goods, made by him while acting in the ordinary course of business of a mercantile agent, shall, subject to the provisions of this Act be as valid as if he were expressly authorized by the owner of the goods to make the same; provided that the person taking under the disposition takes in good faith, and has not at the time of the disposition notice that the person making the disposition has not authority to make the same.

Although the 'factor' must be in possession of the goods or the documents of title with the consent of the owner, and in his capacity as a *seller* (and not, for example, as a repairer or mere custodian), and must have been acting in the ordinary course of business when he sold the goods, it is still perfectly possible for the owner to have his goods sold behind his back and without permission. The most common example of the use of this section is that of the motor dealer who is left in possession of a customer's car with instructions not to sell below a certain price, who does in fact sell below that price. The 'log book' is not a document of title, and so the dealer must have possession of the car itself before the section will work; even then, the courts tend to take the view that a sale below the price demanded by the seller is not 'in the ordinary course of business' which is very harsh upon the innocent purchaser.

Market Overt

Section 22 of the Act, which applies only to England and Wales, states that when goods are sold in 'market overt', according to the usage of the market, to an innocent purchaser who has no knowledge of any defect in the title of the seller, then the sale is binding on the true owner even though he has not authorized it.

'Market overt' means a recognized market established by long standing, custom or royal charter, or under an Act of

Parliament. All shops in the City of London are regarded as markets overt on every day except Sunday.

Voidable title

Section 23 of the Act states that 'when the seller of goods has a voidable title to them, but his title has not been avoided at the time of the sale, the buyer acquires a good title to the goods, provided he buys them in good faith and without notice of the seller's defect of title'.

This really gives effect to the Common Law rule, examined more fully in Chapter 3, to the effect that where A has the right to rescind a contract with B, he loses that right once he resells to an innocent purchaser, C. This will happen, for example, where there has been a misrepresentation by B, but not where there has been a *mistake*, since this would render the contract *void*, and not even an innocent third party can obtain rights arising under a *void* title. The case of *Lewis* v. *Averay* dealt with in Chapter 3, illustrates the distinction perfectly.

Buyer or seller in possession

Section 24 of the Act states that where the seller (A), having sold the goods, remains in possession of either the goods themselves or the document of title to them, an innocent purchaser may acquire valid title from him if he receives from him either the goods or the documents of title thereto in good faith without notice of the rights of the original buyer.

In short, A, having 'sold' goods to B, can 'sell' them to C, D, E or any number of people, and the one who actually gains possession of the goods or the documents of title has the best legal title. As with the rules of market overt and factors, the philosophy behind the rule is that of protecting the innocent purchaser who cannot be expected to know whether A has the authority to sell the goods or not, and can only take matters at face value. B may sue A, but he cannot insist on getting the goods he bought. Thus, if A takes B's money in respect of a car in his showroom, and agrees to continue garaging it until B has fixed up the insurance, he may sell it to C five minutes later; if C drives away in it, it is his, and B can only sue A for damages.

By the same token, s. 25 of the Act allows the buyer, once he has obtained the possession of the goods or the documents of title with the consent of the seller, to sell them to an innocent third party and pass good title to them, even though the seller has not authorized him to do this. Thus, once A allows B to take the goods away under an agreement to purchase, B may validly sell them to C, even if he never pays A for them.

Section 25 will not cover a resale by a 'purchaser in possession' who has in fact taken under a sale or return agreement, or someone who is in possession under a hire purchase agreement, unless the goods take the form of a motor vehicle, in which case under the Hire Purchase Act, 1964, s. 27, an innocent private purchaser from a 'buyer in possession' gets a valid title to the vehicle even if it is subject to a hire-purchase agreement.

Nor will s. 25 cover goods held under a 'conditional sale agreement' which is a 'consumer credit agreement' under the Consumer Credit Act, 1974 (see Chapter 5), apart from under the exception provided by the 1964 Act in relation to cars.

The description of the goods

As will be seen in Chapter 5, the seller who misdescribes his goods may well be committing a criminal offence under the Trade Descriptions Act, 1968. But quite apart from that, he may also entitle the buyer to rescind the entire contract, since s. 13 of the Act states that whenever there is a sale of goods 'by description' there is an implied condition in the contract that the goods must comply with that description; also, if the sale is by sample, both the sample and the bulk of the goods must comply with the description.

There will clearly be a 'sale by description' when the buyer has not seen the goods, and is relying on the description applied by the seller (e.g. in a catalogue), but there will equally be a sale by description when the goods describe themselves by their very appearance. Thus, in *Grant* v. *Australian Knitting Mills* (1936), it was held that a piece of woollen underwear sold across a shop counter was a 'sale by description'.

Even where the buyer has seen the goods for himself, and had a chance of examining them, and in fact selects an item for himself, this will still not prevent the sale being one by 'description'. This is specifically stated in s. 13(3) of the Act, and is well illustrated by the facts of *Beale* v. *Taylor* (1967), in which a buyer examined a car described as a 1961 Triumph Herald. It later transpired that only the rear half of the car was a 1961 model, the front half being an earlier model which had been welded to it. It was held that the sale had been by 'description' even though the buyer had examined the car, and that therefore there had been a breach of s. 13.

The quality of the goods

Section 14 of the Act begins by stating that as a general rule, in a contract of sale, there is no implied condition or warranty concerning the quality of the goods, or their fitness for any particular purpose. The section then goes on to lay down two implied conditions by way of exception to this general rule, the first dealing with quality, the second with fitness for purpose!

Merchantable Quality

By virtue of s. 14(2), a person who sells goods in the course of a business does so, in the absence of a clear contractual term to the contrary, subject to an implied condition that the goods are of 'merchantable quality'; this will not cover defects specifically brought to the buyer's attention beforehand, or which ought to have been revealed when and if the buyer examined the goods prior to making the contract. If the goods are not of 'merchantable quality' when they should be, the buyer may either rescind the contract or settle for damages.

It will have been noted that those who are bound by s. 14(2) are those who sell goods in the course of a 'business'; there are thus no implied conditions as to merchantable quality in 'private sales' (e.g. of a family car), but government departments and local authorities are classed as businesses for the purposes of s. 14.

'Merchantable quality' is defined by s. 14(6) of the Act so as to include goods which are 'as fit for the purpose or purposes for which goods of that kind are commonly bought as it is reasonable to expect having regard to any description applied to them, the price (if relevant) and all the other relevant circumstances'. This definition is notoriously vague, and has given the courts a good deal of difficulty, but it would seem that goods are merchantable if they are fit for one of their ordinary uses (and one only). Even then, the test of merchantability is a flexible one in terms of price, age, and so on, and the court will expect a second-hand, five-year-old car to be less merchantable than a brand new one.

A good example of the principle in practice was *Brown* v. *Craiks* (1970), in which a buyer bought some industrial fabric which he then found to be unsuitable for making into dresses, although it was suitable for other purposes, and could be sold for those purposes at a slightly lower price. It was held to be of merchantable quality because it was saleable without any substantial reduction in price.

If, in fact, the buyer wishes the goods for some specific purpose, then his remedy may well lie under the next subsection.

Fitness for purpose

Section 14(3) of the Act states that where the seller sells goods in the course of a business, and the buyer, either expressly or by implication, makes known either to the seller or to his agent the particular purpose for which the goods are required, then there is an implied condition in the contract of sale that the goods are reasonably fit for that purpose. This is so even if the goods are not normally supplied for that purpose, unless the facts suggest that the buyer was not relying on the seller's skill and judgement. The definition of 'business' is the same as in s. 14(2).

Where goods only have one normal use, then their mere display for sale is an automatic undertaking by the seller, that they are fit for that use, without any words passing between buyer and seller. If, for example, I buy a hot-water bottle, I am entitled to assume that it will not burst in bed when full of hot water (*Priest* v. *Last*, 1903), if I buy underwear, I may assume that it is fit to wear next to the skin (*Grant* v. *The Australian Knitting Mills*, 1936), and if I buy milk, I may assume that it is fit for human consumption (*Frost* v. *Aylesbury Dairies*, 1905).

Where, however, the goods have more than one normal use, or they are required for some unusual purpose, or by some abnormal purchaser, the special circumstances or use must be made known to the seller specifically, and he must give an assurance that the goods are fit for this special purpose, before s. 14(3) will apply; this assurance may, of course, be implied from his actions in handing over the goods and taking the money. In *Griffiths* v. *Peter Conway* (1939), for example, it was held that a woman who purchased a tweed coat and contracted dermatitis from wearing it, whereas a person with a normal skin would not have done so, could not hold the seller liable under s. 14(3) because she had not made her special condition known to him.

It will be noted that the goods need only be reasonably fit, and the courts are entitled to take all the circumstances into account so that, for example, one would expect less from a second-hand item than from a new one. But even then, the seller must comply with certain basic standards, and in *Crowther* v. *Shannon* (1975), it was held that the seller was liable under s. 14(3) when a Jaguar car with 82,000 miles on the clock sold for £390, suffered a total engine seizure after just over three weeks and 2,300 miles.

Sales by sample

Section 15 of the Act states that where there is a sale of goods by sample, there is an implied condition in the contract that the bulk will correspond to the sample in quality, that the buyer will have a reasonable opportunity of comparing the bulk with the sample, and that the goods will be free from any defect rendering them unmerchantable which would not be apparent upon reasonable examination of the sample.

Before there can be a 'sale by sample', there must be an express or implied term to that effect in the contract, and if the contract is a written one, this term must also normally be written. 'Unmerchantable' is defined as in s. 14(2).

A good illustration of the interrelation of sections 14 and 15 is provided by *Godley* v. *Perry* (1960), in which G, a six-year-old boy, bought a catapult from P, a local shopkeeper. It broke upon use, and G lost his left eye. It was held that P had supplied a catapult which was sold by description, but which was not merchantable and was not reasonably fit for the purpose for which it was supplied, and concerning which G had relied upon P's skill and judgement. But since P had bought the catapult as part of a consignment, and since the consignment had been tested by pulling the elastic on the sample catapult, the wholesalers who had supplied P were liable to him under s. 15 of the Act. Thus, both P *and* G were entitled to damages from their respective sellers.

Exclusion of liability

We dealt in Chapter 3 with the general nature of the exclusion clause, and the legal rules which govern them. Until 1973, the greatest weakness in the Sale of Goods Act was that the implied terms laid down under ss. 12–15 might be simply circumvented by an exclusion clause. In other words, the seller included a clause in the contract to the effect that he was not to be bound by any of the implied terms imposed by those sections; since the sections only took effect in the absence of any stipulation to the contrary in the contract, this was perfectly feasible from a legal point of view.

The Supply of Goods (Implied Terms) Act, 1973, put a stop to this, and its provisions were later incorporated into the much wider Unfair Contract Terms Act, 1977. As we have seen above, this Act prohibits any term in the contract which purports to exempt the seller from the consequences of a breach of the implied undertaking as to title imposed by s. 12 of the Act. The Act's approach to ss. 13–15 is slightly different.

By virtue of s. 6 of the 1977 Act, it is impossible, legally, for the seller to exempt himself from the provisions of ss. 13–15 of the 1979 Act where the buyer 'deals as a consumer'. This phrase is defined elsewhere in the 1977 Act as describing a situation in which the buyer does not make the contract in the course of any business, and does not purport to do so, whereas the seller does make a contract in the course of a business and the goods are of a type ordinarily supplied for private use or consumption. A buyer cannot 'deal as a consumer' where the sale is by auction or competitive tender, but otherwise the burden of proof is on the seller to show that the buyer is not a consumer.

The 1977 Act goes on to list certain types of sale which will not be regarded as consumer sales whatever the circumstances. These include sales of goods in which the buyer will be re-selling to a wholesaler, retailer or distributor, sales for the purpose of some industrial process, and sales for the running of a business. It was held, however, in *Rasbora Ltd* v. *J.C.L. Marine Ltd* (1977) that it is still a 'consumer' contract where the purchaser is a company set up by a private individual in order to purchase an item for him for his own private use.

When the buyer does *not* deal as a consumer, then s. 6 of the 1977 Act states that the seller may only exempt himself from ss. 13–15 of the 1979 Act where he can show that the exclusion clause was a 'fair and reasonable one to be included having regard to the circumstances which were, or ought reasonably to have been, known to or in the contemplation of the parties when the contract was made'. The Act lays down guidelines as to what may or may not be considered 'reasonable', under which the court may have regard to the relative bargaining strengths of the parties, any 'inducement' given to the purchaser to accept the term, the means used to acquaint the purchaser with the existence of the term, and whether or not the goods were made to the buyer's specification.

Performance of the contract

So far as the details concerning the time and place of the delivery and the manner and timing of payment are concerned, the parties are free to negotiate such terms as they wish, which then become binding upon them in the same way as any other contractual term. If they do not make such provisions, then the 1979 Act will imply the following terms into their contract.

First and foremost, that the delivery of the goods and the payment of the price are to be concurrent conditions. In short, that the buyer will not receive the goods until he pays for them, and that the seller will not be paid until he delivers. At the very least, before the buyer may sue for non-delivery, he must show that he is ready and willing to pay (or has been offered credit facilities), while the seller may not sue for the price without showing that he is ready and willing to deliver.

Delivery by seller

'Delivery' may, in law, take several forms, such as handing over the goods, handing over a document of title, handing over a warehouse key, or instructing an independent carrier to transport the goods to the buyer. What is required in law is a 'voluntary transfer' from seller to buyer.

In the absence of any agreement to the contary, the place of delivery is the seller's place of business, or his home if he has no business premises. If the sale is of specific goods which are known to both parties to be in another place, then that other place is the place of delivery. In other words, it is for the buyer to collect the goods, and not for the seller to deliver them. If the seller does agree to deliver, then he must do so within a reasonable time.

So far as the timing of delivery generally is concerned, the 1979 Act presumes that time is not 'of the essence of' the contract (i.e. vital to its validity). The parties are, however, free to make it so, and an agreed delivery date in a commercial contract will normally be sufficient to make the validity of the contract dependent upon punctuality by the seller and allow the buyer to rescind the contract for late delivery. Alternatively, he may accept late delivery and simply sue for damages for the loss or inconvenience. Where there is no stipulation as to time, delivery must be within a reasonable time.

The Act is very specific concerning the seller's duty to deliver the correct quantity. Thus, if the seller delivers less than he contracted to sell, the buyer may reject the entire consignment or pay for what is delivered at the contract rate. If the seller over-delivers then the buyer may again reject the entire consignment if he so wishes, or simply accept what he ordered and reject the rest. As another alternative, he may accept the entire consignment at the contract rate. Finally, if the seller delivers goods of a different type it goes without saying that the buyer may reject them; alternatively, where the unordered goods are mixed in with the contract goods in the same consignment, the buyer may simply accept the goods which he ordered and reject the rest, or reject the entire consignment.

The courts will not concern themselves with trifling deviations from the original agreement, and in *Shipton, Anderson* v. *Weil Bros* (1912), the court refused to allow the buyer of 4,950 tons of wheat to reject the consignment where the seller in fact delivered 4,950 tons 55 lb!

In the absence of prior agreement, the buyer is not obliged to accept delivery by instalments, so that the seller may not make up for an initial short delivery by a second delivery. Where there is a contract specifying delivery by instalments, it will be a question of fact and interpretation whether or not each delivery must be paid for separately. If so, then rejection of one instalment does not preclude acceptance of a later one, and vice versa. But before a failure in one instalment may be used by the buyer as an excuse for rejecting the entire contract, it must be shown that the instalment in question was of vital importance to the entire contract, or that there is a likelihood of a repetition of the default.

If the buyer agrees that the seller may make delivery by independent carrier, then the delivery by the seller to the carrier is deemed to be the equivalent of delivery to the buyer, provided that he has made the best contract which was reasonably possible with the carrier on the buyer's behalf. Even when the seller agrees to deliver at his own risk, the buyer will normally, in the absence of specific agreement, run the risk of accidental loss or damage, or deterioration in transit.

Acceptance by buyer

Once the seller has 'tendered' (i.e. offered) delivery, the buyer is under an implied obligation to accept and pay for the goods, once he has had a reasonable opportunity of examining them, to ensure that they comply with the contract. If he unreasonably refuses to accept delivery, he is liable in damages to the seller.

Once the buyer has accepted the goods, he is obliged to pay for them, so 'acceptance' is clearly an important process. It may consist of formal intimation of acceptance, allowing a 'reasonable time' to elapse after delivery without complaint, or the performance of some act which indicates that the buyer has accepted the goods as his (e.g. resale). Although the buyer has a right of examination, it must be exercised within reasonable time; however, even when the goods were bought in circumstances in which they could not be fully tested (e.g. deep freezers from a discount centre), the buyer is allowed a reasonable time period for 'home trial' before being deemed to have accepted the goods.

Where the buyer rejects the goods, he need only notify the seller of the rejection, and need not actually return the goods himself.

We may now look at the remedies available to the buyer and the seller when the other party fails to honour his obligations.

Rights of the seller

Where the buyer has defaulted (i.e. refused to accept delivery, or failed to make payment), there are two sets of remedies available to the seller, depending upon the precise circumstances. One set of remedies is against the buyer himself, and the second against the goods.

Remedies against the buyer

Where the buyer has actually accepted the goods, but simply refused or failed to pay for them, then the obvious remedy is for the seller to sue him for the price of the goods. Before he may do so, the buyer's failure or refusal to pay must have been wrongful in the sense that he has accepted the goods, and therefore has no complaint about their quality, etc. Clearly, the seller may not, in the absence of special agreement, sue for the price unless he has at least tendered delivery, and that delivery has been wrongfully rejected, nor may he sue for the money until any agreed period of credit has expired.

It is of course possible for the parties to agree that the price shall be payable on a certain day, regardless of whether or not delivery has been made, and whether or not 'the property in the goods' has passed to the buyer. In the absence of such an agreement, the property must actually have passed to the buyer before the seller may sue for the price (see above). In short, in the absence of special agreement, before the seller may sue for the price, the property must have passed to the buyer, and he must have accepted the goods, or at least refused valid tender of delivery.

A claim for the price may also, where the buyer has refused to accept the goods but the property has already passed under the terms of the contract, include damages for storage, inconvenience and additional loss caused by that refusal.

If the seller is unable to raise an action for the price because, e.g. the property in the goods has not passed (which will be the case where there is no special agreement and the buyer has simply refused to accept delivery), he may sue the buyer for damages for non-acceptance, where the refusal to accept has been 'wrongful' (see above). The 'measure' of damages will normally be the difference between the contract price and the market price at the date of the breach by the buyer. See Chapter 3 for further details on the assessment of damages.

Remedies against the goods themselves

The seller who in the eyes of the law is 'unpaid' has certain remedies against the goods which make up the subject matter of the contract. A seller will be regarded as 'unpaid' when the whole of the purchase price has been neither paid nor tendered, or a cheque or other negotiable instrument given in purported payment has been dishonoured. In such a situation, assuming that the property has not passed to the buyer, the seller may of course withhold delivery of the goods until he is paid, since delivery and payment are, in the absence of special agreement, 'concurrent' (see above).

Apart from this right to retain the goods, the unpaid seller also has the right of lien, stoppage *in transitu*, and resale, which may now be examined in more detail.

Right of lien
The seller has what is called a *right of lien* (i.e. a right to detain the goods, similar to the right of retention above) even though ownership of them has passed to the buyer under the contract, provided that he, the seller, has not yet parted with possession of the goods. This is another example of a situation in which possession and ownership are not concurrent, and this right of lien may be exercised by the seller whenever goods have been sold without any stipulation as to credit, or the credit period has expired, or the buyer has become insolvent.

The right of lien clearly cannot operate once the goods have been delivered to the buyer, and the seller will equally lose his right of lien if he delivers the goods to a carrier for transmission to the buyer without reserving a right of disposal, or if the buyer or his agent lawfully acquires possession of the goods, if the seller waives his lien, or if the documents of title come into the possession of a bona fide purchaser.

The lien extends only in security of the price of the goods themselves, and not to any other indebtedness of the buyer to the seller. But unless the contract is severable, the seller may retain any part of a full order in order to secure payment of the rest; where it is severable, each consignment, once paid for, belongs to the buyer, and cannot later be withheld in security for non-payment of another instalment.

The right of lien does not of itself include a right of resale, and the seller may well be liable to the buyer if he sells goods to someone else while he has them under his lien (see above).

Stoppage in transit

An unpaid seller, who has parted with physical possession of the goods, may nevertheless get them back by stopping them *in transitu*, if the goods are indeed in the course of transit and the buyer has become insolvent. The period during which goods are in transit is in effect the period between them being handed by the seller to an independent 'middle man' for transmission to the buyer and their being actually received by the buyer. Obviously, if the buyer collects them himself, it will not apply, while if the seller delivers them himself, he still has possession for the purposes of lien, and does not need rights of stoppage.

'Transit' ends when the buyer obtains delivery, or when the carrier acknowledges that he holds the goods for and on behalf of the buyer, or when the carrier wrongfully refuses to deliver the goods to the buyer. Even where there has been part delivery, the remainder may still be stopped in transit. The right of stoppage will also be lost where the documents of title to the goods come into the hands of a bona fide purchaser.

The actual stoppage is effected by the seller taking

repossession of the goods or giving notice of his claim to the carrier, who must comply with this request. The right is obviously exercised whenever the seller has not been paid, and is to place him in the position from which he started before parting with the goods. The sale itself is not rescinded, and the seller has no right to resell the goods simply because he has the right to stop them in transit.

Modern systems of finance such as bankers' confirmed credits and government backed export guarantees have rendered stoppage in transit somewhat academic, and it never did apply to the Post Office anyway.

Resale

The point has already been made that the mere existence of rights of lien and stoppage in transit do not of themselves give the seller the right to sell the goods to someone else. There is still a contract between A and B, and A cannot simply sell the goods to C, particularly since in many cases, actual ownership may have passed to B, although he does not yet have possession.

The seller may in fact resell the goods in the following circumstances:

1 Where the right of resale was expressly reserved in the original contract of sale itself; or
2 Where the goods are perishable; or
3 Where the seller notifies the buyer of his intention to resell and the latter does not pay or tender the price within a reasonable time thereafter.

In each of these cases, having resold the goods, the seller may claim damages from the defaulting buyer for any loss on resale; at the same time, he may keep any profit.

Even where the seller does not have a right of resale, he may pass a valid title to any innocent second purchaser (i.e. C in the example above), since he is normally the *seller in possession* (see above); even where he is not, s. 48 of the 1979 Act confers a good title to the goods upon C. B may of course sue A for breach of contract.

Rights of the buyer

The most obvious legal right available to a buyer whose seller has failed to deliver the goods which he has contracted to deliver (in the correct quantity, etc.) is an action for damages for non-delivery. If the seller has totally failed to make any delivery at all, the buyer can recover any payments he may have made. Alternatively, if the buyer is accepting part of the consignment but the remainder has not been delivered, or if the contract is a 'severable' one (see p. 143), he may secure the return of any part of the purchase price which relates to the rejected or undelivered part of the whole consignment.

In rare cases, the court will, instead of awarding damages to the buyer, order the seller to physically hand over the goods as he contracted to do (known as an order of 'specific performance', or, in Scotland, of 'specific implement'). This will only be done where damages for non-delivery would be inadequate, and the goods themselves are of special significance to the buyer (e.g. a family heirloom).

Where the seller is in breach of condition, of course, the buyer may rescind the entire contract, refuse to accept the goods and refuse to have anything more to do with the transaction. The buyer's right to reject goods which do not comply with the contract was noted above, and it need hardly be said that a failure to deliver at all within a reasonable time or the contract time will entitle the buyer to regard the contract as being at an end.

Even where there has been a breach of condition the buyer may, if he wishes, allow the contract to continue and simply sue for damages for the breach. Where there has been merely a breach of warranty, then suing for damages is all that the buyer may do, since he cannot rescind the contract.

5 Protecting the consumer

In this chapter, we shall be examining, in outline at least, some of the major provisions enacted in the past decade or so in an attempt to protect the consumer from some of the more serious dangers which he faces when purchasing goods or services.

Consumer credit

It is one of the clichés of modern life that it is all too easy for the weak and gullible to be seduced into credit agreements which they simply cannot afford. At the same time, the credit market has become particularly complex, with hire purchase, bank loans, credit cards, credit sale agreements, budget accounts and whole host of other forms of 'never-never' all too available.

In 1971, the Crowther Report on Consumer Credit recommended the simplification of consumer credit under one 'umbrella' definition, and the licensing and closer control of all businesses offering credit to the consumer. The Consumer Credit Act, 1974, was passed to implement those recommendations, and it is designed to come into force in stages; this section is written on the assumption that by the time it is read the 1974 Act will be in full force.

The Act covers all 'regulated agreements', which in turn consists of all 'consumer credit agreements' and 'consumer hire agreements' which are not exempt from the Act.

A 'consumer credit agreement' is one under which the 'creditor' (lender) provides the 'debtor' (borrower) with credit not exceeding £5,000. This credit may be either 'fixed sum' (e.g. a hire-purchase agreement) or 'running-account' (e.g. a bank overdraft or credit card system), but it will not include any interest or deposit – it is simply the amount which is credited to the debtor (roughly speaking, the capital sum advanced to him). The Act only applies where the debtor is an individual, partnership or unincorporated association such as a registered club. Typical consumer credit agreements are hire-purchase, credit sale agreements, bank loans and credit card agreements.

A 'consumer hire agreement' is any agreement for the straightforward hire of goods (i.e. not hire-purchase) which is capable of lasting for more than three months, and does not oblige the hirer to make payments exceeding £5,000. This means, in effect, that a hire agreement will not be covered by the Act if the first three months compulsory rental will amount to more than £5,000 (e.g. £2,000 per month), or the deposit will exceed £5,000. The person hiring the goods is known as the 'hirer', while the person hiring them out is the 'owner'.

Certain agreements are 'exempt' from the Act (even if they are consumer credit agreements or consumer hire agreements), in the sense that the courts have no control over them except in so far as they may be attacked as being 'extortionate'. The most important exempt agreements in practice are building society or local authority mortgages, running accounts with local tradesmen which are settled by a periodic single payment (e.g. the milkman's account), and credit card agreements which require the holder to settle each monthly account with a single payment.

The Director General of Fair Trading (DGFT) requires that every person wishing to conduct a non-exempt 'consumer credit business' or 'consumer hire business' (other than a local authority or a company operating under an Act of Parliament authorizing it to carry on such a business) must apply for and maintain a licence under the 1974 Act. The DGFT maintains a public register of licences.

Licences are issued for six categories (A–F) of business, and a licence is required for each category before business may be conducted in it (e.g. consumer *credit* is in category A while consumer *hire* is in category B). The 'standard' licence will be granted only to a named person in respect of the specified activities (so that, for example, each company within a group will require a separate licence), while the 'group' licence will cover associations of persons already controlled by a common authority (e.g. the Law Society).

The DGFT must be satisfied that the applicant for a licence is a fit and proper person to hold one, and it is an offence to carry on a business requiring a licence without having obtained one. Furthermore, any 'regulated agreement' (see above) made in such circumstances will be unenforceable against the debtor or hirer, unless the DGFT allows it to go ahead. The DGFT may suspend or revoke the licence of any licensee whose behaviour or activities fall below the requisite standard.

We may now examine in greater depth the two types of regulated agreement covered by the 1974 Act.

Consumer credit agreements

Definition
There are many types of transaction covered by the term consumer credit agreement, far more than may be examined in detail in a book of this length. We shall therefore concentrate on the three major types, which must first of all be distinguished from each other.

A 'hire-purchase agreement' is one under which the debtor agrees to hire the goods for a specified period from the creditor, at the end of which he may exercise an option to purchase the goods in return for further payment. It is not regarded in law as a sale of goods.

A 'conditional sale agreement' is one under which the buyer (debtor) takes immediate possession of the goods, but by virtue of which the 'property in' the goods will not transfer to him until some condition (normally the payment of the entire purchase price) has been fulfilled. A 'credit sale agreement', on the other hand, is one under which the buyer obtains both immediate possession and the 'property in' the goods at the very start of the agreement, but the obligation to pay the purchase price is deferred to a later date.

Only in the case of a credit sale agreement may the 'buyer in possession' pass a good title to an innocent third party when the original purchase price remains unpaid, unless the goods in question are a motor vehicle, and are sold to an innocent private purchaser, in which case even goods on hire purchase or under a conditional sale agreement may validly pass, even though the goods have not yet been paid for by the original buyer or hirer.

Formation

As a general rule, a consumer credit agreement is formed just like any other contract, and reference should be made to Chapter 3 for the detailed rules of offer and acceptance. But the Consumer Credit Act, 1974, has introduced special rules for consumer credit agreements, mainly for the protection of the debtor, and these may be summarized as follows. First of all, any dealer with whom the debtor is negotiating prior to making a consumer credit agreement of the type we are considering in this section is acting as agent for the eventual creditor in the agreement. Thus, for example, if A makes a hire-purchase agreement with a finance company, B, to buy a car currently owned by a motor dealer, C, C is B's agent during the course of the negotiations, so that any misrepresentation made by C will be enforceable against B (the creditor) and any deposit paid by A to B will be effective against C. This also means that the normal offer and acceptance rules, when applied in relation to C, apply simultaneously to B.

Either side may withdraw from a proposed consumer credit agreement before it is completed, and in practice the customer (A above) may withdraw simply by notifying either the prospective creditor or the dealer, or any credit broker or other agent employed by the customer. The normal Common Law rules concerning withdrawal of offer apply (see Chapter 3). The customer, once he has validly withdrawn, is in the same position legally as if he had cancelled (see below).

The actual terms of the agreement must comply with any

current regulations concerning, e.g. the size of the initial deposit or the maximum period for repayment. If not, the agreement will be illegal, and unenforceable by any party aware of the illegality at the time the agreement was made.

Statutory formalities

The agreement must comply with a whole host of statutory formalities, which apply to all agreements other than 'non-commercial agreements' (i.e. agreements between private individuals) and 'small agreements' (i.e. where the amount of credit is £30 or less), where the credit is for restricted use (i.e. it is not simply an overdraft or open credit arrangement) and where the supplier and the creditor are connected in business in some way. These formalities are designed to ensure that the debtor is fully aware of what he is taking on, and that his rights and obligations are clearly spelt out.

Section 55 of the Act deals with 'pre-contract disclosure' of information, and gives the DGFT the power to pass Regulations concerning the disclosure to the potential debtor, before he enters into the agreement, of the total charge for credit, the true annual percentage charge for credit, and the cash price equivalent of the goods. Until these Regulations are enacted, almost identical provisions under the Hire Purchase Acts govern this type of transaction.

Section 60 of the Act will be used to enact Regulations concerning the actual form and content of the agreement itself, which will have to be in writing, and is likely to have to show the identities of the parties, the total charge for credit, the amounts payable under the agreement and the intervals between them, the true annual rate of charge for credit, and the debtor's right to pay off the debt earlier than stated in the agreement. All the terms of the agreement must be embodied in it (i.e. there will be no extra oral clauses permitted), and it will require to be signed by the debtor in person and by or on behalf of the creditor. Similar requirements already exist in respect of hire-purchase agreements.

Every debtor is entitled to a copy of the agreement. If both parties sign at the same time, the debtor need only be given one copy of the agreement just signed, but if, as is more common, the debtor signs his half first, and the agreement is then sent away by the dealer for the creditor to sign, then the debtor should be given one copy of the agreement as it stands when he signs it, and a final copy within seven days of signature by the creditor. If the agreement is cancellable, this fact must be clearly stated on every copy. Failure to comply will result in the agreement being unenforceable without the leave of the court.

Cancellation

A consumer credit agreement is regarded as 'cancellable' by the debtor if the preliminary negotiations included oral representations made face to face with the customer by the 'negotiator' (i.e. owner, creditor or dealer) and the debtor signed the agreement elsewhere than on the premises of the negotiator or any party to a 'linked transaction'. These provisions are clearly aimed at doorstep 'pressure' salesmanship, but do not cover land mortgages or other land credit or agreements exempted from the 'formalities' requirements (see above). Thus, for example, small orders by housewives from door-to-door salesmen will not be cancellable.

In order to exercise his right of cancellation, the debtor must serve a written notice of intended cancellation on the creditor or his agent or any other person nominated in the agreement. This notice must be served during the five clear days following the receipt by the debtor of his second statutory copy of the agreement, or where both parties signed at the same time, a notice informing him of his right of cancellation which should arrive within seven days of the making of the agreement.

The parties are then both free from any further commitments under the transaction; the customer is entitled to his money back along with any goods traded in part exchange, or the cash equivalent. The customer must in return hand back the goods when and if the owner calls to collect them, subject to his right of lien over them until he gets his money back. There are special rules where goods or services were supplied to meet an emergency, or the debtor himself has incorporated the goods into something else.

Termination

The 1974 Act is also careful in its control of the termination of consumer credit agreements. So far as hire-purchase agreements are concerned, they are most frequently terminated prematurely (i.e. before all the payments are made, and before the debtor becomes the owner of the goods) by the creditor exercising his right under the agreement to terminate it because the debtor has failed to maintain the payments, although they may also terminate by mutual agreement, or by the debtor giving notice to the creditor that he wishes to terminate in accordance with the agreement.

Most hire-purchase agreements give the creditor the right to terminate the agreement once the debtor is in arrears with his payments, or commits some other breach such as selling or attempting to sell the goods. However, whatever the agreement may say, s. 87 of the 1974 Act requires the creditor to first serve a 'default' notice on the debtor, which specifies the breach of contract, indicates what action is required from the debtor to remedy it (e.g. how much is due in arrears), indicates the amount of any compensation payable and the date by which the breach must be remedied, and spells out the consequences of not complying with the notice.

If the debtor fails to comply with a valid default notice, the creditor may then regard the agreement as terminated, although he will still require a court order to get back the goods if they are on private premises, or are 'protected goods' in the sense that the buyer has paid one third or more of the purchase price. However, even where the goods are protected, the creditor can still get them back if they are in the hands of a third party to whom the debtor has disposed of them, or if the debtor has abandoned the goods.

It is also possible for the debtor to obtain from the court a 'time order', which in effect is an extension of the time period during which the debtor must remedy the breach. But once the final time period has expired, the creditor's rights apply in full. As we have seen, he has the right to recover goods themselves upon application to the County Court (or directly in certain cases), and, where the debtor has been in breach of contract, the right to damages for the breach or the amount (if any) stipulated in the agreement as payable in the event of early termination. The object of the exercise is to place the creditor in the same position he would have been in had the agreement gone through to completion. The court may even at this stage grant a time order allowing the debtor time to pay, or may instead order him to return all or part of the goods to the creditor.

The debtor also has a statutory right to terminate the agreement granted to him under the 1974 Act, which he may exercise simply by giving notice to the creditor or his agent, following upon which he must return the goods themselves, make good all the arrears of payments due up to the date of termination, compensate the creditor for any failure to take reasonable care of the goods, and make a final payment of the minimum amount specified in the agreement, or the amount necessary to bring the total payments up to one half of the total hire-purchase price *or* the amount of the creditor's actual loss, whichever is the smallest of the three.

The above provisions deal with hire-purchase agreements. Where the agreement is a *conditional sale agreement*, exactly the same provisions apply as for a hire-purchase agreement, but a *credit sale agreement* does not give the creditor the right to recover the goods on default by the buyer, since they are the buyer's from the start. Nor may the debtor terminate the agreement prematurely, since he has contracted to buy the goods. The seller/creditor may sue for the entire outstanding balance upon the occurrence of certain specified breaches by the debtor, provided that he first serves a notice on him. The court may grant a time order, but the question of protected goods cannot arise.

Rights of the debtor during the agreement

During the currency of the agreement, and at any time before the final payment has been made, the debtor may request a copy of the agreement and a signed statement of account upon payment of 15p. He is also entitled – without fee – to a written 'settlement statement' showing the amount payable to clear off the debt. Default can result in the agreement becoming unenforceable by the creditor, who also commits a criminal offence by defaulting.

Sections 8–11 of the Supply of Goods (Implied Terms) Act, 1973, in effect introduced into all *hire-purchase contracts* the same implied terms as to title, description, merchantability, fitness for purpose and sample as exist under the Sale of Goods Act, 1979, ss. 12–15 (see Chapter 4). Instead of 'buyer and seller', they apply to 'creditor and debtor', and the Unfair Contract Terms Act, 1977, imposes the same prohibition on the exclusion of these implied terms from hire-purchase contracts as it does in the case of contracts for the sale of goods.

Since a *credit sale agreement* is in effect a sale of goods on deferred payment terms, the normal implied terms under the Sale of Goods Act, 1979, apply. The same is true of *conditional sale agreements*, with the necessary amendments in wording.

Consumer hire agreements

A consumer hire agreement has already been defined above. Since there is no element of credit in such agreements, and it is the owner of the goods himself who makes the contract direct with the hirer, there is therefore no complication with dealers acting as agents for finance companies. However, the same rules apply concerning the formalities of the agreement as apply in the case of consumer credit agreements, for which see above. Similarly, the rules concerning copies of the agreement are the same, as are the rules relating to cancellation of the agreement.

However, the rules concerning termination have to be different, since with a consumer hire agreement it is not normally intended that the hirer will ever become the buyer. Where the hirer either fails to keep up the hire payments, or commits some other breach which it is agreed under the terms of the contract will give the owner the right to terminate, the owner must still first of all serve a default notice on the hirer, which, like those served in connection with consumer credit agreements, give the hirer time to remedy the default or apply to the court for a time order. But the court may not extend the period for which the hirer may remain in possession of the goods, and he must part with them in terms of the agreement.

The hirer himself may terminate the agreement once it has run for eighteen months, by giving as a period of notice either three months or the time period between the due dates of hire payment. The agreement itself may allow a shorter period.

The owner of the goods may recover repossession of them following termination of the agreement, which will in most cases be upon the expiry without remedy of the default notice. No court order is required, but the owner may not enter any premises in order to take repossession without the permission of the owner of them, or a court order. In such cases, the court may take steps to ensure that the hirer is not also charged excessive amounts for periods during which he no longer has the goods.

Advertising and canvassing

Of the many powers given to the Director General of Fair Trading under the 1974 Act, the powers to control advertising and canvassing for credit customers are among the most important. A breach of the controls laid down in this area can result in the offender being prosecuted.

Advertising

The Act covers advertisements issued by anyone carrying on a consumer credit or consumer hire business, or a land security business (thus, even building societies are covered here). The type of advertisement covered is that which indicates that the advertiser is willing to provide goods on credit or hire, but the controls will not cover advertisements for credit transactions in which the credit must exceed £5,000. Also included in the advertising controls are those advertising credit brokerage services or debt adjustment or counselling facilities.

In all these cases, the advertiser commits a criminal offence if he publishes an advertisement which contains information which is false or misleading in a material respect, or offers credit terms without the 'cash' option being available, or infringes any of the Regulations enacted to deal with advertisements. These cover matters such as the detail which may appear on advertisements, and the provision, without request, of additional information to the consumer.

Among those who may be convicted of any infringement of the advertising laws will be the person running the business, the author of the advertisement and the advertising agent. The main defence will be that the violation was caused by someone else, and that he (the accused) used all due diligence to prevent it happening. There is also the threat that anyone convicted of an advertising offence will be deemed unfit to hold a licence from the DGFT (see above).

Canvassing

We have already seen that when the debtor enters into an agreement elsewhere than on 'trade premises' (e.g. on his own doorstep), he may *cancel* the agreement during the five-day 'cooling off' period. But apart from that, and completely separate from it, is the possibility that by indulging in doorstep selling of credit, the creditor is infringing a Regulation.

The Act is concerned with what is termed 'canvassing off trade premises', and this consists of making oral representations to a consumer in an attempt to persuade him to make a 'regulated agreement' during a visit by the canvasser for just that purpose which is unsolicited by the debtor and is conducted elsewhere than on business premises occupied by the creditor, debtor, supplier, consumer or canvasser.

Where the activity may be classed as 'canvassing off trade premises' as defined above, then it is totally prohibited where it involves mere straightforward cash loans or other loans which are unconnected with particular goods. To attempt such canvassing will constitute a criminal offence. Other types of regulated agreements (e.g. hire-purchase) may be canvassed even on a doorstep basis, provided of course that the canvasser has an appropriate DGFT licence. It is also a criminal offence to send a person under eighteen any circular inviting him to obtain credit or to hire goods, or to make further inquiries about them, or to issue a credit token (or credit card) to someone who has not asked for it in a written application signed by himself.

Before leaving this section on Consumer Credit, the reader is reminded that the subject is vast, complex and in a state of change. Only the barest outline of certain selected topics has been given here, and detailed advice should be sought before credit transactions are entered into.

Fair trading

Reference has already been made to the Office of the Director General of Fair Trading, established under the Fair Trading Act, 1973, with the power to increase economic efficiency through the regulation of monopolies and restrictive practices (dealt with in Chapter 6) and to protect consumers against unfair trading practices. It is this latter function which is the concern of this chapter, and we have already seen how this objective is achieved in the sphere of consumer credit regulation.

But the powers of the DGFT are much wider than this, and under the Fair Trading Act, 1973, he may not only take action to prevent unfair trading practices which are already prohibited by law, but also take steps to regulate any new and undesirable practice which he comes across, or which is reported to him. It is this aspect of his work which we will be examining in this section.

The regulation of 'consumer trade practices'

A 'consumer trade practice' is one in which the supplier is acting in the course of a trade or business and the customer is not, which is carried out in connection with the supply of goods or services to consumers, and which relates to the terms and conditions upon which, or subject to which, the goods or services are supplied, the manner in which those terms or conditions are communicated to potential customers, the promotion of goods or services, salesmanship methods, packaging, or the method of securing payment for goods or services supplied. Although this lengthy remit is fairly comprehensive, it excludes certain professional services (e.g. those of solicitors and dentists) and does not include the nationalized industries.

When the DGFT becomes aware of a trade practice which he feels should be investigated further, he will first collect as much information as he can on its prevalence, damaging effects, costs to the consumer, effect on commercial morale, etc., and will formulate a proposed policy for control. He will then report to the Consumer Protection Advisory Committee (CPAC), an independent body of specialist advisers from consumer and manufacturing circles. The CPAC may then conduct its own investigation, calling for representations from all interested parties, and considering carefully the report of the DGFT. The CPAC then reports to the Government of the day, and legislation may or may not result, carrying criminal sanctions with fines of up to £1,000 for a first offence and two years' imprisonment following conviction upon indictment.

The DGFT is in any case limited in the type of trading practice which he may refer to the CPAC. Not only must it be one which adversely affects the economic interests of UK consumers, but it must also be likely to mislead them, pressurize them into transactions or force them into contracts on terms inequitable to them. The legislation which may follow the CPAC report may include controls such as total prohibition, exclusion of certain parties or types of transaction, requirements for the inclusion of certain 'safety clauses' in all such consumer agreements, detailed Regulations covering the style and format of notices, agreements, etc., and insistence that certain items of information be given to the consumer.

Up to the end of 1979, there had been several important references to the CPAC by the DGFT, four of which were (briefly) as follows.

(1) Misleading statements concerning consumer rights

Despite the passing of the Supply of Goods (Implied Terms) Act, 1973, which made it unlawful for a retailer to attempt, by means of a clause of a contract, to deprive a consumer of his implied rights under ss. 13–15 of the Sale of Goods Act, 1979 (see Chapter 4), many retailers continued to display notices such as 'no refunds' and 'sale goods may not be returned'. Not only that, but dealers continued to include in their contracts clauses which appeared to take away the customers' rights under the Act, although by law, this could not longer happen. Certainly, very few traders considered it their duty to advise consumers positively about their rights.

Unless the consumer happened to know the law, or sought legal advice on the matter, he might well be fooled by such statements, which were clearly contrary to the economic interests of the consumer, and likely to mislead him. The DGFT therefore referred the whole range of such practices to the CPAC, and after some deliberation, the result was the Consumer Transactions (Restrictions on Statements) Order, 1976, which makes it an offence to display, in any place where consumer transactions take place, any notice containing a term which is outlawed by s. 6 of the Unfair Contract Terms Act, 1977 (which took over from the Supply of Goods (Implied Terms) Act, 1973). Section 6 is explained in Chapter 4. It is an offence to include the same sort of notice in any advertisement, even in a catalogue, or on the goods themselves or their containers. Likewise, it is now a criminal offence to issue any document or statement along with any goods concerning their defects, fitness for purpose or correspondence with description without also stating that the consumers' statutory rights are not affected. Equally illegal is any form of 'guarantee', even direct from the manufacturer, which does not also indicate to the consumer that his statutory rights are not affected.

(2) Prepayment mail order

The big risk to the consumer where he sends 'money with order' is that he never sees the money or the order ever again, either because the mail order firm goes bankrupt in the meantime, and secured creditors take the lot, or because the whole process was a confidence trick in the first place. The risk is particularly acute when the firm is advertising, not from its own established catalogue (e.g. Mothercare and Marshall-Cavendish), but via a newspaper or magazine.

It does not require much stretch of the imagination to see how this sort of practice is contrary to the economic interests of the consumer, and likely to mislead him, and the DGFT referred the practice to the CPAC. The disappointing outcome was the almost useless Mail Order Transactions (Information) Order, 1976, which simply requires that mail order firms requiring payment before dispatch should give their name and address (how else would the victim know where to send the money?). Even this does not apply to advertisements by radio, television or film.

(3) Trader posing as a private seller

It is by no means novel for a trader to advertise articles for sale by means of small, separate entries in, for example, a local newspaper or a specialist magazine which give the impression that he is a private seller. There are several advantages for the trader in getting the customer to believe that he is a private seller, not the least of which is that the customer will be less on his guard, and less likely to pursue any legal remedy he may have.

The Business Advertisements (Disclosure) Order, 1977, makes the practice illegal, and requires businessmen to make it clear in all advertisements designed to attract consumers that they are in fact dealers, and not private individuals. The two exceptions cover auctions and sales by tender, and sale of agricultural produce or game.

(4) Bargain offers

Everyone is familiar with the 'normal price £10, our price £7.50' type of advertisement, and the consumer often has little or no means of checking the validity of the 'normal price' claim. After acquiring special powers, the DGFT reported direct to the Secretary of State on this problem, and the attempted solution is the Price Marking (Bargain Offers) Order, 1979, the general effect of which is to make it illegal for any retailer to indicate that his price for a particular item is lower than any other price for the same item unless the comparison is with his own previous or future prices (e.g. 'special introductory price'), or with the price charged by some other identified person. Equally, the retailer may make comparisons with the price charged in other circumstances (e.g. when indicating the advantages of 'bulk buying'), or to another class of persons (e.g. '50 per cent reduction for OAPs'). Finally, he is allowed to compare his price with that recommended by another person who is not a retailer (e.g. with the manufacturer's recommended price), and although the Secretary of State has the power to ban this type of advertisement in all cases, he has so far only done so in the case of beds. All other forms of reduced price claim are illegal.

Control of persistent offenders

Where the DGFT is satisfied that a particular businessman has persisted in a course of conduct which is contrary to the interests of consumers in the UK (be it economic interests or the interests of health and safety), and which is unfair in the sense that it is a breach of the criminal law, or of a duty owed to the consumer, he has several powers of action.

He must first of all attempt to secure an undertaking from the offender that the practice will cease, failing which he will apply for a court order from the Restrictive Practices Court, or from the County Court (Sheriff Court in Scotland) in the case of 'small traders'. If such an order is granted, and then breached by the trader, he will be in contempt of court. These orders are known as 'cease and desist orders' at least in popular parlance.

Trade descriptions acts

The Trade Descriptions Act, 1968, was one of the first of the modern consumer protection statutes, and its general aim (which has on the whole succeeded) was to make it a criminal offence for suppliers of goods or services to falsely describe what they had on offer. There was another, smaller, Act of the same name passed in 1972, but the basic Act is still that of 1968.

It will already have been noted that the Act applies both to goods and services, although they are dealt with in different sections of the Act. Taking goods first, s. 1 of the Act makes it a criminal offence for any person, in the course of any trade or business, to either apply a false trade description to any goods, or supply or offer to supply any goods to which a false trade description has been applied. Thus, no offence is committed if the offender is a private individual (although it does not matter whether or not the customer is a private consumer), and s. 1 only covers 'goods', a term defined in the Act so as to include ships, aircraft and crops growing in the ground.

The offence may be committed by either supplier or buyer, as in *Fletcher* v. *Budgen* (1974), in which a garage proprietor was convicted for telling a customer that his car was only worth £2 in scrap, then reselling it at a large profit. It will also have been noted that there are two separate offences under s. 1 of the Act, those of *supplying* or *offering* to supply goods to which a false trade description has been applied, and applying a false trade description in the first place; the latter offence could be committed, for example, by an advertising agent. The 'application' of the false trade description may be written or oral, and may be on the goods themselves, on the container, in the shop or in an advertisement.

'Trade description' covers a whole host of statements, including those relating to size, quantity, composition, fitness for purpose, strength or performance, testing or approval by any person. It also covers matters such as a method of manufacture, and any previous history. In order to constitute an offence, the statement must be 'false to a material degree', and this will clearly be a question of fact in the circumstances of each case.

It is in theory possible for the supplier to prevent a particular statement from constituting a false trade description by displaying a 'disclaimer' (e.g. in a car sales forecourt to the effect that 'mileometer readings are not guaranteed'). But it must be displayed to the consumer before the 'supply' takes place, and must, in effect, negate any effect which the trade description might have had. A 'false trade description' can take almost any form, of course, even simple appearances. Thus, a picture on the packet of an item on sale is a description of what is inside the packet.

Section 11 of the 1968 Act made it a criminal offence to indicate that the price at which goods are being offered is less than that which is recommended by the manufacturer, or that at which the same goods were previously offered. This latter provision is intended to prevent the bogus 'sale' items in the shops, and the section requires that before the seller can claim that the goods are genuine reductions, he must have had them on offer at a higher price for a continuous period of not less than twenty-eight days in the preceding six months. But disclaimers are permitted.

We may now look at the control of services before moving on to look at the enforcement of the Act and the defences available under it. Section 14 of the Act in fact states that it is an offence for anyone, in the course of any trade or business, 'knowingly or recklessly' to make a false statement concerning the provision of services, accommodation or facilities, the nature, time and manner in which they are provided, and their examination, approval, location or amenities. A typical area involving s. 14 would be package holidays abroad, and indeed there have been many prosecutions of travel firms under s. 14. It would, of course, cover other service industries such as repairs, cleaning, maintenance and consultancy. It is believed to cover the professions as well.

It will have been noted that offences under s. 14, unlike those under s. 1, may only be committed 'knowingly or recklessly', and this means that no one may be convicted under

s. 14 unless he at least made the statement without caring whether it was true or false. If the maker of the statement honestly believed it (whether that belief was reasonable or not) then he has committed no offence under s. 14, whereas under s. 1 the offence is complete once the statement is made, regardless of motivation.

Again, if the statement was true when it was made, no offence is committed by the maker if the circumstances subsequently change; thus, in *Sunair Holidays Ltd* v. *Dodd* (1970) travel agents were acquitted of a charge under s. 14 involving a hotel room which did not have a terrace which was advertised, because at the time of the making of the statement, that type of accommodation had been booked by the agent with the hotel.

The 'statements' which constitute the alleged offence must be false to a material degree (as with s. 1 offences with relation to goods), and also in line with s. 1 offences, they must be made in the course of a trade or business, and may be avoided by a disclaimer. Statements can take the form of pictures or diagrams, as in *R* v. *Clarksons Holidays* (1972), where C were fined for passing off as an existing hotel an artist's impression of what the unbuilt hotel would look like.

Whether the offence concerns goods (s. 1) or services (s. 14), there are certain defences available under s. 24 of the Act. To summarize, a person charged under either section will be acquitted if he can show that the commission of the offence was due to a mistake, to reliance placed on information supplied to him, to the act or default of 'another person', to an accident or to some other cause beyond his control, and that in each case, the accused himself took all reasonable precautions and exercised all due diligence to avoid the commission of the offence.

Any mistake used as a defence must be the mistake of the accused himself, and no one else; where the defence claimed is the 'act or default of another person', it may even include a person in a managerial position. Thus, in *Beckett* v. *Kingston Brothers* (1970), the firm was acquitted of selling Danish turkeys as Norfolk King Turkey, once it was shown that the labelling had been undertaken by a branch manager. An example of 'some other cause beyond his control' might include, for example, a customer in a supermarket going around altering price labels.

So far as taking all reasonable precautions and exercising 'all due diligence' are concerned, this requirement seems to be satisfied once the employer shows that he has established an effective chain of command for control and supervision, as was the position in the leading case of *Tesco Supermarkets Ltd* v. *Nattrass* (1972), where, by using this defence and showing that they had established a proper system of control, the employers escaped liability for a false 'special offer' poster displayed (contrary to instructions) by a branch manager ('another person' as explained above).

Where an innocent supplier merely supplies goods to which a false trade description has already been applied, he has a special defence where it can be shown that he did not know, and could not reasonably have found out, that the description had been applied to the goods, or that the goods failed to conform to their description. A similar defence is available to some person in the publishing industry who innocently publishes a false advertisement.

The enforcement of the Act is in the hands of the local authorities (normally through Environmental Health or Consumer Protection Departments) under the general supervision of the DGFT. Each local authority will normally appoint inspectors under the Act. These inspectors have a wide variety of powers, including those of test-purchase, seizure, inspection, entry, spot-check and analysis. It is possible for an ordinary member of the public to bring a prosecution, but the vast majority are by local authorities, who notify the DGFT before each prosecution, in order that some national balance may be maintained.

The fact that an offence has occurred under the Act does not give the 'victim' any civil rights (e.g. to sue for damages), although the criminal court may award compensation to the victim.

Unsolicited goods

One insidious form of 'salesmanship' which has also been challenged in recent years is that of 'inertia' selling, whereby goods are delivered to a person who has not ordered them, and he or she is informed that unless the goods are returned by a certain date, it will be assumed that the goods are being purchased. Even without any Act of Parliament to protect him, it is extremely unlikely that any consumer would ever become liable to purchase goods simply by failing to reject them when they are imposed upon him. But this fact was not generally known, and many nervous, elderly and unsuspecting people who could ill afford, for example, a set of books, suffered genuine miseries in the belief that they were legally obliged to pay for goods which had been dumped on them.

To prevent this sort of exploitation, Parliament passed the Unsolicited Goods and Services Act, 1971, which states, in effect, that where a person receives unsolicited goods which it is intended by the sender that he shall acquire, and there is no reason to believe that the recipient was sent them for acquisition for the purposes of trade or business (i.e. the recipient is a private individual with no business use for the goods), then the recipient may regard the goods as a free gift to him once certain further conditions are satisfied.

First of all, the recipient must not agree to keep or return them. Secondly, he must either wait six months, at the end of which the sender has not repossessed the goods and has not been unreasonably prevented from doing so by the recipient, or he may give written notice to the sender that the goods are unsolicited and unwanted, specifying where they may be collected. Thirty days after the sending of such a notice, assuming that there has been no repossession and no unreasonable obstruction by the recipient of any attempted repossession by the sender, the goods become a free gift, just as they do after six months where no such notice has been sent by the recipient.

It is, furthermore, a criminal offence for the sender of unsolicited goods, in the course of any trade or business, to make a demand for payment for what he knows to be unsolicited goods. Any threat of legal proceedings, collection proceedings or the placing of the recipient on a 'debtors' register' is also a criminal offence.

Consumer safety

It has taken politicians a long time to realize that in order to protect consumers from the sort of shoddy product which can cause death or serious injury, it is not enough simply to require particular manufacturers of specific products to compensate victims once the accident has occurred. What is required is some system to ensure that faulty goods will not be manufactured in the first place.

The process began with the Consumer Protection Act, 1961, which at the time of writing (January 1981) is still partly in force. This gave the appropriate Secretary of State the power to enact 'product standards' legislation to ensure that certain identified and potentially harmful products comply with minimum standards of manufacture. Manufacturers may also be required to publish warnings or operating instructions, and a failure to comply with the relevant Regulations becomes a criminal offence.

Regulations under the 1961 Act which still remain in force cover items such as carry-cot stands, nightdresses, electrical appliance colour codes, electric blankets, toys, hood cords on children's clothing, oil heaters, babies' dummies, and prams and push chairs.

The Consumer Safety Act, 1978, when fully implemented, will repeal the 1961 Act, which has in any case been amended from time to time. Like the 1961 Act, it gives power to the Secretary of State for Prices and Consumer Affairs to make Regulations to ensure that goods are safe to be used by the consumer, and to prohibit the circulation of those which fail to comply with these Regulations. These Regulations may also demand that warnings and instructions be issued with the goods, and may dictate design and production standards.

Both manufacturers and suppliers may be caught by such Regulations, and the breach of any Regulations will be a criminal offence. Those Regulations noted above in the context of the 1961 Act are still in force, until overtaken by new Regulations issued under the 1978 Act.

By way of enforcement, the Secretary of State is given three main powers to take swift and effective action against the marketing of items which fall foul of the Regulations. The first of these, the 'prohibition order', is a general ban on all traders which prevents the manufacture, import or supply of unsafe goods or components. A 'prohibition notice' will have the same effect, but will be selective in the sense that it will be directed simply at one trader or group of traders. A prohibition order was passed in 1978, for example, to prevent the use in the UK of a particular form of flame-resistant chemical which was used in the process of manufacture of children's night-wear, but was found to be carcinogenic.

Once the defective goods are on the market, the Secretary of State relies on the efficiency and goodwill of the retailers themselves in securing the recall of the goods, and not even the 1978 Act gives the Secretary of State the power to order recall. Under the 1978 Act, any individual trader can receive a 'notice to warn' which requires him to take steps to warn consumers about the dangers of goods he has already supplied. The nature of the warning will be specified in the notice itself.

It is a criminal offence for a trader to fail to comply with the terms of a prohibition order, prohibition notice or notice to warn. Enforcement is in the hands of the local authority, whose inspectors have the same types of powers as those available to inspectors under the Trade Descriptions Act – they are frequently the same individuals anyway.

The 1978 Act is unusual for a statute which sets out primarily to impose criminal liability for failing to comply with prescribed standards, in that it imposes civil liability on offenders, and affords a right to damages to any consumer who has suffered because of an infringement of any Regulation under the Act, or a failure on the part of a trader to comply with a prohibition notice or order. There will be no need to prove negligence, nor need the 'victim' have bought the item himself.

Liability for negligence

So far, we have noted the major ways in which a businessman (be he manufacturer or retailer) may be liable under some criminal statute (for example the Trade Descriptions Act, 1968, or the Consumer Safety Act, 1978) for supplying inferior goods or services. He may also, as was noted in Chapter 4, be liable in breach of contract if his goods or services fail to live up to the desired standard. The final point to be noted is that both manufacturer and retailer (but mainly the former) may also be liable to a consumer for any injury or loss sustained as the result of their *negligence*. This topic takes up the remainder of this chapter.

The history of *manufacturer liability* for defective products is, so far as the law of negligence is concerned, a short one. The first test case, and still the leading authority on the subject, was that of *Donoghue* v. *Stevenson* (1932), in which the House of Lords found itself considering a case in which two ladies went into a café in Paisley and ordered ginger beer. The bottle which Mrs D received had been bought for her by her friend, and manufactured by S. She drank half the contents of the bottle and then, while in the act of pouring the remainder into her glass, noticed the decomposing remains of a snail in the bottle. She suffered both shock and gastro-enteritis.

The action was a novel one in law, because Mrs D was attempting to sue the manufacturer of the ginger beer directly, on the basis of his negligence in allowing the snail to get into the bottle. She clearly could not sue the café owner, since she had not bought the bottle, and therefore had no contractual relationship with him, nor could he be said to have been negligent in not noticing the presence of a snail in a sealed opaque bottle over whose contents he had little control. Either the manufacturer was liable, or no one was.

Their Lordships in fact found the manufacturer liable, in

an historic judgement which applies to both England and Wales and Scotland, and which formed the basis for our entire law on negligence. So far as the liability of manufacturers is concerned, the following extract from the judgement of the House of Lords sums it up admirably.

A manufacturer of products, which he sells in such a form as to show that he intends them to reach the ultimate consumer in the form in which they left him, with no reasonable possibility of intermediate examination, and with the knowledge that the absence of reasonable care in the preparation or putting up of the products will result in an injury to the consumer's life or property, owes a duty to the consumer to take that reasonable care.

It will be noted immediately that the 'duty of care' which the manufacturer owes to the ultimate consumer is only that of 'reasonable care'. The manufacturer need only guard against those dangers which are reasonably foreseeable, and need not worry about the exceptional case (e.g. to refer to the case of *Griffiths* v. *Peter Conway*, quoted in Chapter 4, p. 135, the manufacturer of tweed coats need not worry about the occasional exceptional customer with a highly sensitive skin).

But once the risk is apparent, and is of the sort which should be guarded against, the manufacturer 'takes his victim as he finds him' in the sense that he will be liable for all the losses, injury, etc., flowing from the foreseeable damage to the customer. If, for example, a person with a stomach complaint dies as the result of mild food poisoning which would have caused lesser symptoms in a fit person, the manufacturer will be fully liable for all the consequences, once it is shown that the food poisoning itself was a foreseeable consequence of negligence by the manufacturer.

So far, the examples have been drawn from the sphere of food and drink, where the risk of injury through negligence is perhaps the most easily appreciated. But what is being written is equally applicable to, for example, deck chairs which collapse unexpectedly, electrical appliances with faulty wiring, hot-water bottles which leak and cars with defective steering. If a manufacturer is negligent in circumstances in which it is reasonably foreseeable that such negligence could cause loss or injury to someone, then if loss or injury do occur, the manufacturer will be liable to pay damages for negligence.

Donoghue v. *Stevenson* as well as dealing specifically with the question of *manufacturer* liability, also proved to be a watershed in the law of negligence generally, and the principles of 'duty of care' and 'foreseeable loss' now apply in a whole host of business and commercial situations. For example, a retailer may be liable to a customer for his negligence in failing to pass on a manufacturer's warning, or for his failure to store goods correctly. A professional man such as an accountant or stockbroker may be liable for giving negligent advice to a client, and a contractor may be liable to his client for the negligent performance of a maintenance job.

In short, everyone in the world of business and commerce undertakes some sort of legal obligation towards his client and customer, the general tenor of which is that he will act with reasonable care to protect them from foreseeable loss or injury arising from his statement or actions. The loss or damage may be physical, emotional or financial, and may involve damage to the person or to property. Every occupier of premises owes a duty of care to everyone invited to make use of those premises, to ensure that the premises are reasonably fit for the purposes for which that person is being invited on to them.

There are two possible lines of defence open to any person sued for negligence. The first (known by the Latin term *Volenti non fit injuria*) is to allege that the victim 'volunteered' for his injury (an unlikely contention in most cases, unless the victim deliberately ignores, for example, warning notices), and the second, and more common defence, is that the victim was 'contributorily negligent' (e.g. by being drunk on duty, or not wearing safety equipment) and that therefore the damages awarded should be reduced by the proportion to which the victim was at fault.

6 Controlling competition

The great majority of business enterprises exist by selling something or other, be it goods or services. As a general rule, it is in the best interests of the business (and the personal interests of those who work within it) to secure as many sales as possible, while at the same time keeping costs to a minimum. Both objectives can be furthered by increasing the share of the available market which falls to one's own organization, and the elimination of trade rivals, by agreement or by some restrictive means, lawful or otherwise.

This chapter examines some of the ways in which the law influences and controls the activities of those whose task it is to market the firm's product or services. First of all, we shall look at the ways in which statute aims to ensure that no one entrepreneur secures the entire market for himself, and then we may examine some legal devices open to the individual to prevent his product from being copied or unfairly exploited.

Monopolies

As we saw in Chapter 3, the Common Law is only concerned with one trader or manufacturer acquiring a monopolistic position in a market when he attempts to do so by means of a contract which is in 'restraint of trade'. Even then, only when they are 'unreasonable' will the courts refuse to enforce such controls, and in theory, one entrepreneur could acquire a dangerously high share of a given market before a court of law got around to regarding his activities as 'unreasonable'.

Since the Second World War, Parliament has publicly acknowledged that Common Law, with its *laissez-faire* leanings, is inadequate to the task of preventing and controlling cartels. A series of statutes ranging from the original Monopolies and Restrictive Practices Act, 1948, through to the most recent Competition Act, 1980, has been enacted with the express purpose of subjecting to close scrutiny, and if necessary, prohibiting, commercial agreements which threaten to 'tie up' a particular market too closely than is consistent with the public interest. Most of these are dealt with in the next few sections, and we will first concentrate briefly on 'monopolies' strictly so called.

The 1948 Act established the body now known as the Monopolies and Mergers Commission, which is a body of between ten and twenty-seven members whose principal task is to consider the desirability of monopoly situations referred to it by the Department of Prices and Consumer Protection. Since 1965, the authority of the Commission has extended to cover not only monopolies in the supply of goods, but also in the provision of services, in addition to proposed company mergers which threaten to create a monopoly, and monopolies in exports of goods of any description from the UK. Many 'referrals' will now in fact come from the Director General of Fair Trading, whose office is now the main fact-finding agency in connection with alleged monopolies.

Either the Secretary of State or the DGFT may refer a suspected monopoly to the Commission where it appears to them that:

1 in the case of the supply of *goods*, either at least one quarter of all the goods of that description which are supplied in the UK or any part thereof (e.g. one city) are supplied to or by any one person (or group of persons whose affairs are conducted in such a way as to restrict or distort competition) *or* that agreements or arrangements have been made which result in those goods not being supplied at all in the UK or any part thereof.

2 in the case of the provision of *services*, either the supply of at least one quarter of services of that description in the UK or any part thereof is made by or for any one person

(or group of persons as above) *or* that agreements or arrangements are in operation which result in those services not being available at all in the UK or any part thereof.
3 in the case of *exports*, at least one quarter of the goods in question which are produced in the UK are produced by one person or group of interconnected companies, or agreements are in operation which affect at least one quarter of goods of that description produced in the UK and prevent, restrict or distort competition in relation to exports, or to a particular market.

The calculation of one quarter may be by value, size or any other criterion which the Department or the Commission may choose. The Commission may be asked simply to give a ruling on the facts (e.g. 'Is there a monopoly situation?'), or it may be asked to comment on the 'public interest' aspect of such a state of affairs (as most economists will tell you, some monopolies can be in the public interest).

A Report is sent to the Department, which is then laid before both Houses of Parliament, except where the 'public interest' requires secrecy. Where this has happened, and the Report in question finds a particular monopoly to be contrary to the public interest, the Department may make a variety of orders to prevent it continuing; typical of these might be an Order prohibiting the enforcement of a monopoly by the threat of withdrawal of supplies, or an Order rendering unlawful any price discrimination. Breach of such an Order will not be a crime, but may be enforced by civil proceedings. Undertakings may also be secured from parties concerned.

Company mergers fall to be considered by the Commission where the result will be to create or strengthen a monopoly situation as defined above, or the assets taken over will exceed £5 million in value. Under the 1980 Act, the Director may make preliminary inquiries into *suspected* monopolies, and if his suspicions are confirmed, may either seek an 'undertaking' from the offender, or refer the matter to the Commission. Also under the 1980 Act, public sector bodies may be subjected to an 'efficiency audit'.

Restrictive trade practices

A 'restrictive trade agreement' is one which is made between two or more persons carrying on business in the UK in the production or supply of goods, or the application of any manufacturing process to goods, which is designed to fix prices and/or regulate the supply of goods in any way. This can even include 'information agreements' under which manufacturers or suppliers inform each other of prices, delivery conditions, processes of manufacture, etc., a device which could obviously be used as an indirect restrictive trade agreement.

By virtue of the Restrictive Trade Practices Act, 1976, and the Competition Act, 1980, all such agreements must be registered with the DGFT, and even then will be regarded as void unless and until it is proved to the satisfaction of the Restrictive Trade Practices Court (RTPC) that they are in the public interest. An injunction may be sought by the DGFT to prevent a void agreement being implemented.

Certain types of agreement are exempted from the registration requirements, and are valid without reference to the RTPC; they include arrangements for the exploitation of a patent, copyright, trade mark or design, agreements on terms and conditions of employment of staff, sales agency agreements and information agreements on processes relating solely to the export trade.

The type of matter which will come under consideration in the 'public interest' includes public safety, levels of employment in an area of the UK, export potential and public policy. Any agreement must also be shown to be 'reasonable' in all the circumstances. To quote a few decided cases by way of illustration; in *Re Chemists Federation Agreement* (1958), a claim that a movement to restrict the sale of proprietary medicines to registered pharmacies was in the public interest because some retail chemists might be driven out of business was rejected, while in *Re Net Book Agreement* (1957), the 'reduction in retail outlets to the detriment of the public' argument was accepted in the case of an agreement to enforce minimum retail prices in connection with the sale of certain books.

In *Re Yarn Spinners Agreement* (1959), an agreement not to sell yarn below a certain price in order to preserve jobs in certain less efficient mills was set aside because although it had this laudable effect, this was outweighed by the harm which resulted in the way of higher export prices and excess capacity in the industry.

The 1976 Act also re-enacts those provisions of the Fair Trading Act, 1973, which for the first time gave the DGFT the power to exercise control over restrictive trade practices relating to services other than for the production and supply of goods. Once again, 'information agreements' are included.

Resale price agreements

Since 1964, Parliament has sought to prevent traders from agreeing upon, and subsequently enforcing, minimum prices for goods, in the interests of economic efficiency. Ironically, it is alleged in some economic circles that this process has decreased efficiency, and led to the creation of monopolies, by allowing price-cutting wars which have driven more marginal traders (notably retailers) out of business.

The latest Act is the Resale Prices Act, 1976, which makes it unlawful for two or more suppliers to make any agreement to withhold supplies from dealers who fail to comply with minimum or other resale price conditions, or to deal with such recalcitrant dealers in any other way less favourably than those who do comply. Conversely, dealers may not agree to refrain from ordering from suppliers who do not enforce Retail Price Maintenance (RPM).

However, these provisions apply only to collective agreements, and *individual* buyer and seller agreements *re* price may be enforced. Similarly, an *individual* supplier is free to recommend minimum prices for his goods, even though such an agreement to recommend minimum prices would be unlawful if made among suppliers generally. Where an *individual* agreement does exist, it may be enforced by the supplier against any business retailer who was aware of the condition when he bought the goods, even though he was not a party to the contract. Thus, for example, an RPM agreement between manufacturer and wholesaler can be enforced against every retailer who was aware of it when he bought the goods for commercial resale.

Where a contractual term is employed which contravenes the Act, the effect of the Act is simply that it is void in so far as it relates to the establishment of a minimum price for goods to be resold in the UK, and any attempted trade reprisals against a dealer who fails to observe such a restriction may be challenged by civil proceedings by either the trader concerned or the Crown.

The RTPC may grant an exemption from the normal provisions of the Act to either an individual supplier or an association of suppliers, where it may be shown that otherwise there would be a reduction in quality, a reduction in the number of retail outlets for those particular goods, a price increase, a danger to health resulting from a misuse of the goods, or a reduction in associated services. In each case it must also be shown that such an eventuality would be detrimental to the public, even taking into account the benefits to be obtained from an immediate price reduction.

Under these provisions, the Court in 1969 allowed an exemption in favour of books, and in 1971 an exemption in favour of proprietory drugs. In both cases, the price agreement was justified on the grounds of the reduction in retail outlets which might otherwise result.

Competition in the European Economic Community

Britain's entry into the EEC resulted in the laws of that Community becoming part of UK law under the European Communities Act, 1972. Articles 85 and 86 of the Treaty of Rome are intended to prevent the stifling of competition within the EEC, and they are dealt with below. An agreement or decision reached in breach of either Article is automatically void under EEC law, and could not be enforced in a Community court. The Commission may also impose a fine.

But within the UK, although the DGFT and the RTPC are required to take account of Articles 85 and 86, they could apply one of the exemptions under the 1976 legislation even though the agreement still contravenes one of the Articles. This exemption would, of course, only apply within the UK, and would be unenforceable anywhere else within the Community.

Article 85 is primarily concerned to prohibit agreements which have the tendency to distort competition between Community members. Thus, in 1966, the European Court of Justice declared unlawful the system whereby Grundig sought to secure territorial distribution rights over their products for their French agents by arranging for the latter to register a special trade mark, and in 1969, two price-fixing cartels were broken up, one dealing with dyestuffs and the other with proprietary drugs.

Where it is likely that a particular agreement will infringe Article 85, the parties may well wish to obtain a ruling, which they may do from the Commission. Again, there are major exemptions from the Act, notably where the agreement contains parties who are all from the one member state and does not involve trade outside that state, or where only two organizations are involved, and the agreement concerns only the fixing of prices or conditions of trading in the resale of goods, the application of a manufacturing licence, or the cooperation of two organizations in joint research and development.

Article 86 is concerned with the acquisition of a 'dominant position' in a particular market by some organization, and seeks to prevent such a position being abused, where this abuse has affected trade between member states. 'Dominant position' has been defined by the European Court of Justice as 'a position of economic power held by an undertaking which gives it power to prevent the maintenance of effective competition on the market in question by lending to the enterprise the chance of behaving on the market substantially independently of its competitors, its customers and lastly of consumers'.

In the case involving *Hoffman La Roche* in 1979, the Court held that possessing a very large share of the market could itself constitute a 'dominant position'. This particular case was concerned with the manufacture and supply of vitamin tablets, and it was held that Hoffman La Roche had a 'dominant position' in that they held 80 per cent of the B2 market, each vitamin being a separate market. In this case, they had secured agreements with twenty-two major customers to the effect that the latter would take all or a large percentage of their supplies from Hoffman La Roche. This was held to be an abuse of a dominant position and likely to affect competition between member states. They were fined £180,000.

Copyright

Copyright may be defined in general terms as the right to prevent another person from making use of one's own invention, but the term is confined, in modern usage at least, to 'inventions' of a literary, dramatic, musical or artistic nature. Unauthorized use may consist of public performance, dramatization, recording, broadcast, translation, use as an advertising gimmick, or reproduction on a manufactured article – the list is almost endless. To infringe a copyright in such a way is to give the copyright owner the right to sue for damages.

The law is now controlled by the Copyright Act, 1956, and it is to this Act that one must turn for basic definitions. 'Copyright' is defined as the 'exclusive right' to do 'certain acts' in relation to copyright works, or to authorize other people to do them. In short, if I write a novel, I may either translate it into French myself, or authorize someone else to do the job. If some other person does it without my knowledge or consent, and attempts to sell the result to a publisher, I may sue him for infringement of copyright. The translator also has a copyright of his own, when it is completed.

The owner of the copyright will frequently be the author or composer, or his employer (as, for example, where a feature is written for a Sunday newspaper by a staff reporter, in which case the newspaper copyright remains with the employer). Alternatively, the composer may have assigned his right to enforce the copyright to some organization which represents his interests, and those of others like him (see Performing Right Society, etc., below).

Before copyright may exist in any literary, dramatic or musical work which is original, it must be unpublished. Once it is published, copyright continues to subsist in work if it was first published in the UK or a country in which the Act applies under a reciprocal agreement, or if the publisher was at the time of first publication a British subject or domiciled or resident in the UK or any other country to which the Act extends. 'Publication' consists only of the issue of reproductions to the public, and the copyright will continue until fifty years after the end of the calendar year in which the author died, or fifty years after the date on which the work is thereafter first published, performed in public or offered for sale as a record or broadcast.

Control over copyright music is very tight; thus, in *Performing Right Society* v. *Rangers FC Supporters Club, Greenock* (1974), it was held that it was a 'public performance' for copyright music to be performed to members of a private club, while in *Performing Right Society* v. *Harlequin Record Shops* (1979), it was held to be an infringement of copyright to play music in record form to patrons of record shops without first obtaining a Performing Right Society (PRS) licence, since there was no implied licence to perform simply because the proprietors were promoting the records.

After the fifty-year period has expired, the work is said to be in the 'public domain', although any new arrangement will be the copyright property of the arranger.

There is also a copyright in sound recordings, films and broadcasts. Thus, a recording may not be played or broadcast to the 'public', at least not without the consent of the copyright owner. However, in *Phonographic Performance Ltd* v. *Pontins Ltd* (1968), it was held not to be a public performance for records to be played to residents of an hotel or holiday camp. Nor is it unlawful to play copyright recording to members of a private club, although in all these cases, the position may be different if a special charge is made for admission to that part of the premises. The copyright period for recordings is fifty years from the end of the calendar year in which the recording or film was first made.

It will have been noticed that so far as music recorded on disc is concerned, there are at least two separate copyrights involved, one in the music itself and another in the recording of it. The musical copyright is controlled by the Performing Right Society, and the recording copyright by Phonographic Performance Ltd (PPL), both of whom require a fee before a licence to perform copyright works controlled by them will be granted. Both organizations represent the great majority of copyright owners in their particular field, and the copyright fees thus obtained are redistributed among their members. This is certainly a more efficient system than each copyright owner pursuing each individual hotelier, restaurateur, shopkeeper, disco operator, etc., for a separate licence fee. The payment of the block fee to either PRS or PPL authorizes the payer to perform all the copyright music represented by that organization.

A person whose copyright is infringed may sue for damages, or may seek an injunction (in Scotland, interdict) to prevent further abuses. Any unlawful copies, plates, stencils, recordings, etc., will be regarded as the copyright owner's *own* property. A deliberate infringement of copyright may even be prosecuted as a criminal offence before the magistrates' courts.

A copyright may be *assigned* to someone else, provided that this is done in writing and signed by the owner or his agent. A copyright may be *bequeathed* under one's will, and it may be transferred upon bankruptcy. The owner of a copyright may licence someone else to make use of the work which is under copyright (see PRS and PPL above).

Patents

We have seen that the law of copyright seeks to protect a person's legal right to an 'invention' of artistic or literary merit. More directly industrial and commercial inventions are likely to be covered by patents, which basically ensure that once a person has produced a novel process, material, etc., he or she will be free to make the most of it for a given period, without fear of plagiarism by trade competitors.

A patent is, in law, an agreement under which the state, in return for full disclosure of some new machinery, industrial process or product, allows the inventor a monopoly of exploitation of it. The law is now governed by the Patents Act, 1977, which as well as reforming certain aspects of UK law on the subject, also allows the UK to participate in reciprocal patent agreements both within the EEC and elsewhere. In time, a British inventor will be able to patent an invention for the whole of the EEC by registering in the UK Patents Office.

Dealing first with the patent position solely in the UK, no one may register for the grant of a patent unless his invention is new, involves an 'inventive step', and is capable of industrial application. An invention will be new if it does not form part of what is termed 'the state of the art' in the particular field of industry to which it relates, which in effect means whether or not the invention has already been made available to the public in the UK or elsewhere. It will be an 'inventive step' if the process, machine, etc., was not obvious to anyone skilled in 'the art', and it will be 'capable of industrial application' if it can be employed in any kind of industry, including agriculture. One item excluded from the category of items capable of industrial application is any method of diagnosis or treatment of the human body or of animals.

Among other matters which will not be patentable because they do not satisfy the above tests are scientific discoveries, theories or mathematical methods, computer programmes, systems or rules for performing a mental act or playing a game, and any aesthetic creation.

Applications for patents are made to the Patents Office, and the first stage is for a full specification to be lodged, and this will be checked to ensure that there is something in it which is patentable. The specification is then published, and the public has three months in which to lodge objections. After this, assuming that there have been no objections, etc., 'Letters Patent' will be granted which will cover the UK for four years, or may be renewed on an annual basis for the next twenty years (thirty years with the leave of the High Court). Thereafter, the owner of the patent may either exploit the invention himself, or licence others to do so. Alleged infringements give the owner the right to sue in the courts, resulting in injunction and damages.

One frequent problem with patents is that the invention is that of an employee, and it is the employer who is claiming the right to exploit the invention. The 1977 Act made considerable changes in this area, and the rule now is that the invention is that of the employer if it was made by the employee in the normal course of his duties, and that an invention might reasonably have been expected to arise from those duties (e.g. the man was a research physicist), or the employee had a special obligation to further the employer's interests. In such cases, the employee may well still be awarded compensation by the employer on the order of the Comptroller of Patents or the court, and in all other cases, the patent may be taken out by the employee himself.

The European Patent Convention of 1975 provides for the granting of twenty-year patents on essentially the same basis as the 1977 Act in the UK, except that examination will be by the European Patent Office. The patent will extend only to the country of origin, but the possession of a European Patent (UK) will eventually be the only way to patent an invention in the UK, as the laws of member states are drawn together under the Convention.

The Community Patent Convention set out to establish a patent for the whole Community, although it is handled by the European Patents Office just as if it were a European patent. It will cover the exploitation of inventions throughout the whole of the EEC.

Registered designs

A 'design' is defined under the Registered Designs Act, 1949, s. 1 as:

Features of shape, configuration, pattern, or ornament applied to any article by any industrial process or means, being features which in the finished article appeal to and are judged solely by the eye, but does not include a method or principle of construction, or features of shape or configuration which are dictated solely by the function which the article has to perform.

They are therefore essentially something artistic added to something practical. The motif on a set of pillow cases, the pattern on wallpaper and the configuration of a line of lace may all be thought of as examples of design.

They may be protected by their inventor in one of two ways. First of all, they may be registered under the 1949 Act, which until 1968 was the only way of protecting them, or they may be treated as copyrights under the Design Copyright Act, 1968.

The effect of registration under the 1949 Act is to give the proprietor what is in effect a copyright in the design for the next five years; before it may be so registered, the design must be 'new or original'. Although damages are awardable against infringers, these will not be granted unless the infringement was dishonest. The article which contains the design must also carry the registered number of the design.

The Design Copyright Act of 1968 gave the owner of an industrial design the right to enforce it as a copyright for fifteen years after it is first marketed, after which the copyright runs out and the design may be used without infringement. Anyone seeking to enforce the copyright must produce examples of both the original, protected design and the alleged copy; if he succeeds in his action, he may demand the surrender of the article as well as damages.

Trademarks

A trademark is defined under the Trade Marks Act, 1938, as:

A mark used or proposed to be used in relation to goods for the purpose of indicating, or so as to indicate, a connection in the course of trade between the goods and some person having the right either as proprietor or as registered user to use the mark, whether with or without any indication of the identity of that person.

Clearly, the primary purpose of a trademark is to identify a particular brand of goods for the convenience of the customer, and the ultimate profit of the manufacturer. Golliwogs on jam jars and storks on margarine packets are obvious modern examples. No one is obliged to register a trademark, and many do not do so, although the effect of registration is to confer a monopoly in the use of that particular mark in relation to goods. The 1938 Act in fact only applies to trademarks used in relation to goods.

The Register of Trade Marks is kept in the Patents Office, and is divided into Class A and Class B. Class A trademarks are those which are sufficiently distinctive as to be in effect unique, and in order to be registerable in Class A, a trademark must include or consist of a name represented in a special or particular manner, or a signature of the applicant or his predecessor in the business, or an invented word or words, or a word or words which have no direct reference to the character or quality of the goods, or some other distinctive mark, such as for example a colour scheme.

The effect of registration in Class A is that the applicant acquires the exclusive right to make use of the trademark, but it will not be granted if the above tests are not satisfied, or the proposed mark is deemed to be too close to an existing one, or illegal, indecent or misleading. If the application passes the Registrar, it will be advertised in the Trade Marks Journal, and objections may be lodged.

A Class B trademark may be registered where it is capable of distinguishing the goods of its owner from those of other manufacturers, but is not sufficiently distinctive to merit inclusion in Class A. The protection afforded to Class B owners is not so complete as for those in Class A, and in particular, infringement will be permitted where the infringer can show that the public is not likely to be confused.

Infringement consists of another proprietor making use

of the same mark, or something very similar, in relation to his own goods, and certainly in the case of Class A marks, it is no defence to show that the public was not likely to be deceived, etc. A Class A trademark is the exclusive property of the owner, and that is that. The question of whether or not the public will be deceived will in fact be relevant on the question of whether or not the offending mark is sufficiently similar to the registered mark.

Once a person has a trademark registered, he is in a position to defend himself against potential trade competitors, by making use of the 'passing off' and 'trade libel' laws, which may now be examined.

Attacks involving business reputation

This deliberately general title has been chosen for the last section of this chapter, in order to illustrate that an attack on a rival manufacturer or supplier can be both positive and negative, and that each concerns his business reputation. The positive side takes the form of misleading the public into believing that when they buy goods manufactured by A, they are in fact buying the product of manufacturer B; A is said to be 'passing off' his goods as those of B. Alternatively, A may attempt to malign the product of his competitors; if he does so unfairly, and beyond the bounds of recognized competition, he commits a form of defamation known as 'trade libel'.

Passing off

'Passing off' is the name given by lawyers to that form of activity which consists of A selling or attempting to sell goods by pretending that they were made by B when in fact they were not. This may be done in a variety of ways, as indicated below, but the legal effect is the same – the person whose goods they are being passed off as has the right to challenge such action in the courts and obtain both damages and an injunction to prevent further abuses.

One obvious way in which 'passing off' might occur would be for A to attach to his goods a trademark belonging to B; it is not necessary for the trademark to be registered as such before there can be a 'passing off' action at Common Law, but where it is so registered, then the injured party can also bring an 'infringement' action in the manner indicated above.

Once a particular trademark or name has become particularly well known in industry or in a particular trade, then it would seem that other, newer entrants into the market cannot make use even of their own names if there would be a risk of confusion with an existing brand leader. Thus, in *Wright* v. *Wright* (1949), it was held that a Mr Wright could not carry on a cosmetic business in his own name, nor could he market any toilet goods, so long as there was a risk that his products might be confused with the firm marketing the famous Coal Tar Soap.

Again, a particular word may become associated with the particular trader or manufacturer in such a way that he is ultimately able to claim it for his own; thus, in 1924, the Havana Cigar and Tobacco Company laid claim to the word 'Corona' even though it is generally believed to refer, not to a particular brand but to a particular size of cigar, while in 1961 the Bollinger family successfully opposed the use of the phrase 'Spanish Champagne', since the term 'Champagne' was held to refer to the produce of the region of France with the same name. More recently, in 1974, the English firm of H. P. Bulmer were similarly restrained from using the word in connection with cider or perry, while in 1979 it was held that 'egg flip' could not be marketed as 'advocaat'.

The passing off may be more underhand in its nature and may, for example, take the form of an imitation which at a quick glance makes a product look like that of a leading manufacturer, when in fact a closer inspection shows that it is not. One might, for example, produce a near-copy of a logo or symbol associated with a product, or use the same colour scheme on the packaging, and this might be sufficient to imitate the 'get-up' of the established product. In *Hoffman La Roche* v. *DDSA Pharmaceuticals* (1972), it was held that drugs might be fully identified by the colour coding on the tablets.

The simplicity with which passing off can be accomplished is readily appreciated if one takes a standard item from the larder (e.g. a tin of beans) and studies the label. Anyone buying, for example, a tin of beans with the number '57' on it could think of only one manufacturer, while the outline silhouette of a stork on a margarine packet normally means only one thing. If a dishonest trader were to arrange for near imitations to appear on his own identical produce, a lot of busy shoppers might be deceived.

Trade libel

If, instead of attempting to identify his own goods with those of a trade rival, a manufacturer sets out to demolish that rival's reputation by casting doubts on the quality of the product, he runs the risk of committing a 'trade libel'. Also known as 'injurious falsehood', the activity takes the form of making false statements about the goods (NB not the manufacturer, trader, etc., himself), to some third party with the malicious intent to cause damage. If the words are in some permanent form (e.g. written in an advertising brochure) then there is no need to prove actual damage before the injured party can claim compensation; the same is true of any statement which is calculated to injure the plaintiff's trade or business.

In short, any scurrilous abuse or derogatory statement directed at the product of a trade rival, once communicated to a third party, is actionable by the maligned manufacturer without proof of actual loss. Where it is falsely and maliciously stated that a particular trader has ceased to carry on business, the latter will receive damages if he can show that his business was damaged as a result.

Clearly, there is a thin line between trade libel and the sort of advertising which suggests that 'in exhaustive tests', Product A consistently performed better than Product B. The advertising executive has the author's heartfelt sympathy in his search for that line.

7 Using business premises

It often comes as a surprise to the business entrepreneur, who is accustomed to being in complete control of his operations, to find that when it comes to the use to which he puts his own business premises, he cannot do simply as he wishes. For one thing, of course, he may not own the premises, but may simply hire them from a landlord, in which case he is subject to the terms and conditions of the lease. But even where he is the true owner of the premises, his activities on them may be severely hampered.

He cannot, for example, simply take a large detached property in a quiet residential area and turn it into a discotheque or a glue factory – a combination of the planning laws and a group of irate neighbours will make sure of that. Nor can he pollute the environment with impunity, nor create sufficient noise to drive out the neighbours. He may be restricted in his use of the premises by some local by-laws, or by restrictive covenants which 'burden' the land. Someone else may have rights over the land by virtue of an 'easement'. He is liable for the safety of not only those who work on the premises (see Chapter 10) but also those who visit them. As a final indignity, he is called upon to pay rates.

These matters are looked at in outline in the following sections; however, it must be emphasized at the outset that the law relating to 'real property' is complex, and in places irrational, and that legal professional advice should always be sought before entering this difficult area.

It is also regretted that the complexity of the subject matter, and restrictions of space, make it impossible to deal effectively with the many differences in this area between the laws of England and Scotland. This chapter is therefore restricted to a consideration of English law.

Business tenancies

Much has been written in recent years, and many new Acts of Parliament have been concerned about the problems of the tenant, and the imposition of rent control and security of tenure. A large proportion of this has passed over the heads of business tenants, although in many cases they are just as much in need of protection. The business tenancy is still very largely a matter of free negotiation, of contract, between the 'landlord' (the owner of the 'freehold' in the land or buildings) and the 'tenant' (the person who is to occupy the land as a tenant under a 'leasehold' agreement).

The lease itself, like any other contract, will deal with several matters in 'clauses', and these will normally concern the size of the rent, the intervals at which it is to be paid, the duration of the tenancy, and the rights and duties of the parties concerning rates, repairs, etc. The lease may also carry other restrictions, known as 'covenants', under which the tenant agrees that he will not conduct certain types of activity on the premises, or behave himself in a particular way. Thus, in *Egerton* v. *Esplanade Hotels, London Ltd* (1947), the tenants of hotel premises in Paddington were evicted under a covenant in the lease against conduct likely to annoy the landlords or their other tenants after the manager and porter were convicted of brothel keeping.

The lease may also contain what is called a 'rent review clause' under which the rent may be adjusted (invariably upwards) from time to time; the longer the lease the more likely it is to contain a rent review clause, which is perfectly lawful, provided that it is clearly drafted and leaves little doubt as to how the new rent will be calculated. Other terms and conditions may concern the liability of the tenant to comply with the licensing laws, the planning laws, etc., and the agreement of the tenant not to change the use to which the premises are put. There may also be prohibitions on assignment or subletting of the premises, and the carrying out of improvements and alterations.

Where a tenancy is for three years or more, it must be in deed form, but it is in any case hard to envisage a situation in which a businessman would wish to embark on any substantial occupation of premises belonging to someone else without 'something in writing' anyway.

Although, as mentioned above, tenants of business premises do not enjoy the comprehensive statutory protection now afforded to domestic occupiers of residential property (notably in the matter of controlled rents), they are, under the Landlord and Tenant Act, 1954 (which applies only to England and Wales), given statutory protection when it comes to eviction. In short, the tenant may apply to the court for the creation of a new tenancy at the end of the old at a rent and for a period to be fixed by the court, assuming of course that the lease is not forfeit for, for example, non-payment of rent or a breach of a covenant in the lease.

The landlord, if he wishes to repossess the premises, must first serve upon the tenant a written notice to quit in the special form prescribed by the 1954 Act, and this must be given between six and twelve months before the expiry date of the lease. The tenant then has two months in which to notify the landlord of his desire to obtain another lease. If the landlord does not wish the tenant to have another lease, then he must say so in his original notice to quit. Under the 1954 Act, there are only seven main grounds upon which the landlord may oppose the grant of a new tenancy, and he must specify his chosen ground in the notice to quit. Alternatively, the tenant may, without any sign of a notice to quit from the landlord, serve notice upon him that he requires a new tenancy, and it is for the landlord then to justify refusal on one of the seven grounds laid down by the Act, and referred to above. These seven grounds are as follows:

1 that the tenant is in breach of an obligation to repair the premises, and that this has led to a serious deterioration in the condition of the premises;
2 that the tenant has been guilty of persistent delay in the payment of rent;
3 that the tenant has committed other substantial breaches of his obligations under the lease;
4 that the landlord has offered and is willing to provide suit-

able alternative accommodation for the tenant on reasonable terms;

5 that the landlord requires the whole of the premises so that they may be let or relet as a whole;

6 that the landlord intends to demolish or reconstruct the premises, and cannot reasonably be expected to do so without obtaining possession of the whole of the premises;

7 that the landlord intends to occupy the premises himself for the purpose of some business to be carried on there, or as a residence.

All disputed questions under the 1954 Act may be dealt with either by the County Court or by the High Court, according to the rateable value of the property which comprises the tenancy (£5,000 or over to the High Court). If the landlord is successful in proving his grounds, then the court may not grant a new tenancy, but if the grounds for refusal of a new tenancy are as specified in 5, 6 and 7 above, the court may award compensation to the outgoing tenant, based on the length of the previous occupancy and the rateable value of the premises.

Where the landlord does *not* succeed in making out his grounds for repossession of the premises, then the court may grant a new tenancy for a period of up to fourteen years. The actual period granted will take into account the length of the previous period, although the two need not be identical. The property to be covered by the new lease will normally be the same as in the old one, but not necessarily so. The rent will be fixed by the court, using 'open market' tests, taking into account any improvements made by the tenant himself.

So far as repairs and improvements are concerned, an outgoing tenant may also be entitled to compensation in respect of these where they have increased the letting value of the premises. This may occur either where the tenant obtained the prior consent of the landlord to the repairs, etc. (by serving notice on him and not having received objections within three months), or where he obtained from the County Court a certificate authorizing the repairs, etc., on the grounds that they were proper improvements which would add to the value of the premises, and not detract from the value of any other property owned by the landlord.

Local authority powers

A great deal of Parliament's day-to-day power is delegated by it to other authorities under its general control (see Chapter 1) and one of the best examples of this is the degree of control exercised by local authorities (in the name of Parliament) over premises within their jurisdiction. This is obvious enough even to the domestic owner/occupier who cannot even erect a garage on his own land without seeking permission from the town hall, and whose rate demands get higher as his dustbins get fuller. It is even more obvious to the business manager, who actually wishes to do more with his premises than live on them, since this brings him into even closer contact with the network of controls operated by local authorities. In this section, an outline sketch of these controls is attempted.

Planning

First of all, of course, there is the question of planning. Since 1947, the government has not been prepared simply to let every occupier of premises do what he wishes with them, and in the process destroy the environment. Every local authority is charged with the duty of making the best use of all the land within its area, and this will normally entail 'zoning' of land for particular purposes. The Town and Country Planning Acts of 1947 and 1977, and their Scottish equivalents, take the matter even further.

Under these Acts, no one may, without planning permission, develop the land which he occupies, that is, conduct building, mining or engineering operations upon it, or make any 'material change of use' of the land. Purely internal alterations will not require planning permission (although they may be subject to other controls) unless they alter the use to which the buildings are to be put, but otherwise (and this will include even, for example, luminous signs on the outside walls) permission must be sought for any material change in the external appearance of a building.

The question of 'change of use' is even more complex, although it exists as part of a laudable attempt to ensure that the character of certain localities is retained (as rural, industrial residential, and so on). The system proceeds on the basis that all activity is divided into a series of 'classes', and that while one may proceed from one use to another within a given class without planning permission, one cannot change from one class to another without full planning approval.

Shops and hotels are in different classes, and offices are kept in a different class from, for example, cinemas. But, for example, dance halls and swimming pools are within the same 'use class' and one may therefore change from one to the other without planning permission. The classes are organized according to their effect upon the locality, and one can readily appreciate why planning permission should be required for a conversion of a private house in a residential area to an insurance company office, while a change from, say, a cinema to a theatre involves no appreciable change in effect upon the neighbourhood.

Rating

Another aspect of local authority control which often comes under fire is the system of rating. This is, of course, the method by which local authorities finance their services and activities, and it certainly appears on the surface as if the heaviest rates are paid by those occupying business premises. While this is true in absolute terms, it ignores the mathematical basis upon which rates are levied.

The amount of the rate is of course expressed as a certain amount 'in the pound' upon what is called the 'rateable value' of the premises. This in turn is fixed by a local valuation officer who calculates first of all the 'gross value' of the premises, being an estimate of the annual rent which the property could reasonably be expected to command on the open market. From this is deducted the estimated annual cost of maintaining the premises in their existing state, and this produces the 'net value' upon which the rates are actually levied. Appeals may be made against the size of the rateable value thus arrived at.

Rates are payable by the person or organization in 'rateable occupation' of the premises, unless that organization can show that some other person (for example, the landlord) has agreed to pay them. Only when premises are completely unoccupied are rates not levied, and even then the local authority has discretionary power to levy rates on even empty property after three months. Rates may be reduced for seasonal occupation and apportioned as between two or more occupiers. Rate relief is also available for charities.

Public Health

There have been statutes charging local authorities with the duty of guarding public health for well over a century, and as life has become more complex technically, so the risks have become greater. No one set of Regulations can cover the lot, and in the exercise of its public health functions, the local authority draws from a variety of sources for its powers and responsibilities.

First of all, there is the question of safety of buildings. Under the Building Regulations, all new buildings, and all alterations to existing buildings, must comply with certain standards of structure, and under the public health aspect of their powers, local authorities can prohibit or modify any new proposals which do not comply with Building Regulations. There is obviously a close connection here with the whole issue of planning, and Building Regulations deal with matters such as types of construction, the materials used, lighting, ventilation, height, drainage, water supply and fire precautions.

Fire precautions may also be dealt with in connection with existing buildings, and local authorities may insist on adequate exits and fire escapes, etc., both under the Public Health Acts and most recently under the Fire Precautions Act, 1971, which may, by Regulation, be extended to cover all premises upon which staff are employed. Shops are already covered by such Regulations, and offices are covered anyway by the Offices, Shops and Railway Premises Act, 1963, which allows local authority inspectors to lay down requirements for fire safety, as well as dealing with matters such as floor space per employee, minimum working temperatures, ventilation and lighting levels.

Whenever a fire certificate is required, under the 1971 Act (for example for hotels and boarding houses, shops which employ more than twenty staff on the premises at the one time or more than ten above ground level, or offices covered by the 1963 Act), then it is the local fire authority which decides whether or not to grant one, after they have approved the system employed on the premises to secure escape in the event of fire, the fire-fighting equipment provided on the premises, and the fire alarm system.

Public health also includes matters such as fresh water and garbage disposal, and it will come as no surprise to learn that the local authority is involved in this area as well. Thus, under the Water Act, 1973, it is the responsibility of the local authority to ensure that a 'wholesome' supply of water is available to all premises, although the actual responsibility for supply rests with the Regional Water Authorities or the remaining private water companies.

Each local authority is legally obliged to collect household waste from all premises within its area, and, as part of the wider public health duty, to collect other more directly industrial or commercial waste, for which it may charge separately. Also, under the Control of Pollution Act, 1974, those who amass large quantities of industrial or commercial waste which could prove harmful or annoying to the general public can be required to place it in suitable receptacles. The 1974 Act is, of course, a much wider piece of legislation which gives enforcement powers to each local authority on a variety of local environmental matters such as pollution of streams, noise nuisance and emission of smells and fumes.

The Clean Air Acts also deal with the emission of pollutants into the atmosphere, and all these Acts (including that of 1974) proceed on the enforcement basis of 'abatement notices' or similar documents, giving the occupier one final opportunity to improve matters before a summons is taken out.

Finally, the local authorities are charged with the duty of preventing the spread of infectious diseases, and have a wide variety of powers open to them in the pursuit of this duty. Most local authorities now appoint 'community physicians' to advise and coordinate the fight against disease, and the worst of such diseases are classified as 'notifiable' (e.g. cholera, smallpox and typhus). They are notifiable to the local authority, as is food poisoning, in order that fast and efficient steps may be taken. These last points are of particular relevance to medical officers employed by large industrial organizations, who may be the first to become aware of a new outbreak within their own work force.

Covenants and easements

The word 'covenant' is used in general parlance to indicate a form of undertaking, and lawyers use the word in a very similar fashion. We have already noted the possible existence of covenants in a lease, whereby, for example, the tenant covenants not to license the premises for the sale of alcohol, and it now remains to consider, how covenants may arise between two owners of freehold land. We may then consider 'easements', which are in effect more direct rights which a land owner may have over the land of another.

NB that the section on restrictive covenants is not applicable to Scotland, and that in Scotland, 'easements' are known as 'servitudes'.

Restrictive Covenants

We have noted above the use of the word 'covenant' as a form of undertaking; the addition of 'restrictive' indicates that the undertaking is one which in some way cuts down A's use of his own land. The phrase might also have been used in Chapter 3 (Contract) to describe another sort of situation under which a person (in that case an employee) limits his activities (his choice of future career) by means of a contractual undertaking. The phrase should, however, be confined to the situation in which use of land is limited by agreement.

If we take the simplest form of restrictive covenant first, we can readily appreciate a situation in which A, a local farmer, sells land to B upon which he intends to build a house. B agrees, as a term of the contract of the sale of land, not to develop or construct any business or business premises, but to maintain the land for ever as a residential site. It does not require much imagination to appreciate that the courts will uphold this covenant, if only because it is a term in a solemn contract. B, the *covenantor*, is bound to A, the *covenantee*, under a *restrictive covenant*; B's land is called the 'servient land' and A's the 'dominant land'. All fairly straightforward.

But what if B sells his house and land to C? Is C still bound (under a contract which after all was between A and B, and to which he was not a party) not to develop the land for any business purpose? And what if farmer A sells his land to D? Can D, as the new farmer, enforce the covenant against B, the original covenantor, or C his successor? For over a century, the answer in all cases has been 'Yes, subject to certain conditions'.

Whatever may be the normal rule concerning 'privity of contract' (see Chapter 3) the position regarding restrictive covenants is that they may be enforced by any assignee of an original party to it, provided that the latter owns some land which is benefited by the covenant, and therefore has some interest in enforcing it. In other words, the benefit of the covenant 'runs with' the land which it was originally intended to benefit, and whoever is the proprietor for the time being is entitled to the benefit of it. Thus, in the example above, anyone who buys A's farm will be entitled to enforce the restriction against building or developing a business on B's land, or whoever else's land it may become.

But – and this is an important qualification to the general rule – where the land which forms the 'servient' land is sold to a bona fide purchaser in good faith who has no knowledge of the existence of the covenant, it may not be enforced against him. Nor may the burden of a covenant travel with the land at all unless it is negative in nature (i.e. it prohibits certain actions being taken), and it would therefore not apply, for example, to a covenant to build a house. And before the covenantee or his successor may enforce the covenant against a new servient owner, he must at the time of the covenant have retained land which was intended to benefit by or be protected by the covenant.

This rather complex set of statements can be illustrated more simply by returning to the original example. For as long as B is owner of the servient land, and farmer A is the owner of the dominant land, there can be no question that the covenant may be enforced. If farmer A sells his land, equally there will be no problem over the new farmer, D, enforcing the covenant of which he now has the benefit. It is only when B, the original covenantor, sells his land that the limits are placed on the travelling of the burden of the covenant. If the assignee of the servient land is a bona fide purchaser unaware of the existence of the covenant, he will not be bound by it; even if he is aware of it, he will only be bound by it where it is negative in nature, where the original covenantee retained land which was intended to be protected by the covenant, the benefit of which has validly been transferred to the party now seeking to enforce it.

Covenants – the existence of which could obviously be highly inconvenient to a business organization wishing to expand or diversify – may be modified or discharged altogether in certain cases, apart from the obvious situation in which the parties to a covenant simply agree to discharge it. Covenants may, for example, be discharged by the covenantor breaching the covenant and not being challenged by the covenantee. More properly, they may be discharged by means of an application to the Lands Tribunal for a ruling that by reason of changes in the character of the neighbourhood or the property itself, or any other circumstances which may seem material to the Tribunal, the covenant should be regarded as obsolete. Alternatively it may be shown that the continued existence of the covenant would impede some reasonable use of the land, that all those entitled to the benefit of the covenant have agreed to the discharge or modification, or that the proposed discharge or modification will not injure them anyway. More recently, 'public interest' has been introduced as a major ground for allowing the modification or discharge of a covenant.

Easements

An 'easement' is a right which A has over the land of B which does not involve the removal of anything from the land – it has been described as a 'privilege without profit', and classic examples are a right of way, a right to light, a right of support, and a right to draw water.

In order for a right to be an 'easement' there must be both dominant and servient 'tenements' (i.e. pieces of land), they must be owned by different persons, the easement must be for the benefit of the dominant tenement, and the subject matter of it must be something capable of being in a direct grant by deed. We may now look in outline at the more common examples.

A *right of way* entitles A to cross the land of B, either for some specific purpose (e.g. to reach a stream) or generally. The actual route which he is to take may or may not be defined. A *right of water* may either be a right to take water (e.g. from a tap or from a stream) or it may be the right to pollute water (subject of course to any statutory prohibitions such as the Control of Pollution Act, 1974).

A frequently quoted easement is the *right of light*, which is in effect the right not to have the natural daylight to one's windows obscured or reduced by neighbouring buildings. This is an automatic right once the right has been enjoyed for twenty years, hence the rather inaccurate use of the phrase 'ancient lights' as an occasional description of this particular easement.

All manner of other items can come within the category of easement, and over the years this legal rag-bag has included the right to use a letter-box, the right to use a lavatory, the use of a wall to fix a sign, and the use of sheds on the servient tenement for the storage of equipment from the dominant tenement.

Taking easements and restrictive covenants together, it can be readily appreciated that to proceed with, for example, the purchase of an old building for a new factory without very careful checks on the state of play *vis-a-vis* the neighbours is a very hazardous enterprise indeed. It is even conceivable that there is a covenant against the building being used for business purposes (which the incoming proprietor may be deemed to have knowledge of, whether he has or not). Less dramatically, a neighbouring proprietor may have acquired the right to turn his delivery vans in the yard, or run his power cables under the premises. Alternatively, the new factory which was planned may be blocked by the simple fact that to build another storey might interfere with the 'ancient lights' of a neighbour.

Occupier's liability

At Common Law it was established for many years that the occupier of premises owed a legal duty to those who entered his premises to ensure that they were reasonably safe for them to do so, and the Occupier's Lability Act of 1957 merely put it in statutory form and tied up a few loose ends in the process. For this reason, much of the 'case-law' pre-dates the Act, but is still perfectly relevant.

Basically, the Act states that the 'occupier' of premises owes a 'common duty of care' to all visitors to his premises. What this means in less formal language is that the occupier must take such care as is reasonable in the circumstances to ensure that the premises are reasonably safe for the purpose for which the visitors are invited or permitted to be there. 'Visitors' includes everyone coming on to the premises with the consent (express or implied) of the occupier, and means in effect just about everyone except a trespasser.

The 'circumstances of the case' will depend upon the purpose for which the visitor was invited on to the premises in the first place. Thus, while the delivery driver is entitled to assume that the premises are reasonably safe to make deliveries to, the window cleaner may assume that the premises are reasonably safe for cleaning windows. Where the visitor is a child, then special precautions must be taken, not only because most children are more vulnerable to accidents, but also because many of them will not benefit from warning notices. Even when the child is a trespasser, the occupier may still be under a duty of care to him, where something owned by him has acted as a 'lure' to the child (e.g. an open lorry in the yard).

Despite the Unfair Contract Terms Act, 1977, it is still theoretically possible for the occupier to absolve himself from liability for death or bodily injury by means of some suitable clause in a contract. Alternatively he may be able to show that the visitor knew of the danger but deliberately took the risk. Warning notices may be effective here, but it will depend upon the circumstances – they are more likely to be effective where they were intended to warn the visitor against doing something which he had not been invited to do in the first place (e.g. enter a forbidden area of the factory).

Where the accident or injury arises from the work of some *independent contractor* (who, for example, left some loose roof tiles where they could be dislodged by a high wind), then the occupier will only be liable where he himself has been negligent (in, for example, failing to check that the job had been done). Thus, whereas in *O'Connor* v. *Swan and Edgar* (1963), it was held that the proprietor was not liable when a piece of roof recently repaired by independent contractors fell on a customer, the occupier in *Woodward* v. *Mayor of Hastings*

(1945), was held liable for failing to check that ice had been cleared from a doorstep by a cleaner employed on a contract basis.

The care which the occupier must take need only, of course, be reasonable in the circumstances, and this will clearly vary from case to case. With the possible exception of children, the occupier is certainly under no obligation to make his premises 'idiot proof' and in most cases, a simply worded warning notice should suffice, provided of course that the visitor has an option whether to obey the notice or not. And the more remote the risk, the less precaution need be taken against it; there is, for example, the infinitesimal risk that a building may be struck by a crippled airliner, but that hardly obliges the proprietor to issue all visitors with tin hats.

Even where it is held that the occupier is liable to pay damages, there is still the possibility that the injured party was himself partly to blame for what happened, and that the full amount of the damages will therefore be reduced by the proportion to which he was at fault. This may happen, for example, where the visitor was drunk, or failed to notice a warning which was not displayed to maximum effect anyway.

A good modern example of this principle was *Stone* v. *Taffe* (1974), in which a gentleman leaving a function in the upstairs room of a public house via a narrow unlit staircase fell and was killed. The brewery, as occupiers, were found liable in damages, reduced by fifty per cent because of the deceased's condition at the time. In *Wood* v. *Moreland* (1971), however, it was held that the management of an hotel was under no obligation to remove all the snow and ice from the car park for the benefit of guests leaving a function at one o'clock in the morning. It was not even held to be reasonable to expect the management to scatter ash or sand at that time in the morning. Clearly, the circumstances can make all the difference.

Nuisance

Nuisance may best be defined as the unlawful interference with the use or enjoyment of another person's land and/or property. It can take many forms, such as noise, smells, vibration and visual obstruction. If, for example, I attempt to practise the bagpipes at three o'clock in the morning on a residential housing estate, or if I allow my restaurant to launch offensive odours into the street, I may well be committing a nuisance.

Nuisance may be both 'public' and 'private' and we may examine them in that order.

Public nuisance

A public nuisance is an unlawful interference with the enjoyment of property by the public in general (e.g. in a street or a public park). A classic example would be the obstruction of the highway. Since it extends well beyond private interests, and is in effect an attack on the rights of the public as a whole, public nuisance is a crime as well as a civil wrong. If the owner of a discotheque pollutes the night air at one hundred and twenty decibels, he may well be committing the crime of nuisance as well as a crime under the Control of Pollution Act, 1974, in addition of course to exposing himself to actions for 'private' nuisance (see below).

A private individual may sue in respect of a public nuisance, but only where he can show that he has suffered some loss or harm *over and above* that suffered by the public at large. A good example was *Rose* v. *Miles* (1857) where M obstructed a waterway, and in addition to the general inconvenience to the public, forced R to have his goods delivered overland, for which R was awarded damages.

Private nuisance

Before A may sue B for private nuisance, he must be able to show that B unlawfully and unreasonably interfered with his enjoyment of his land by something more than just an isolated act, and that he, A, suffered actual damage as a result.

Provided that the action complained of is lawful, it cannot be a nuisance, however maliciously intended it may have been; thus, in *Mayor of Bradford* v. *Pickles* (1895), it was held not to be a nuisance for one landowner to remove water from under his own land, even though it was done with the intention of causing subsidence to the land of a neighbour.

The action complained of must be a 'state of affairs' rather than an isolated incident. Thus, whereas the occasional escape of a cricket ball from a cricket field will not be a nuisance (*Bolton* v. *Stone*, 1951), it will be a nuisance to allow electrical wiring to deteriorate to the point at which a fire destroys a neighbour's house (*Spicer* v. *Smee*, 1946).

The 'interference' must also be unreasonable, and a variety of factors will be considered in this context. For example, what will be a nuisance in one locality may not be in another, and the complainer will not obtain damages if he is hypersensitive to, for example, noise, or if he has chosen to carry out some special activity next door (for example mink farming or glass blowing). Again, the purpose for which the actions are taken will be relevant, assuming that they do not fall into the category of 'lawful' in the first place (as in *Bradford* v. *Pickles* above). Thus, in *Christie* v. *Davey* (1893), a neighbour who created as much noise as he could in order to disrupt a musical evening next door was liable in nuisance, although the actions themselves might have been reasonable had they merely been necessary in order for the guilty party to be heard above the noise of the music (for example turning up the stereo unit).

The only person who may sue in respect of a *private* nuisance is someone with a legal interest in the land affected. This can lead to unjust results, as in *Malone* v. *Laskey* (1907), in which vibrations from an engine dislodged a lavatory cistern in the house next door which fell on the owner's wife. Since she did not own the house, it was held that no damages were awardable; had the cistern fallen on her husband, presumably they would have been.

8 Hiring and firing

The employer/employee relationship

There are many contexts in which it is vitally important to know whether one man is the 'employee' of another. To take only the more obvious ones, the owner of a business will normally only be required to deduct PAYE and National Insurance from the money paid in wages to an employee, and not the fee paid to an independent contractor. Only an employee is entitled to redundancy payment in certain circumstances at the end of the job, and only an employee has the right not to be unfairly dismissed. A higher duty of safety is owed to an employee than to an independent contractor.

In addition, an employer is 'vicariously' liable for the negligent actions of an employee (e.g. a van driver employed by him who knocks down a pedestrian) committed during the course of his employment, but will not be liable at all if the accident is caused by an 'independent contractor' (e.g. a maintenance engineer driving to the factory to service a tea vending machine).

For these reasons, two major tests have been devised over the years to establish whether or not A is the employee of B. The first, or 'control' test, states that A will be an employee if B may tell A not only which job to do, but how to do it. This test is not very appropriate in an age of technical specialization (e.g. it does not apply comfortably in the case of NHS medical staff, who are employees but at the same time specialist experts), and the more modern test is the 'organizational' test, under which A will be an employee if the work he performs is 'an integral part of' B's business. This test was sufficient to confer 'employee' status on a circus trapeze artist in *Whittaker* v. *Minister of Pensions* (1967).

In practice, the modern courts do not stop merely at applying those two tests, but employ a whole host of others, and look at the entire situation realistically. It may well be that A is an employee for one purpose (e.g. the Health and Safety at Work Act, 1974) but not for another (e.g. income tax). Combining all these factors together is not easy, and can sometimes lead to startling anomalies. Thus, a company director who is the sole shareholder of the company may be employed by it, whereas a partner in a firm can never be, unless as a salaried partner. Business consultants can be employees, despite their apparent independent image, but there is serious doubt as to whether judges and police officers are employees in the normal way. It is uncertain to what extent agency staff are employees, but the better opinion seems to be that they are employed by the agency. Part-time or casual staff are perfectly eligible to be classed as employees, as indeed are outworkers in industries such as garment manufacture, hosiery and footwear.

The contract of employment

Once it has been decided that A is the employee of B, there will be a contract of employment between them, if only one 'implied' by the courts because of their relationship. Where A and B set out to *form* the relationship of employer/employee (i.e. they do not leave it to the courts to imply such a relationship), this contract is usually a little more obvious, although its terms are often to be gleaned only by adding together what was said at the initial interview, agreed by subsequent correspondence, and confirmed by a more formal document once the employee commenced work.

Legally, a contract of employment may take any form (e.g. oral, written, or a mixture of the two), and, subject to certain special rules, is governed by exactly the same principles as an ordinary contract. In theory, the parties are free to negotiate such terms as they wish, but in reality, statute and union pressure have combined to ensure that a significant proportion of the terms in a contract of employment are dictated to the parties from Acts of Parliament or collective agreements.

One of the most important of these Acts of Parliament is the Employment Protection (Consolidation) Act, 1978 (EPCA), s. 1 of which states that every employee must receive, by the end of the thirteenth week of his employment, a written statement containing the following information:

The names of the parties;
the date of the commencement of the contract;
whether or not any period of employment with a previous employer will count as part of the employee's 'continuous period of employment', and if so, the date of commencement of that period;
the rate of pay, or the method by which it may be calculated;
the intervals at which payment falls due (i.e. weekly, monthly, etc.);
the hours of work;
what arrangement exists (if any) for holidays and holiday pay, sickness and sick pay, pensions and pension schemes;
the length of notice required to terminate the contract on either side;
the title of the job which the employee is employed to perform; and
whether or not the employer is contracted out of the state pension scheme.

In addition, this document must contain details of (or a reference to) any disciplinary code to which the employee will be subject, and must in addition identify some person to whom the employee may refer if he is dissatisfied with any disciplinary decision relating to him, and some person to whom he may apply for the purpose of redressing some grievance in connection with his employment, and the manner in which such an application should be made. Matters relating to health and safety at work are not included in this requirement.

Instead of detailing all these provisions in a special document, the employer may simply refer the employee to a document reasonably accessible to him (e.g. a collective agreement or a pensions booklet) which contains that information. If no provisions are being made on certain matters (e.g. sickness benefit, pension schemes), this fact should be stated. If there is already in existence a formal written contract containing all these provisions, then s. 1 is of course complied with. A simple s. 1 notice is not itself a contract, but is evidence of its terms.

Section 1 does not apply to staff normally employed for less than sixteen hours per week (eight hours after five years' service), staff who are married to their employers, Crown employees, staff whose employment will be wholly or mainly outside the UK, registered dock workers and merchant seamen. Any change in terms must be communicated to the employee within four weeks. Failure to provide a s. 1 notice can lead to a referral to an industrial tribunal.

The implied terms of a contract of employment

Quite apart from the express terms which the parties actually include in the contract of employment, there are other terms which are 'imported' or 'implied' into the contract, either as a result of a statute, or by the courts over the years. Statutory implied terms (e.g. the right to equality of treatment regardless of sex, the right not to be unfairly dismissed, etc.) are dealt with in Chapter 9, and we will concentrate here on those terms which have in the past been implied into contracts of employment by the courts. They are just as binding as any express term of the contract, and may not easily be cancelled out even by a clear term to the contrary in the contract itself.

Duty to work and duty to provide work

It is sometimes stated as an implied term of the contract of employment that the employee must make himself available for work as agreed, and must be ready and willing to do such work as he was employed to do, and that in return the employer is under a duty to pay him and provide him with work. Certainly, if the employee fails to appear for work on a regular basis, the employer would probably experience no legal difficulty in dismissing him, but at Common Law, the duty to provide work probably only ever extended to piece workers, those training for a particular profession, those seeking to exercise skills and those with an international reputation to maintain (e.g. chefs).

The provisions concerning guarantee payments (see Chapter 9) have in any case largely taken over in this area.

Employee's duty of obedience

This somewhat Dickensian-sounding phrase is still employed to convey the fact that in every contract of employment, there is an implied undertaking by the employee to obey all reasonable instructions given to him in the course of his employment. Failure to do so will probably always be a disciplinary matter, but will not always entitle the employer simply to sack the employee; before he may do that, the refusal must be so serious and fundamental to the contract that in effect it is a rejection of it, as in *Pepper* v. *Webb* (1969), in which a gardener was dismissed by his employer when, after a lengthy record of unsatisfactory behaviour, he refused to carry out instruction with the words 'I couldn't care less about your bloody greenhouse and your sodding garden'. His dismissal was upheld as valid by the Court of Appeal.

But an employee is only obliged to carry out such orders as are reasonable, relate to his work, and come to him through the correct chain of command. It goes without saying that he is not obliged to perform any act which is unlawful, or would expose him to an unreasonable risk of injury; thus, in *Morrish* v. *Henlys (Folkestone) Ltd* (1973), it was held that an employee was perfectly entitled to refuse an instruction to falsify petrol consumption records.

Employee's duty of good faith

There is an implied term in every contract of employment to the effect that the employee will perform his duties to the employer in 'good faith', in the broadest sense of that term. This includes not only the more obvious aspects such as dishonesty, undermining the employer's business, and so on, but also persistent idleness or deliberate lack of effort.

Thus, to take a few examples, in *Sanders* v. *Parry* (1967), it was held to be a breach of faith for a salaried solicitor to leave the firm he had worked for and set up on his own after 'poaching' the employer's secretary and his best client, while in *Sinclair* v. *Neighbour* (1967), the court felt that it was a breach of faith for a betting shop manager to borrow £15 from the shop till on an IOU when he knew that this was expressly forbidden by the company regulations.

One aspect of the duty of good faith involves not disclosing trade secrets or exploiting customer contacts acquired confidentially during one's employment, unless to do so is in the public interest, as in *Initial Services* v. *Putterill* (1968), in which it was held to be in the public interest for a former sales manager of a laundry company to reveal details about his former employer's pricing structure which disclosed evidence of a price-fixing ring. Again, while there is no general duty to disclose the activities of one's fellow workers, it is generally assumed that there *is* such a duty where to fail to do so would affect the employer's business interests, or endanger the staff.

Good faith also involves doing only the employer's work in the employer's time, and this fact has been given some recognition by the requirements of the Patents Act, 1977, s. 39, to the effect that any invention created by an employee in the normal course of his duties is the property of the employer (see Chapter 6). This is occasionally extended so as to prevent employees from behaving outside normal working hours to the detriment of the employer, as in *Hivac Ltd* v. *Park Royal Scientific Instruments* (1946) in which it was held that employees could not take spare-time jobs with a direct trade competitor on work which competed with that of their regular employer.

An interesting development of the 'good faith' concept was *Secretary of State for Employment* v. *ASLEF* (2) (1972), in which ASLEF members 'worked to rule' and caused severe disruption to the railways. Having established that the rule book was regarded as part of the terms of the contract of employment, the Court of Appeal nevertheless held that the manner in which it was done was with a lack of good faith, and with the object of disrupting the employer's business, and it was therefore a breach of contract.

Employee's duty to account

Every employee is under a duty to account to the employer for all money and property handled by him in the course of his employment. Thus, not only is the receptionist or cashier responsible for her 'float' and the sales assistant for her stock, but the manager is answerable for the car, the lathe operator for his machine, and so on.

In particular, no employee may make any secret profit from his position, since any extra financial benefit which emerges belongs to the employer; thus, in *Boston Deep Sea Fishing and Ice Co.* v. *Ansell* (1880), it was held that the managing director of a trawler company who was a shareholder in the company supplying ice for the ship's holds, and who received a bonus for each order which he placed for ice, had been justifiably dismissed for making secret profits.

In return for the employee's duty to account, the employer is under a duty to reimburse him for expenses incurred, or to indemnify him against losses incurred, in the course of his employment.

Employee's duty to excercise reasonable care and skill

Every employee owes a duty to himself, his fellow workers and his employer to carry out his duties carefully and competently. Where he fails to do so, and his negligence causes injury, he may be liable to compensate the injured party directly, or to reimburse the employer in respect of damages which he has had to pay by virtue of his 'vicarious' liability for the actions of employees. Thus, in *Lister* v. *Romford Ice and Cold Storage Co. Ltd* (1957), the driver of a lorry owned by R who injured his mate by his negligent driving was required to indemnify his employers against the damages which they had been obliged to pay to the mate.

If an employee's negligence injures only himself, then any damages which he might have received from the employer (see below) will be reduced to take account of his 'contributory negligence'.

The employer's duty to provide for the employee's safety

This term is implied into the contract of employment by Common Law, but is best considered in the light of safety law as a whole, and therefore appears in Chapter 9.

Quite apart from the above implied terms, which have been well established for many years, a series of new 'implied terms' has begun to emerge under the pressure of cases now being dealt with by industrial tribunals under recent employment protection legislation. For example, there now seems to be an implied term that every employer will treat every employee with respect and consideration, will not victimize him and will not subject him to intolerable strain in order to drive him out. He must also make every effort to ensure that his induction and training go as smoothly as possible.

It is arguable that the rules of decency, equality and good manners always required such behaviour from an employer, but hitherto the law simply required him to comply with the letter of the law. Industrial Relations Codes of Practice (see below) now require him to adhere to its spirit as well, and a failure to do so may result in an action for unfair dismissal. Also, when assessing whether or not it was reasonable for an employer to sack an employee for failing to comply with certain instructions (e.g. to move to another factory, to change shift duties), the courts will usually ask whether such an obligation could be reasonably implied into the contract, by reference to the practice in the rest of the industry or otherwise.

Vicarious liability of the employer

The point has already been made that an employer is 'vicariously' liable for negligent actions performed by his employees in the course of their employment. He may even in some cases be liable for their deliberate actions where it may be said that his negligence led to them being employed in the first place, as in *Morriss* v. *Martin* (1966), in which the employers were held to be vicariously liable when an assistant in a dry-cleaning shop stole a fur coat belonging to a customer.

So far as vicarious liability for negligent acts is concerned, the law is that not only will the employee himself be directly liable for what he has done, but his employer will be also. Thus, the pedestrian knocked down by a refuse lorry may sue either or both the driver or the local authority which employed him. As we have seen, the employer may claim a 'contribution', or even a total indemnity, from the employee, but that does not prevent the injured party from recovering from the employer in the first instance.

But before the employer will be liable, the acts complained of must have been committed 'during the course of the employee's employment', and this requirement is the one which in practice causes most of the difficulties. If the employee goes off on what the law calls 'a frolic of his own' (as would be the case, for example, if a van driver were to use the van during his day off to help his brother move house), then the employer bears no responsibility for what he does, but he may be liable when the action is committed in the general course of the employee's duties, although not specifically authorized. The real problem arises where the action is within the general scope of the employee's employment, but specifically *prohibited* (e.g. giving lifts to hitch-hikers). The position here seems to be that the employee is not acting within the scope of his employment, and that the employer is therefore not liable.

A neat illustration of the distinction arose in *Daniels* v. *Whetstone Entertainments Ltd* (1961), in which a dance hall steward employed by W assaulted D. He was ordered to return to his other duties but shortly afterwards assaulted D again. It was held that the first assault was within his duties (keeping order) but the second one was not, and the employers were therefore liable only in respect of the first assault.

'The course of employment' may well include journeys to and from work, and actions performed during meal breaks; thus, in *Harvey* v. *O'Dell* (1958), the employer of two electricians was liable in respect of a road accident which occurred while the men were returning from a café from their lunch break, since he had sent them on a distant all-day job with no instructions regarding food, and the journey was therefore 'reasonably incidental to' their work.

Employers may occasionally, under statute, be liable in respect of *crimes* committed by employees, in which the crime becomes that of the employer. A good example of such a statute is the Trade Descriptions Act, 1968, which is dealt with more fully in Chapter 5.

Dismissal

There is, of course, much more to the relationship between employer and employee than simply a contract of employment, the implied terms, and the laws on dismissal, as reference to Chapter 9 will show, but this early opportunity is being taken of dealing with dismissal (a) because it is partly based on contract; (b) because it helps to complete the framework upon which the various 'employee rights' of Chapter 9 are based.

Until 1971, dismissal was simply a matter of contract. Although the Common Law recognized that some dismissals might be unlawful where they were grossly unreasonable, it was still fairly true to say that provided an employee was supplied with the correct amount of notice, or payment in lieu of notice, the employer had validly dismissed him, and his motives for doing so were his own affair. Even these minimum periods of notice were dispensed with where the employee had done something to warrant 'summary dismissal'.

From 1971 onwards, the paramount factor has been the 'fairness' of not only the grounds for a dismissal, but also the method by which it was carried out. Every employee has a statutory right not to be unfairly dismissed, which takes precedence over anything in the Common Law. But it is still necessary to examine the old Common Law; (a) because not every employee is covered by the statutory code (e.g. staff with less than a year's service); (b) because it still governs the way in which a contract of employment may come to an end; (c) because before a tribunal can determine that there has been an 'unfair dismissal', it must first establish whether or not there has been a 'dismissal'.

Dismissal at Common Law

At Common Law, a contract of employment may come to an end in one of four ways.

(1) By the giving of notice

It is still very common indeed for a contract of employment to be brought to an end by one party giving notice to the other. Simply because the employer has given the employee the requisite amount of notice does not make the dismissal fair, but at least it clearly brings the contract to an end, and is clear evidence of dismissal.

It will be recalled that the period of notice required from either party in order to terminate the contract is one of those factors which under s. 1 of the EPCA must be recorded in writing at the outset. In fact, the Act goes further than that, and insists on certain *minimum* periods of notice, which will apply in the absence of any longer period specified by the parties themselves (e.g. under a collective agreement).

Thus, under s. 49 of the Act, the employee is entitled to at least one week's notice until he has completed two years' 'continuous' service (i.e. working for more than sixteen hours per week, or eight hours per week after five years' service), after which he becomes entitled to a further week's notice for each year of service up a to maximum of twelve weeks' notice after twelve years' service. Under this system, for example, the employee with five years' service would be entitled to five weeks' notice, while the fifteen-year man would receive the maximum of twelve weeks' notice.

By comparison, an employee need give only one week's notice to terminate the contract, regardless of his length of service, unless the contract provides for longer. The parties may clearly stipulate for longer periods under the contract, and in theory, either party may give salary in lieu of notice (i.e. the need to actually work the period is commuted to the payment of the wage which would have been earned during that period).

There are some employees for whom these periods are not applicable (staff in the first four weeks of employment, or staff working for less than sixteen or eight hours per week), and in such cases, the Common Law requires a 'reasonable period' of notice. While an employee is working out the amount of notice laid down under the 1978 Act, he is entitled to his normal pay for working his normal hours, or to be paid for a normal week where he is ready and willing to work, but no work is provided, or where he is off sick or on holiday. If he is being laid off on the grounds of redundancy, he will also normally be entitled to time off to seek other work (see Chapter 9).

(2) By summary dismissal

Under the Common Law, an employer might, on certain grounds, dismiss an employee 'summarily', i.e. on the spot, without notice and without payment in lieu of notice. Section 49 of EPCA preserves this right when the behaviour of the employee has merited it. But the point must be re-emphasized that the sort of behaviour on the part of the employee which might be sufficient at Common Law to justify 'summary dismissal' may not be enough under EPCA to make the dismissal 'fair'.

The sort of ground upon which, at Common Law, the employer could validly dismiss an' employee summarily included 'gross misconduct' (whatever that may mean), disobedience, gross neglect and dishonesty. Already in this chapter, we have seen two examples of successful summary dismissals, those in *Pepper* v. *Webb* and *Sinclair* v. *Neighbour*. To these may be added the examples of the night watchman in *Ross* v. *Aquascutum* (1973) who regularly left his post for two hours at a time, the factory hand in *Dalton* v. *Burtons Gold Medal Biscuits* (1974) who falsified a fellow employee's time card, and the airline pilot in *Alidair* v. *Taylor* (1976) whose less than perfect landing of a plane-load of passengers destroyed the entire nose-wheel assembly.

(3) By automatic operation of law

There are certain events which, by the operation of a rule of law, have the effect of bringing the contract to an immediate end. An obvious example is the death of the employee; the same is probably true of the death of the employer, where he is a human being. The biggest employers are, however, companies, and an order for the winding up of a company operates as notice of dismissal to all the employees. Where the employer is a partnership, it is a breach of contract of employment for the partnership to be dissolved, but the contract is not necessarily thereby dissolved.

The most obvious legal event which can bring the contract of employment to an end is one which may be classed as a 'frustrating' event. These were dealt with in general terms in Chapter 3, and the reader is referred back to the case of *Condor* v. *The Barron Knights* (1966), see p. 114. The illness of the employee is an obvious potentially frustrating event, as in the above case, and in *Hart* v. *A. R. Marshall* (1978), in which it was held that after twenty-one months off through illness, an employee who was a key maintenance fitter could be regarded as dismissed by virtue of a frustrating event. The relevant factors to be considered in each case are the nature and duration of the illness, the prospects of recovery, and the importance of the worker to the overall operation run by the employer.

Another problem which can face an employer is that of the employee who is unable to attend work because he is in prison. Under the Advisory, Conciliation, and Arbitration Service (ACAS) Code of Practice, 1977, s. 15(a) (see p. 227), an employee should not normally be dismissed simply because he has committed an offence outside his employment, although the tribunal must recognize a frustrating event if a prison sentence keeps him from work for an excessive period. Thus, in *Moore* v. *CEGB* (1974), it was held that a month in custody awaiting trial was not long enough to justify dismissal, but in *Hare* v. *Murphy* (1974), it was held that a twelve month sentence was a frustrating event.

(4) Expiry of a fixed term
When it is agreed by the parties beforehand that the contract of employment shall only continue for a given period, then, so far as the law of contract is concerned, it will validly come to an end at the expiry of that period. If the contract is not renewed by the employer, it may be classed as an unfair dismissal, but it will still mean that the contract is at an end. It will be recalled that when laying out in written form those essential terms of the contract required to be in writing under EPCA, s. 1, the employer must include the termination date of any fixed-term contract.

Unfair dismissal

These, then, are the ways in which an employment contract can come to an end at Common Law; if one were to add to those the situation in which the employee simply walks out, then this accounts for all the ways in which a period of employment may end.

Whatever the Common Law may say, under EPCA, s. 54, most employees have 'the right not to be unfairly dismissed';

the only employees who are denied this right are those who have been 'continuously employed' (i.e. for sixteen hours a week or more) for less than fifty-two weeks with the same employer (two years where the employer employs twenty or less staff), employees who are married to their employers, registered dock workers, the master and crew of any 'share fishing' vessel, and employees over the normal retirement age. Those normally employed outside Great Britain are also excluded, as are employees working under a fixed term contract of two years or more who have excluded their right to claim by written agreement with the employer before the period has expired.

The fifty-two week period is calculated by reference to the 'effective date of termination', i.e. it includes any period of notice which may have been given or, where this is longer, the period of notice which should have been given as the maximum required by EPCA. The fifty-two week qualifying period does not apply at all where the principal reason for dismissal was an 'inadmissible' one, namely dismissal as a result of a wish on the employee's part to become a member of an independent trade union, or to take part in its activities, or a refusal on his part to join or remain in a trade union which was not an independent trade union. Again, there are no qualifying periods of employment to be satisfied where the alleged grounds for dismissal is racial or sexual discrimination (see Chapter 9), or a previous conviction which is 'spent' in terms of the Rehabilitation of Offenders Act, 1974.

If an employee is dismissed for a reason which he feels is unfair, he has three months in which to complete form IT1, supplied by the Department of Employment, and lodge his claim before an industrial tribunal. He is assisted in this by s. 53 of EPCA which gives most dismissed employees who have fifty-two weeks' continuous service the right to demand from the employer, within fourteen days, written grounds for the dismissal. These grounds may be used in evidence in any subsequent proceedings, and any failure of the employer to supply them when requested can lead to an award of compensation to the employee amounting to two weeks' pay.

Having been dismissed, and having brought his employer before an industrial tribunal (see Chapter 1 – these tribunals now have exclusive jurisdiction in dismissal cases) and proved the dismissal, the employee may now call upon the employer to show that the dismissal was a 'fair' one. There are in fact six separate categories laid down under s. 57 of the Act which will constitute 'fair' dismissal, and it is for the employer to bring himself within one of them. Once he has done that, he must still show that in all the circumstances of the case, he set about applying the dismissal procedure to the employee fairly, and in a reasonable manner.

The employer must therefore satisfy three tests.

1 He must identify the reason for dismissal.
2 He must show that it was a 'fair' reason per s. 57.
3 He must show that he acted 'reasonably' towards the employee.

We may now look more closely at the 'fair' grounds for dismissal.

The capabilities of the employee
No tribunal will expect an employer to put up with a worker who is incompetent, but it will first of all require evidence that the worker in question was given every opportunity for training, retraining, transfer and so on. Supervision facilities and staff support must be adequate, and several warnings would normally be required before final dismissal, although these may perhaps be dispensed with where the incompetence is overwhelming and particularly disastrous (e.g. public transport, as in *Alidair* v. *Taylor*, above).

Along with 'capabilities' in the sense of skill or aptitude may be classed 'availability'. No employer is forced to continue on his books (even without pay) an employee who is likely to be absent for a long time due to ill-health or some other reason such as a prison sentence. The same considerations also concern the employee who is fit for work, but unfit for his normal job. The employer must make reasonable efforts to relocate him where possible, but there will come a point at which he may 'fairly' dismiss him, even if the contract has not become 'frustrated' anyway (see above).

The qualifications of the employee
Where a person is appointed on condition that he already has certain qualifications, or will acquire them in a specified period of time, then again the employer is justified in dismissing him if it transpires that he does not possess them, or cannot possibly qualify, as in *Blackman* v. *Post Office* (1974), in which a trainee postal officer was dismissed after failing an aptitude test for the maximum number of occasions permissible under the regulations.

Again, however, the tribunal will expect to find that the employer gave the employee every assistance and consideration, and that no suitable alternative post is available.

The conduct of the employee
This category is very wide, and is frequently quoted as the one under which it is alleged the employee was 'fairly dismissed'. In the past few years, it had become more and more obvious that one must distinguish between misconduct within the workplace, and misconduct during the employee's own time, unconnected with work.

It is fairly obvious that certain serious misdeeds by the employee (e.g. theft, violence, drunkenness, obscenity and malicious damage) if committed while at work, will leave little room for doubt that the employer may fairly dismiss the employee. Reference to the section above on summary dismissal will recall a few examples. This is not to say that dismissal should follow a first offence; this will normally only happen where there has been 'gross misconduct' (see below, ACAS Code of Practice). The employer must show that he investigated the incident thoroughly, interviewed the witnesses, allowed the worker concerned to state his case, and so on. Where a particular action is to be visited with more serious consequences than one would normally expect (e.g. smoking in a food preparation area), it must be well publicized, preferably in a disciplinary code handed to the worker upon his arrival at the firm.

The ground of misconduct which in practice causes the greatest difficulty is, of course, dishonesty. It is now firmly established that an employer may 'fairly' dismiss an employee for, e.g. theft, even though he may not have proof 'beyond reasonable doubt' of his guilt (the standard required for a conviction in court), provided that he has reasonable grounds for believing the employee to be guilty. If he has, then he may dismiss the offender, even if his guilt is never established in court, as in *Conway* v. *Matthew Wright and Nephew* (1977), in which an employer was held to have validly dismissed a night watchman suspected of malicious damage to company property, even though it was later decided that there was insufficient evidence for a prosecution.

The question is, therefore, not whether the employee was guilty, but whether or not the employer has reasonable grounds to believe he was. The employer must be seen to make some investigation for himself; thus in *Tesco* v. *Hill* (1977), it was held to be insufficient simply to dismiss a cashier suspected of theft and then call in the police without giving her the opportunity of explaining her side of the affair. Once the police investigations have begun, of course, the employer is limited in his investigative powers anyway, and many industrial relations advisers feel that the appropriate action here is suspension on full pay pending the outcome.

So far as conduct outside the employment is concerned, the employer will not normally be able to use this as conduct justifying a 'fair' dismissal unless it in some way casts doubt on his suitability for the job, or his reliability or honesty, as in *Singh* v. *London CBS* (1976), in which it was held that the operator of a one-man bus was validly dismissed for a fraud on a building society. In *Fowler* v. *Cammell Laird* (1973), it was held that an employer could dismiss an employee who stole a fellow worker's wing mirror, since this was disruptive of working relationships, but in *Norfolk County Council* v. *Bernard* (1979), the tribunal held that the mere fact that a teacher had been convicted of possessing and cultivating cannabis did not necessarily justify dismissal. In other words, it is a question of fact in each case, and one normally requires evidence that the behaviour outside the workplace affects relationships inside, or reflects adversely on the employer's business.

One form of 'misconduct' which may conveniently be touched upon here is that of striking. Section 62 of EPCA states, in effect, that an employer is immune from any possibility of unfair dismissal proceedings if he dismisses an employee who is on strike, or in respect of whom a lockout is in operation. The main qualification is that the employer must treat all such striking workers in the same way (otherwise those discriminated against may claim unfair dismissal), and in *Stock* v. *Frank Jones (Tipton) Ltd* (1978), it was held that it *was* discrimination, and therefore a potential unfair dismissal, for the employer to fire only those who remained on strike, and to keep those who had a change of heart after coming out initially. In *Marsden* v. *Fairey Stainless Ltd* (1979), it was held that s. 62 applies even where the strike was engineered or provoked by the employer.

Redundancy

If the employer can show that the reason for the dismissal was genuinely that of redundancy, then the dismissal will not be classed as unfair. However, the employer must be able to show that he acted fairly in selecting a particular employee for redundancy in the first place, and that he explored all the other possibilities before resorting to redundancy. The employer must also be able to show that he consulted with the trade unions in the manner required by EPCA; he will also, of course, be obliged to make redundancy payments to the employee concerned. This latter point is taken up in more detail in the final section of this chapter.

Under the detailed provisions of EPCA, selection of a particular individual for redundancy will be regarded as automatically unfair, if he was selected whereas others equally qualified for redundancy were not, and either the reason was an 'inadmissible' one (see above) or he was selected contrary to an agreed system or procedure without justification.

Statutory restriction

It will be a 'fair' dismissal where to have retained the employee would have led to the contravention of some 'enactment' (i.e. either an Act of Parliament or regulations made under it). An obvious example would be the continued employment as a driver of someone who had been disqualified (*Appleyard* v. *Smith*, 1972), or the continued employment in a meat processing plant of a person who refuses to shave off a beard, contrary to the Food Hygiene Regulations (*Gill* v. *Walls Meat Co*, 1977).

Again, the employer must be able to show that he gave the employee in question every consideration and, where relevant, that he considered him for an alternative post.

Some other substantial reason

The Act contains this final safety net provision in the hope that any justifiable reason for dismissal which does not fall under one of the more specific headings will come under this one. As might be expected, there have been many cases brought under this provision and it has been held, for example, that a substantial and fair reason for dismissal is that a secretary is married to a trade rival and in a position to give him valuable information (*Foot* v. *Eastern Counties Ltd*, 1972), that a manager refuses to live within a reasonable travelling distance of his premises (*Farr* v. *Hoveringham Gravel*, 1972), that an employee will not accept a change in working hours (*Storey* v. *Allied Brewery*, 1977), and that an employee, in his letter of application has concealed a criminal conviction which is highly relevant to the nature of his or her job (*Debaughn* v. *Star Cinemas*, 1976).

There are, of course, many other reasons for which an employer will consider dismissing an employee, and some are dealt with by the Act. For example, where there is a union 'closed shop' operating within the organization, s. 58 of EPCA states that to dismiss someone who is not, and who refuses to become, a member of that union will not be unfair, provided that the agreement is always enforced without exception, and that the refusal to join is not prompted by a genuine religious objection against union membership or on the grounds of conscience or a deeply felt personal conviction. But at the same time, s. 63 of EPCA states that it may be an unfair dismissal for an employer simply to give in to union pressure against an employee on grounds other than the 'closed shop' grounds outlined above. In such cases, the union itself may be taken before a tribunal as well.

Dismissal on the grounds of sexual or racial discrimination, or pregnancy, will also be regarded as 'unfair' in many cases; these are dealt with in Chapter 9.

Constructive dismissal

Where the behaviour of the employer is such that he is in effect indicating to the employee that he no longer regards the contract of employment as binding upon him, the employee is entitled to resign and claim damages for 'constructive dismissal', just as if he had been unfairly dismissed. The law was in some confusion for several years, and some quite amazing decisions were reached as to what might constitute constructive dismissal, but in *Western Excavating* v. *Sharp* (1978), the Court of Appeal finally ruled that the behaviour must constitute a positive breach of contract on the part of the employer. Examples might be a failure to pay wages, a reduction in the wage rate, a refusal to provide protective clothing on a dirty job contrary to shop floor agreements, and a failure to reimburse an employee for expenses genuinely incurred during the course of his employment.

The breach in question may be of an implied term, as in *Keys* v. *Shoefayre Ltd* (1978), in which it was held to be constructive dismissal for an employer to refuse to guard shop staff against gangs of youths robbing local shops, since it was in breach of an implied duty of safety (see Chapter 9). But there must be a breach of some contractual term; it is not enough simply that life has become intolerable for the employee.

Dismissal procedures

The point has already been made that even if the employer has what the tribunal would regard as a 'fair' reason for dismissal, he may still be liable to compensate the employee for unfair dismissal where he acted unreasonably in implementing the dismissal procedure. In short, he must show that the method of dismissal was as fair as the reason.

Neither EPCA nor any other Act of Parliament actually specifies what will be a 'fair' method of dismissal, and each case is treated on its own merits. However, since 1971, the Advisory, Conciliation and Arbitration Service (ACAS) has issued 'Codes of Practice' for the guidance of employers in 'disciplinary practices'. These codes are not rules of law, and not legally binding; the fact that a particular employer has failed to comply with the Code does not mean that he has acted unfairly, nor will the fact that he has followed it necessarily absolve him. But they tend to be used as yardsticks against which the behaviour of the employer is judged.

The latest such Code dates from June 1977, and its main provisions, in outline, are as follows:

1 Every employer should operate a comprehensive disciplinary system, and its details should be communicated to every employee (*see* EPCA, s. 1, above). In fact, in *Royal Naval School* v. *Hughes* (1979), it was suggested by the Employment Appeal Tribunal that the ACAS requirement for grievance procedures did not necessarily apply to firms with less than forty employees, since it was more directed 'with industry and large enterprises in view'. It would seem, therefore, that where the firm is small enough for there to be daily freedom of contact between staff at all levels, it will not strictly be necessary for the employer to draw up a tightly defined disciplinary code.

2 Disciplinary procedures should be regarded as a means of encouraging improvement as well as imposing sanctions.

3 Detailed procedures should identify the parties, specify the levels of management with disciplinary powers, provide

for individuals to be informed of complaints against them and afford them an opportunity of refuting them, allow for trade union representation, or for the employee to be accompanied by a fellow employee of his choice, ensure that no employee is dismissed for a first offence except for 'gross misconduct', ensure that no disciplinary action is taken until the case has been carefully investigated, provide an opportunity of explaining to the employee what penalty is to be imposed, and specify an appeal procedure.

4 Consideration should always be given, in serious cases, to suspension with pay while the matter is being investigated.

5 In the case of a minor offence, following an informal warning from a supervisor, any repetition should be met with a formal oral warning. For a more serious offence, the first formal warning will be a written one. Further misconduct may result in a final, formal written warning clearly indicating that a recurrence may lead to dismissal, fine or whatever.

Tribunal procedures

It was explained above that every action for unfair dismissal will commence when the employee fills in a form IT1 (within three months of the dismissal) and sends it to the nearest Tribunal Office. The IT1 will contain the bare facts of the claim, and this will be communicated to the ex-employer on form IT2, sent by the Tribunals Office. An attempt will then be made by an ACAS officer to bring the two parties to an amicable agreement (the latest figures suggest a 50 per cent success rate at this stage), but if that fails, the case is set down for a tribunal hearing.

Every tribunal consists of three people; a legally qualified chairman, a representative chosen from a panel nominated by trade unions, and a corresponding 'management panel' member. Proceedings are kept as informal as justice permits, and the normal rules of evidence may be waived in an endeavour to get at the truth. Either party has the right to be legally represented, but in practice some of the best representations are made by union officials on behalf of the employee and personnel executives for the employer.

Once the employee has shown that there has been a dismissal (not always a foregone conclusion), it is for the employer to show that it was a fair one, and that he went about implementing it in a fair way. If not, the tribunal may make awards against the employer, based on the weekly pay earned by the employee before his dismissal (maximum £120 per week). The 'basic award' is calculated by reference to the length of continuous employment (maximum twenty years) and the age of the employee during that period (one and a half weeks for each year over forty-one, one week for every year over twenty-two, and half a week for every year over eighteen). In addition to that is a possible 'compensatory award' to take into account the actual loss sustained by the employee as the direct result of the dismissal (e.g. loss of wages and benefits, the manner of dismissal, and the loss of job security). But the tribunal may also deduct from the award a sum in respect of any amount which it is felt the employee contributed to his own dismissal.

The tribunal may, in suitable cases, also order the employer to either reinstate an employee (i.e. place him back in his exact previous job, with no loss of pay, seniority, etc.), or *re-engage* him (i.e. re-employ him in some comparable capacity), with or without arrears of pay. Before taking such a step, the tribunal will ensure that the employee wishes it, and will also have to assess the likely impact on the place of work of such an order. If the employer fails to comply with such an order, the tribunal cannot enforce it, but can make an additional award of fifty-two weeks pay or less. By adding together all these awards, it is possible that the employee could emerge with over £14,000.

A right of appeal on a point of law lies to the Employment Appeal Tribunal, and from there to the Court of Appeal and House of Lords.

Redundancy

Under the Redundancy Payments Act, 1965 (now largely replaced by EPCA), an employee is entitled to compensation when he is genuinely made 'redundant', i.e. not only is he dismissed, but he is never replaced because the job itself is being phased out. If he is replaced, of course, it is not a redundancy, although it may well be an unfair dismissal (for which see above). Redundancy payment is compensation for the loss of a job, and nothing else; it is therefore payable regardless of whether the employee starts in another, better, job on the following Monday, or whether he is receiving an adequate amount in unemployment benefit.

In order for a dismissal to be on the grounds of redundancy, it must be shown that the employer has ceased, or intends to cease, carrying on the business in which the worker was employed, or in the place where he was employed, or that demands for the type of activity in which the employee was engaged have diminished, or are expected to. This will cover internal reorganization or economy, and will cover changes in job specification; it does not seem to include a change in the hours of work, as can be seen from *Johnson* v. *Nottinghamshire Combined Police Authority* (1974), in which it was held not to be redundancy (nor was it an unfair dismissal) for clerical staff in a police station to change to shift working.

The definition of redundancy will also cover any full 'lay-off' (i.e. no work and no pay) or any 'short-time' working (i.e. no opportunity to earn at least half a normal week's pay). In both cases, the reduction must have lasted for either four consecutive weeks or for any six weeks in any thirteen before the employee may give notice that he intends to leave and claim redundancy pay. The employer may serve a counter-notice, claiming that a period of at least thirteen weeks' full work will commence within the next four weeks.

Certain employees are not entitled to redundancy payments, namely those who have less than 104 weeks' 'continuous service' with the employer, those who work for less than sixteen hours per week (eight hours after five years' service), those who are under eighteen or over the normal retirement age, those who are married to their employers, those employed under a two-year or more fixed-term contract who have 'signed away' their rights, Crown employees, those normally working outside Great Britain, and employees covered by a separate redundancy scheme approved by the Department of Employment.

One important factor in a claim for redundancy payments is clearly the length of continuous service credited to the employee (it also directly affects the size of the award; see below). This service is measured in weeks, and any 'non-qualifying week' may break the chain of continuity. There are obvious exceptions to this, such as where the employee is absent through illness (maximum twenty-six weeks), where there is a temporary cessation of work, or where the employee is off work for reasons connected with pregnancy. A strike week will not break the continuity of employment, but neither will it be counted as a week of 'continuous service', but an employee may, at the discretion of a tribunal, lose all his redundancy entitlement if he goes on strike while working out redundancy notice.

It is also possible for employment with employer A to be added to a period of employment with employer B so as to make one continuous period, when employer B takes over the business of employer A as a going concern, and retains members of staff in their posts on substantially the same terms. The new contracts will (or should, under EPCA, s. 1) contain a statement that periods of continuous employment with employer A will be honoured and count as periods of employment with employer B. The same may happen when the representatives of a deceased employer take over his business as a going concern, and in both cases, an employee who unreasonably refuses an offer of re-employment on substantially the same terms as before loses all rights to redundancy payment.

It is, of course, necessary for the business to be taken over *in toto* before this sort of provision may apply, and it is not enough that B has taken over A's physical assets, if he does not intend to employ them in the same sort of business. This is what happened in *Woodhouse* v. *Peter Brotherhood Ltd* (1972), in which it was held not to be a full takeover for B to take over A's diesel engine plant and use the staff and facilities to make spinning machines. The employees, when finally made redundant, found that they could only claim in respect of their period of employment with the second employer, and could not add to it employment periods with the first (they could have claimed from the former employer at the time of the takeover).

Similar principles apply where the same employer, instead of making E redundant, offers him a different job. If the offer is of reasonably suitable employment, and it is to take effect within four weeks of the termination of the old contract, then it will provide continuity of employment, and in any subsequent redundancy claim, E may add together the two periods in the two different jobs. If the offer is not reasonably suitable, E may refuse it and claim redundancy payment there and then; if it is, and he unreasonably refuses it, he may claim nothing. Separate periods of employment with the same employer but in different capacities will be assumed to constitute 'continuous employment' unless the contrary is proved.

Whether considering the suitability of an offer by a new employer or of a new job by the same employer, the tribunal must weigh a variety of factors in assessing whether or not refusal by an employee was reasonable. They must consider the capacity, status, remuneration and other benefits payable to the employee, the location of the job and the nature of it. Unless the original contract required him to be mobile, he cannot be expected to move to another town, although a move from one office or factory to another in the same town might well be reasonable. Domestic and social considerations will be taken into account, but not mere personal aversions; thus, in *Fuller* v. *Stephanie Bowman Ltd* (1977), a secretary who refused to move to an office above a Soho sex shop was held to have unreasonably refused alternative employment.

Where the employee does agree to try a new job offered by the employer, he is entitled to a four-week trial period (or longer if agreed between the parties) for retraining purposes. If either party terminates the new contract during that period the employee is treated as having been dismissed on the date of the termination of the original contract.

An employer may no longer simply declare redundancies

without consulting with anyone. Under EPCA, he must now consult with the unions. In particular, if an employer recognizes an independent trade union he must, at the earliest opportunity, consult with that union's representatives before making redundant any employee covered by that recognition agreement. If he intends to make redundant more than one hundred employees at the same establishment within a period of ninety days or less, he must begin the consultations at least ninety days before the dismissals occur; for redundancies of between ten and a hundred employees at the same establishment, within thirty days, he must commence the consultations at least thirty days beforehand. In all other cases the period is 28 days.

In his consultations, the employer must disclose details about the number and descriptions of those whom it is proposed to dismiss, the method of selection, and so on, and he must consider and reply to any representations made by the union. If he rejects them, he must give reasons, but he is under no legal obligation to accept them. A failure on the part of the employer to make the necessary consultations entitles the union to seek a 'protective award' from the industrial tribunal; this is in effect a sum of money based on the affected employee's salary and the number of weeks' consultation which should have occurred but did not.

Redundancy payment is calculated in an almost identical manner to that payable in respect of 'basic award' dismissal compensation. In other words, it is based upon length of service (twenty years maximum), weekly salary (maximum £130) and age during the period in question. The maximum is in fact £3,900 at the time of writing (January 1981). The whole of the initial payment must be met by the employer, but he is then entitled to recover approximately forty per cent of that from the Redundancy Fund, in the form of a rebate. This Fund is financed from National Insurance contributions.

Payments may be made direct to ex-employees where the employer either cannot or will not make payments; it is then for the administrators of the Fund to attempt to secure reimbursement from the employer.

References

No employer is under any legal duty to supply a reference to an outgoing employee, unless he has unwisely agreed to do so as a term of some contract. If he does decide to give a reference, he owes a legal duty both to the former employee, who may sue him for defamation of character if he makes any statement which is both untrue and derogatory, and the new employer, who, if he acts upon a falsely favourable reference to his detriment, may sue the giver of the reference for deceit or negligence.

There have also been cases in recent years in which employers have dismissed members of staff for incompetence, dishonesty, etc., and then gone on to give them favourable references. Subsequent industrial tribunal hearings have made much of the references, and have refused to believe that the ex-employee could, in the light of the reference, have deserved dismissal. Obviously, what the employer needs is some means of recording in a reference what he honestly believes to be the truth about an employee without running the risk of a defamation action should it turn out to be untrue.

The law in fact provides him with this in the defence of 'qualified privilege' which is available in any defamation action to an ex-employer who can show that what he put in a reference was what he honestly believed to be true, in furtherance of his duty to the next employer to be as frank and honest as possible. Provided that there is no evidence of malice, and he appears to have had reasonable grounds for his belief, the employer will be protected in any defamation action, even if it transpires that his opinion was not correct.

9 ... And other employee rights

During the course of the contract of employment, every employee is protected in a variety of ways from unfairness, discrimination, exploitation and physical danger by a variety of statutory provisions which between them represent almost two centuries of legislation. In view of the vastness and complexity of the law in this area, what follows can only be an outline guide to the more important of these 'employee rights'.

Wages

One of the basic duties of the employer towards the employee is to pay the wages which he agreed to pay, and in most cases this will apply whether the employer has actually supplied any work or not. Provided that the employee has made himself available for work, he will be entitled to his wages, unless he has been formally notified in advance of a lay-off by the employer.

This was always generally true at Common Law, and was summed up rather quaintly by one High Court judge, who in 1940 pointed out that 'provided I pay my cook her wages regularly she cannot complain if I choose to take all or any of my meals out'. However, it is also recognized at Common Law that there are special cases in which it is important for the employee to be actually *provided* with work, instead of simply being handed the money. One clear example is an apprenticeship, in which skills are acquired via practical experience; another might be the employment of a chef with a reputation to maintain, a skilled worker on 'piece rate', or a salesman paid on commission. In such cases, there is apparently an implied term in the contract of employment that not only will the employer pay the wages, he will also provide the work.

The question of payment during sickness is one which ideally will be dealt with under the Contract of Employment (see Chapter 8), but in the absence of any such provision, it seems from a leading case in 1960, never subsequently challenged, that wages are still payable even where the employee is off sick.

This, then, is the basic position at Common Law. In practice, this relatively clear picture is obscured by a variety of other factors, not the least of which is the possibility of collective agreements between management and union which lay down completely different rules (e.g. the right to guaranteed overtime payments or the right to payment only during the first two weeks of sickness).

Then there are the many statutory provisions which have been enacted over the years to control the fixing of wages, the level of deductions, 'guarantee' payments and so on. These may now be examined a little more closely.

Wages Councils

Since 1945, there has been a regular network of Wages Councils, and some individual Councils have a much longer history (e.g. in the catering industry). They are all now governed by the Wages Councils Act, 1979.

Under this Act, as under previous Acts, the Secretary of State for Employment has the power to establish Wages Councils for particular industries or sections of industries in which it is felt that the existing machinery for wage negotiation is inadequate. Since the last such Council to be established was over twenty years ago, and since most industries now have a fairly efficient system of free collective bargaining (see Chapter 10), the accent in recent years has in fact been on *reducing* the number of Wages Councils (currently forty-three) by creating a suitable environment for the development of voluntary bargaining.

The industries in which Wages Councils traditionally operate (e.g. retail, catering and garment manufacture) are those in which union representation is weakest, and each Council will consist of equal numbers of representatives from both management and union circles, with independent experts. Originally, such Councils dealt only with matters such as the establishment of minimum wages and holiday entitlement, but under the 1979 Act, they may also deal with other matters concerning terms and conditions of employment. Their recommendations may now become effective without being first submitted for approval to the Secretary of State, as used to be the case.

The minimum conditions laid down by the Wages Councils in the form of Wages Councils Orders are enforced by an Inspectorate, who have the usual powers of entry, search, interview and seizure in relation to employers and premises covered by the Orders. Employers may be fined for failure to comply with minimum requirements, and arrears of pay, etc., may be awarded to employees.

As a sort of 'half-way house' between a full wages council and free wage bargaining, there have since 1975 been Joint Industrial Councils (JICs), which differ from Wages Councils in that they have no independent members, and therefore more basically resemble the free bargaining teams employed elsewhere in industry. ACAS will be available to mediate in any real deadlocks, and it is hoped that the JICs will lead to the eventual abolition of the more rigid Wages Councils.

Truck Acts

The wage which is quoted to an employee when he is taken on, whether it is the minimum wage awarded by a Wages Council, or the result of free bargaining, will be the 'gross wage', i.e. before any deductions are made. Historically, the issue of deductions has given rise to considerable abuse by employers, and has necessitated considerable legislation, most of which seems archaic in the light of modern union strength.

The most important of these Acts were the Truck Acts ('truck' meaning barter or payment in kind), the first of which appeared in 1831, and the last echoes of which could be heard in the Payment of Wages Act, 1960. The term 'truck' in this context refers to the practice (prevalent not only in the pre-industrial revolution agricultural industry, but also in the early factory system) whereby the employer paid the employee either wholly or partly in the form of *goods* (e.g. food and clothing) or *tokens* exchangeable for goods only in certain 'tommy shops' owned in the main by the employers themselves.

Clearly, this system of exploitation cannot survive the emergence of strong unions, and in a modern context, the Truck Acts are chiefly important for the way in which they regulate the purposes for which deductions may be made from the gross wage of an employee. But, in passing, it is worth noting that the Acts require wages to be paid either in current coin of the realm (including bank notes), or by cheque, direct transfer to a bank account, postal or money order. If not in cash, then the employee's written request must be obtained for payment into a bank, etc.

Again, it should be stressed that the Acts apply only to 'workmen', a term which by general agreement is taken to cover all manual workers, but not secretarial or administrative staff. In practice, an employer would be well advised to operate the same system for all employees; it is in any case unlikely that any grade of staff would agree to receive payment in ball bearings or cabbages!

Under the Truck Acts, the employer may deduct from the wages of the employee sums in respect of board and lodging, meals, tools and medical services, provided that the amount deducted is a realistic assessment of their worth, and the worker has agreed in writing to such a deduction. In those industries served by a Wages Council, this 'realistic assessment' is made by the Council, in the sense that it quotes different rates of pay for those provided with accommodation than for those without.

An employer may also 'fine' employees by means of deductions from wages (in respect of, for example, breakages or poor workmanship), provided that the conditions under which he may do so are contained in a readily accessible written notice, or incorporated into a contract and clearly specified, that the 'offences' in question are restricted to those likely to cause loss or damage to the employer or his business, and that the amount of the fine is fair and reasonable. On each occasion when such a deduction is made, the employee must be informed in writing of the reason for it, and the amount. In *Byrd* v. *British Celanese Ltd* (1945), an attempt to challenge the practice of 'suspension without pay' on the grounds that it was illegal under the Truck Acts failed because it was held that the Truck Acts applied only to deductions from wages payable, whereas on suspension, no such wages become payable.

In *Hewlett* v. *Allan* (1894), an employee challenged as illegal a deduction from her wage in respect of a subscription to a sickness and accident club which she had agreed to upon taking up her employment. The House of Lords held that any deduction such as this would be lawful if paid over to a third party at the request of the employee.

It is this case which provides the legal justification for deductions 'at source' from the wages of employees who elect to become members of the firm's sports and social club, or who wish to join some form of savings club or bank scheme to 'save as you earn'. In *Williams* v. *Butlers* (1975), it was held to justify the deduction of union subscriptions. There is, strictly speaking, no need for the agreement of the employee to be in writing, but it is highly advisable.

Any provision in a contract of employment which contravenes the Truck Acts will be a complete nullity, and in addition, the employer commits a criminal offence if he is in breach of the Acts, which are enforced by Wages Inspectors.

Even the Truck Acts have, in their turn, been partly amended by other Acts of Parliament which oblige the employer to make certain deductions from wages not envisaged by the early Truck Acts. Two obvious examples are income tax and national insurance contributions, and a third are 'attachment orders' made by a court of law over the earnings of an employee. These may now be examined separately.

Income tax and national insurance

These two compulsory deductions are classed together for the purposes of this chapter because, first of all, they are now payable to the same government body, the Inland Revenue, and secondly, because they both involve a legal liability for payment on the part of the employer which may be wholly or partly passed on to the employee.

Dealing first with income tax, most readers will be familiar, in general terms at least, with the Pay As You Earn (PAYE) system under which Schedule E tax, due by an employee on his earnings, is deducted at source by the employer. In fact, the law places the initial liability for payment firmly on the shoulders of the employer, who must organize the necessary paper work and communicate regularly with the tax office. It is, technically speaking, up to him whether or not he chooses to reimburse himself from the employee's wages!

The system of tax deduction is fairly straightforward, in outline at least. Every employee is given a tax code by the Inland Revenue, and that code is communicated to the employer. The employer then applies that coding to the gross salary of the employee, to arrive at the tax payable. That sum is deducted from the salary and remitted to the Inland Revenue on a monthly basis. The employee is informed on his salary slip (see below) of the amount deducted.

In practice, wage administration can seem quite a complex physical operation, with P45, P30, P60, deduction cards, etc., but a well-organized wage office can take care of it all, and certain commercial concerns have devised record systems which simplify the operation for the employer while still remaining acceptable to the Inland Revenue. The two important factors to remember are that it is the employer who bears the initial liability for paying tax under the PAYE system, and that he should notify the Inland Revenue of every person who receives a salary from him, and every casual worker who is taken on, for however short a time. Otherwise, the employer could find himself liable to pay money to the Inland Revenue which he has no hope – after a lapse of several months or even years – of recovering from the employee.

National insurance payments are deducted along with PAYE tax, and sent to the Inland Revenue at the same time. Liability for payment of the full amount of national insurance is normally shared between employer and employee, the employer making the initial full payment, then deducting the employee's share from his wages. In some cases (e.g. staff under sixteen) no payment is due at all, while in others (e.g. the case of a 'retired' person still in regular employment) only the employer makes a contribution. Finally, it is possible for married women and widows to pay a 'reduced rate' contribution, which reduces the full amount of the payment, but does not relieve the employer of his liability to pay his share.

The actual size of the deduction will depend upon the level of earnings. No contribution is payable at all until the employee's gross eage reaches a certain level (£23 at 1 January 1981), and when the gross wage reaches £165 (again as at 1 Jan. 1981) the maximum contribution is payable. In between lies a sliding scale which the employer applies via a 'ready reckoner' system called a Contribution Table.

Attachment of earnings

Under the Attachment of Earnings Act, 1971, an employer may be obliged to deduct certain sums of money from the wages of an employee at source. This will arise whenever an Attachment Order is served upon him by an officer of the appropriate court (High Court, County Court or Magistrates' Court), which specifically instructs him to make periodic deductions from the employee's wages of such amounts as may be specified in the Order, and pay the money over at given intervals to an authorized 'collecting officer' of the court.

In short, the employee has been found liable in a court of law to pay money over to another party (the 'creditor'), and this is one way of securing payment. An Attachment Order may be in respect of a number of debts, but will normally specify a 'protected earnings limit', below which the employee's gross wage should not fall – in other words, the employer should not make any deduction which will result in the wage falling below this level. If, by any chance, more than one Attachment Order is served in respect of the same employee, then the employer must give effect to them in chronological order.

If it transpires that the particular debtor is not in the employer's employment, or if he subsequently leaves, the employer must notify the court within ten days. If and when the Order ceases to be applicable, the employer will be informed by the court. An employer may also be required by the court to give a written statement of the debtor's actual and anticipated earnings.

On every occasion upon which he makes a deduction under an Attachment Order, the employer must give the employee a written statement of the deduction (see 'itemized pay statement' below), and may charge fifty pence for his administrative costs.

The Scottish equivalent of an Attachment Order is an 'Arrestment Order'.

Itemized pay statement

Section 8 of EPCA 1978 provides that every employee shall be entitled, at or before the time when he receives his pay, to an itemized statement in writing containing details of the gross wage, the amount of any fixed or variable deductions from the gross wage, and the final net wage. Where different parts of the net amount are paid in different ways, the amount and method of payment of each part must be specified.

If the employer fails to give this statement, or deducts items which are not recorded upon the statement, the employee may refer the matter to an industrial tribunal, which may order the employer to provide the statement or to repay the deduction. In the case of fixed deductions, the employer may discharge his obligations by supplying the employee with a 'standing statement' of the amount of the deductions and the intervals between them.

Guarantee payments

Section 12 of EPCA 1978 gives nearly all workers with four weeks or more of continuous service the right to 'guarantee payments' where they suffer a workless day, that is, in effect a day in which there is a reduction in demand for the type of work which they are carrying out, and the employer is obliged to lay them off. In other words, a temporary redundancy.

The right does not extend to dock workers, share fishermen, those employed outside Great Britain, staff normally working for less than sixteen hours per week (eight hours after five years), and those employed by a husband or wife. Nor do the provisions of s. 12 apply if the workless day arises as a result of a trade dispute involving any employee employed by the same employer or any associated employer, or if the employee has unreasonably refused suitable alternative work, or if the employee fails to comply with reasonable requirements imposed by the employer with a view to ensuring that his services are available.

This last proviso was invoked in *Meadows* v. *Faithful Overalls Ltd* (1977), in which staff who refused to remain at work for an hour or so in the absence of heating, even though they were promised that heat would be restored at a given time, were held to have failed to comply with a reasonable requirement on the part of the employer, and were not therefore entitled to guarantee payments.

The guarantee payment is calculated on an hourly basis, but no one employee may claim more than £8 per day by way of guarantee payment. Nor may the employee claim in respect of more than five workless days in any quarter (less than that if he normally works for less than a five-day week). Thus, the maximum guarantee payment per employee is £40 per quarter (as at 1 January 1981).

Health and safety at work

The law concerning safety in the workplace has undergone considerable change as the result of the Health and Safety at Work Act, 1974, but the Common Law is also still applicable. Basically, we may state as a general rule that the Common Law governs the right of the employee to sue the employer for damages if and when he sustains injury at work which is the fault of the employer, whereas the Health and Safety at Work Act, 1974, sets out to ensure, by means of the criminal law, that accidents do not occur in the first place.

Health and safety at Common Law

At Common Law, the employer is under a duty to take reasonable care for the safety of his employees during the normal course of their employment. This duty covers not only the safety of the premises themselves, but also safe systems of work and competent staff. An injured employee may sue his employer for damages arising out of an act of negligence by a fellow employee just as much as if the accident had been caused by, for example, falling masonry.

Dealing first of all, then, with the working premises themselves, the employer must ensure that they are reasonably safe for the jobs which are being performed there. This entails ensuring not only that the structure of the building is safe, that the electrical wiring is properly maintained, and so forth, but also that the floors are dry and free from obstruction, that emergency exits are kept clear, and that guards and stair rails are secure. Furthermore, this duty covers every set of premises upon which the employee is required to work, whether they belong to the employer or not, and in *Smith* v. *Austin Lifts Ltd* (1959), for example, a maintenance fitter sent to repair a customer's lift was awarded damages against his employers because of injuries sustained through using a defective access door on the customer's premises.

In addition to a safe place of work, the employer must also supply safe machinery and tools with which to do the work.

At Common Law, it was enough if the employer purchased his equipment, etc., from a reputable source and maintained a regular inspection system. This meant that if the injury arose from a defect in the equipment which was the fault of the manufacturer, then the injured employee had recourse only to the manufacturer, and could not sue the employer.

This state of affairs was remedied by the Employers' Liability (Defective Equipment) Act, 1969, which states that where an employee is injured in the course of his employment as the result of a defect in equipment provided by his employer for the purposes of the employer's business, then even though the defect is the fault of some third party (e.g. the manufacturer), the employee may also sue the employer, who may then seek reimbursement from the third party.

An employee is also entitled to protection against the incompetence of his fellow employees, and if one member of staff injures another, then the injured employee may sue the employer. This is sometimes expressed by saying that the employer is 'vicariously' liable for the negligent acts of members of his workforce during the course of their employment, or, where this is inappropriate, by claiming that it is the duty of the employer to make the workplace safe by removing the source of danger (i.e. the employee). This was the line taken in *Hudson* v. *Ridge Manufacturing Co. Ltd* (1957), in which H received damages from his employers for their failure to remove, despite numerous requests, an employee whose practical jokes were positively dangerous, and who injured H by tripping him up.

Even if the premises, equipment and employees are reasonably 'safe', the employer will still be liable if an employee is injured as the result of using an unsafe system of work. Thus, in *General Cleaning Contractors Ltd* v. *Christmas* (1953), an employer who expected his window-cleaning staff to work without safety harness was liable in damages when one of them fell from a ledge. But it seems that, at Common Law at least, provided that the employer makes safety equipment, protective clothing, etc., available, he will not be liable if the employee fails to make use of it, at least not when that employee is fully trained in the job, and aware that the equipment is available.

The 'duty of safety' falls squarely on the shoulders of the employer, and he may not delegate it to anyone else, not even the Safety Committees established under the Health and Safety at Work Act, 1974 (see p. 249). But at Common Law, the employer need take only reasonable care, which means in effect that he must take such precautions as a reasonably prudent employer would take. He certainly does not have to guard against every possibility, however remote.

This last point is well illustrated by *Latimer* v. *AEC Ltd* (1953), in which a factory was overtaken by a flash flood during a freak rainstorm. Oil was swept from a drainage channel on to the floor, and the management spread their entire stock of sawdust down upon it to make it as safe as they could. Some parts remained untreated, and L was injured when he slipped. The House of Lords ruled that the employer had done everything that might be reasonably expected of him; his duty of safety was not an absolute one, and he was not liable.

But the standard of care will increase where the employee is suffering from a disability known to the employer which increases the danger or the likely consequences of injury. Thus, in *Paris* v. *Stepney Borough Council* (1951), it was held that an employer must take greater care to protect the eyesight of an employee with only one good eye than he would for a normally sighted person. Also, once an employee is injured as the result of some negligence on the part of the employer, the latter will be liable for the full extent of the injury, however unforseeable it may have been; thus, in *Smith* v. *Leech Brain & Co.* (1962), the employers were held liable for the death of an employee who contracted cancer after a minor burn.

The Unfair Contract Terms Act, 1977, makes it unlawful for an employer to attempt to evade his Common Law liability for employee safety by means of a suitable clause in the contract of employment. But, in theory at least, it is usually open to an employer to argue (in an appropriate case) that the employee volunteered for the risk (*volenti non fit injuria*), either in the sense that the job is an inherently dangerous one anyway (e.g. deep-sea diving) or because the employee deliberately removed, for example, a safety barrier; such defences rarely succeed.

Alternatively, of course, the employer may argue that the worker was *contributorily negligent* (i.e. partly to blame for what happened), and that therefore the damages should be reduced by the proportion to which the employee was at fault.

Before leaving this section, brief mention must be made of the Employers' Liability (Compulsory Insurance) Act, 1969, which requires every employer to take out and maintain an approved insurance policy to cover all possible claims by the employees in respect of bodily injuries. If he fails to do this, the employer commits a criminal offence.

Health and safety under statute

A variety of statutes has, over the years, been passed in order to improve upon the Common Law, which after all only provides for the possibility of the employee suing after he has been injured, which could hardly be described as an ideal system. Acts such as the Factories Act, 1961, the Mines and Quarries Act, 1954, and the Offices, Shops and Railway Premises Act, 1963, were therefore enacted in order to provide a code for *preventing* accidents in the first place. Each employer covered by each of these Acts is required to comply with the detailed provisions covering matters such as ventilation, working temperatures, dangerous machinery, and so on, and commits a criminal offence if he does not.

The greatest drawback with this system, is, of course, that it is piecemeal and deals with only one industry, or section of an industry, at a time. The Robens Committee, reporting in 1972, recommended one Act of Parliament to cover all employers, and greater participation by the workers themselves in matters affecting their own safety. Both these requirements are met in the Health and Safety at Work Act, 1974, which has not yet replaced the Acts referred to above, although it is in almost full force.

The main provision of the Act is contained in s. 2, which requires every employer to ensure 'so far as is reasonably practicable', the health, safety and welfare at work of his entire workforce. This will cover everything from means of access to the premises to storage of equipment, training and supervision, and a healthy working environment, and the employer is required to prepare a written statement of policy on health and safety matters, which is to be brought to the notice of all employees.

An important extension to the Common Law duty of safety is provided by s. 3 of the Act, which imposes a duty upon all employers (and all self-employed persons) to conduct their activities in such a way as to ensure, so far as is reasonably practicable, that people other than employees are not exposed to risks to their health and safety. This would cover, for example, the lorry driver making deliveries to the factory, or the householders living next door. This provision was added to the Act during its Bill stage, as the direct result of the Flixborough explosion.

The safety of employees is protected in other ways too. For example, all those who make premises available for work (e.g. landlords of factory premises) even though they may not employ the staff who work in them, must at least ensure that access and egress are safe for those using the premises. Also, anyone who designs, manufactures, imports or supplies articles for use at work must ensure, so far as is reasonably practicable, that every article is safe and poses no threat to health. He must conduct such safety testing as is necessary, and provide the ultimate consumer with adequate information on the use of the article. The same rules apply to any substance supplied for work.

Section 7 of the Act imposes upon every employee a duty to take care for the health and safety, not only of himself, but also of any other person who may be affected by his actions, and to cooperate with the employer in health and safety matters. Where the employer is a company, another section of the Act imposes liability on any director or other officer who neglects his duty and thus leads to an offence being committed by the company.

This participation by the workforce is furthered by the requirement under the Act that every trade union recognized by the employer has the right to appoint safety representatives for each place of work, whose function it is to investigate all safety matters and make representations to the employer. The safety representative may also consult at the workplace with Health and Safety Inspectors, and attend meetings of the employers' Safety Committee.

These committees are normally established voluntarily by the employer, but the safety representatives may demand that such a committee be established if it does not already exist. Such a committee can be composed of anyone whom the employer wishes, in addition, of course, to the safety representatives, although the norm seems to be for equal numbers of management and union members. At best, a Safety Committee can only make recommendations to the employer anyway.

The detailed rules of safety have yet to be laid down by means of Regulations issued by the Secretary of State for Employment. However, they are likely to follow fairly closely some of the existing Regulations issued under former statutes such as the Factories Act, 1961. It is in this sense that these earlier Acts have not yet fully disappeared, and in order to comply with the broad requirements of s. 2 of the 1974 Act, employers in, for example, factories, are still required to observe the provisions of the 1961 Act.

The enforcement of the Act and any Regulations issued under it is in the hands of Health and Safety Inspectors, who have powers to enter premises, examine, inspect and remove equipment, photograph, analyse or test any items, take samples, interview staff, remove documents, etc., in fact powers to do just about anything within the general area of health and safety. They also have the power to issue 'improvement notices', which allow the employer to put things right within a specified time, and 'prohibition notices' which require the employer to cease certain activities completely until safety has been restored.

In *Associated Dairies Ltd* v. *Hartley* (1979), an Inspector served an improvement notice on a supermarket, requiring them to supply protective footwear to all staff using trolley jacks. It was held that this notice should be cancelled, since it was not 'reasonably practicable' to require such footwear in view of the relationship of cost to risk.

Serious cases are reported for prosecution, which in England and Wales may be handled by the Inspector himself. In Scotland, the final decision, and the task of prosecuting, falls to the Procurator Fiscal.

Maternity

It is in keeping with the general movement towards the equality of employment opportunities between the sexes which has been a feature of legislation during the past decade, and which is described more fully in the section following this, that employees who are pregnant should be protected by certain legal rights in connection with their employment. These fall into three categories: the right not to be dismissed, the right to maternity benefit from the employer and the right to return to work after the confinement. They may be examined in that order.

The right not to be dismissed

It will be classed as an 'unfair dismissal' (see Chapter 8) for an employer to dismiss an employee simply because she is pregnant, unless he can show either that because of her condition, she is, or will be by the time she leaves, incapable of adequately performing the work which she was employed to do, or that by remaining at work in that condition, either she or her employer would be in breach of some Act or Regulation.

Even if the employer can show that the employee in question is covered by one of those exceptions, it will still be an unfair dismissal if there is some other vacancy open which would be 'suitable' for her in terms of her experience, current job and medical condition, and the employer fails to offer it to her with effect from the termination of her original job. In order to be 'suitable', the job must be substantially 'no less favourable' to her than the old job, in terms of the conditions of employment. The right to an alternative job only applies

to an employee who has been employed for the requisite period
to entitle her to claim for unfair dismissal (see page 220).

Also, even if the dismissal is 'fair', it does not deprive the
employee of her other maternity rights, including the right to
return to work after her confinement.

The right to maternity benefit from the employer

An employee with at least two years' 'continuous employment'
(i.e. for at least sixteen hours per week, or eight hours per week
after five years' service) who is absent from work wholly or
partly because of pregnancy or confinement, is entitled to
'maternity pay' from the employer for a minimum of six weeks.
But she cannot claim this right earlier than the eleventh week
before the expected week of her confinement, and she must
remain 'in employment' with that employer at least until that
eleventh week, whether she is actually turning up for work or
not. Where she has been dismissed for reasons of pregnancy,
however, she is still entitled to maternity pay (see above).

In order to qualify for this payment, the employee must
actually be absent from work for reasons connected with her
pregnancy, and she should notify her employer (in writing if
required) at least twenty-one days before the start of her
absence, or as soon as is reasonably practicable. This same
notice may also be used to intimate her desire to return to
work following her confinement. The employer is entitled to
demand appropriate medical certificates.

The relevant six weeks for the purposes of maternity pay
will be the first six weeks of her absence following the eleventh
week prior to the expected confinement; it could, therefore,
consist of the three weeks before confinement and the three
weeks after it. The amount payable is nine-tenths of a 'week's
pay' (i.e. a normal week working normal hours) less any amount
payable by the Department of Health and Social Security
(DHSS) by way of maternity allowance, whether she is
entitled to it or not. The payment is made initially by the
employer, who then recovers the full amount from the

Maternity Pay Fund, which itself is funded from national insurance contributions.

The right to reinstatement following confinement

An employee who is qualified in terms of length of service to claim maternity pay may also claim the right to her job back once she has had the baby. As we have seen, she must notify the employer at least three weeks before she leaves of her intention to return, and she may then exercise her right to return at any time up to the end of the twenty-ninth week after her confinement. She is required to give at least one week's notice of her intention to return, whereupon the employer may, if he wishes, delay that return by four more weeks by giving the employee reasons in writing, and a definite starting date. The employee herself may postpone her return until the thirty-third week with a suitable medical certificate.

She is then entitled to re-enter the same job, on terms and conditions 'no less favourable' than they would have been had she never left; among other things, therefore, she is entitled to any new salary scale, and does not apparently even lose seniority. If she is denied this right, she may claim unfair dismissal. If, in fact, her job has been phased out during her absence, then she may claim redundancy payment unless the employer can offer her some 'suitable' alternative job. Employers with less than five staff may even escape this requirement.

In many cases, of course, the employer will have found it necessary to take on a temporary replacement for the employee who has gone off to have a baby. The question naturally arises as to what the employer can do so far as dismissing that employee is concerned, but fortunately the 1978 Act, which governs nearly all matters concerning maternity rights, provides that if, at the time when the replacement is taken on, he or she is informed in writing that the contract will end upon the return to work of the person who is being temporarily replaced for reasons of pregnancy, then the employer may 'fairly' dismiss the replacement upon the return to work of the regular employee, provided that it was 'reasonable in all the circumstances' to do so (e.g. there is no other vacancy she can fill).

Under the Employment Act, 1980, the employer may contact the employee at least seven weeks after the expected week of confinement to ask if she still intends to return; she must reply within two weeks (or as soon as reasonably practicable) if she wishes to exercise her right to return. See also p. 261 for the right to time off for ante-natal visits.

Discrimination

There has been a determined movement in the past decade or so to eliminate discrimination from the field of employment. In this section, we shall be examining the three most important manifestations of this new philosophy.

Equal pay

Upon our entry to the Common Market, the UK became subject to the articles of the EEC Treaty, Article 119 of which requires each member state to ensure that men and women 'receive equal pay for equal work'. Since a decision by the European Court of Justice in 1976, every employee in the UK has the right to apply to the UK courts for implementation of this principle, which overrides anything which may appear to the contrary in a domestic statute.

In fact, the UK began to implement the principle of equal pay for equal work in 1970, when it passed the Equal Pay Act, which took five years to come into force, by which time the Sex Discrimination Act, 1975 (see p. 255) had taken away some of the necessity for it. The most important part of the Act is s. 1, which states that in every contract for the employment of a woman, there will be deemed by law to be an equality clause which in effect gives every woman two guarantees.

The first is that where she is employed upon 'like work' with a man in the same employment, then the terms of the woman's contract shall be 'no less favourable' to her than the man's, and shall include all the benefits which exist under the main contract. 'Like work' is defined in s. 1 as being work which is 'of the same or a broadly similar nature', in which any differences between the work done by the man and that done by the woman are 'not of practical importance' taking into account the frequency of the differences and the terms of the contract.

There have already been several important tribunal decisions on the nature of 'like work'. In *Dugdale* v. *Kraft Foods* (1977), for example, it was held that men could not be paid a higher rate simply because they were required to work on the night shift, since the time at which work is performed does not affect the nature of the work, and this is the factor to be considered. The same point was made in *NCB* v. *Sherwin and Spruce* (1978), in which the tribunal held that where the hours worked are inconvenient, they may be compensated by an additional premium but not a rise in the basic rate, that one cannot use the argument that men can only be recruited for a higher wage than women, and that the fact that the man in the case was in sole charge during his shift did not make his job 'materially different' from the women who shared the duties on the other shift.

Secondly, where it can be shown that a woman is employed on work 'rated as equivalent' with that of a man in the same employment, then the woman's contract shall be 'no less favourable' to her than the man's is to him, bearing in mind the rating. In short, the employer is to ensure that even though the two jobs are not identical, they are equally rewarded where they are comparable. The Act in fact defines 'work rated as equivalent' in terms of the demands made upon the worker in matters such as skill, effort, decision-making, etc., following upon a job evaluation exercise.

Whether the female employee is claiming equal pay because she feels that she is performing 'like work' with a man, or whether she feels that her job should be 'rated as equivalent' to a man's, the employer has a defence if he can show that the reason for the inequality in the rewards of employment is a 'material difference' between the two cases which is non-sexual in nature.

A good example of this principle in action was *Handley* v. *Mono Ltd* (1978), in which a lady machinist in a garment factory worked, at her own request, for less than the normal working week at a reduced hourly rate from the other machinists. One of these was a man, and she claimed parity of rate with him. It was held that there was a material difference between her case and that of the fulltime staff, since she was utilizing the machines less fully, and received overtime rates at an earlier level in the working week. This difference was clearly non-sexual, since the fulltime *female* machinists received the same as the man.

Similarly, in *NAAFI* v. *Varley* (1977), a female clerk employed in Nottingham claimed priority of working hours with male clerks employed in London. It was held that the material difference in the two cases was in fact the increased strain of living in London, and it was non-sexual since female clerks in London worked the same hours as male clerks in London, and male and female clerks in Nottingham had no difference in hours either. This last case also illustrates the point, often overlooked, that the Equal Pay Act covers all terms and conditions of employment, and not just pay.

No employee may bring an action under the 1970 Act unless and until she has worked for the employer for at least six months. Nor may 'equality clauses' operate where the law imposes certain restrictions on the employment of women (e.g. under certain provisions of the Factories Acts), or where the law gives women certain rights in connection with pregnancy or childbirth, or where a woman is afforded an earlier retirement age by law.

Claims are brought by the aggrieved employee, or by the Secretary of State for Employment, before an industrial tribunal, which has the power to award compensation to the employee.

Sex discrimination

The purpose of the Sex Discrimination Act, 1975, was to eliminate sex discrimination in most areas of human activity, of which employment is clearly an important example.

Section 6 of the Act states, quite simply, that it is unlawful for an employer to discriminate against a woman in his selection and recruitment of employees, and in the terms and conditions upon which he offers them employment. Once a woman is employed, it is unlawful to discriminate against her in the matter of promotion, transfer, training, or other benefits, facilities or services normally provided. Finally, it is unlawful for an employer to discriminate against a woman when it comes to dismissal, or the application of any other disciplinary procedure.

'Discrimination' consists of treating a woman less favourably than a man would be treated in similar circumstances, or imposing requirements and conditions which are designed to ensure that fewer women than men will qualify for a particular benefit. A good example of this latter type of discrimination arose in *Steel* v. *Union of Post Office Workers* (1978), which concerned a promotional policy within the Post Office which relied heavily on the seniority of the applicants. Mrs S had been a postwoman for more years than the man who was awarded the promotion ahead of her, but he had been on the permanent staff for longer than her, since women had not been granted permanent status until the 1975 Act made it compulsory. It was held that the Post Office was unlawfully 'discriminating' against Mrs S by insisting on seniority based on 'permanence'.

Although the terms of s. 6 of the Act refer to discrimination against women, and the rest of the Act uses the same word, in fact s. 2 extends the whole of the Act to cover men! In other words, it is as unlawful to discriminate against a man as it is against a woman. Thus, in *Jeremiah* v. *MOD* (1979), it was held to be unlawful discrimination to require only men on overtime to work in a particularly unpleasant process, when women on overtime were not required to, even though the work was suitable for them.

By virtue of s. 3 of the Act, it is also unlawful to discriminate against a married person of either sex on the grounds that the person in question is married. Thus, in *Thorndyke* v. *Bell Fruit* (1979), it was held to be unlawful to discriminate against a woman who had three children, since there was no evidence that it would affect her suitability for the job, and less women than men were able to comply with a 'no children' rule.

There are certain exceptions to the application of the sex discrimination laws, and several defences and justifications which an employer may claim. First of all, discrimination is not unlawful where the employment is in a private household, in an establishment with less than five employees, or in an establishment outside the UK. Where the exemption claimed is the second of these three, the employee may still claim where she has been 'victimized' because she sought to enforce her rights under the 1975 or 1970 Acts. The Act also excludes from discrimination any provisions relating to retirement or payment of wages, the latter being covered by the Equal Pay Act, 1970.

The Act also does not apply where the employer can show that the reason why a female applicant was not offered a particular job was that being a man was a 'genuine occupational qualification for the job'. The Act goes on to list as the grounds for finding that a 'genuine occupational qualification' exists such matters as physical strength and stamina (e.g. the fire service), authenticity in entertainment (i.e. casting actresses for female parts), considerations of decency and privacy (e.g. public baths and toilets), the nature and location of the job (e.g. a prison or a lighthouse), legal restrictions on the employment of women, the need for effective counselling or welfare services, or the fact that the job is one of two to be held by a married couple.

One recent case will serve as an example. In *Wylie* v. *Dee & Co. (Menswear) Ltd* (1978), a young lady sent by her local Job Centre for a post as sales assistant with a menswear firm claimed that she was refused the job on sexual grounds. While admitting that this was true, the management claimed that part of her job would have included taking inside leg measurements, and that therefore the 'decency and privacy' provision applied. In finding that there had been unlawful discrimination, the tribunal pointed out that the applicant had worked for five years already in menswear shops, that the taking of inside leg measurements was not necessarily vital to the job, and that even if it were, there would have been male assistants available.

An employee who feels that he or she has been discriminated against on sexual grounds may bring an action before an industrial tribunal. The first stage will normally be an attempted reconciliation by an officer of ACAS, but if that fails, and discrimination is subsequently proved, the tribunal has a variety of powers available to it, including compensation, reinstatement or regrading of the employee. It may also make an order 'declaring the right' of the person discriminated against.

The operation of the anti-discrimination laws generally is the concern of the Equal Opportunities Commission, which is empowered to enact Codes of Practice, investigate alleged discriminatory practices, apply to a tribunal for a ruling on an alleged discriminatory practice, assist individual applicants in special cases, and make policy recommendations to the Government.

Racial Discrimination

There have been laws against racial discrimination in Britain for quite a few years, but the Race Relations Act of 1976 is the latest to deal with discrimination on racial grounds in the field of employment. The wording of the 1976 Act is very similar in places to that of the 1975 Act, dealt with above, and will be familiar to the reader.

Section 4 of the Act makes it unlawful to discriminate against a person purely on the grounds of his colour, race, nationality or ethnic or national origins (referred to collectively as 'racial grounds'). 'Discrimination', as before, consists of treating a person less favourably than another person would be treated, and will also include those situations in which an employer makes certain benefits (e.g. promotion) dependent upon some requirement or condition which a person of a particular colour, etc., will be less likely to be able to fulfil.

But in *Panesar* v. *Nestle* (1979), it was held that chocolate factory regulations could lawfully outlaw the wearing of beards, even though less Sikhs would be able to comply with this requirement than men of other religions. The reason, clearly discriminatory, was justifiable on the grounds of hygiene.

It is unlawful to discriminate on racial grounds in exactly the same circumstances as it is unlawful to discriminate on sexual grounds, that is, in selection and recruitment, training, promotion, any other facilities, services or benefits normally extended to employees, and in the matter of discipline and dismissal.

As with sexual discrimination, there are exceptions and special cases. It is not, for example, unlawful to discriminate on racial grounds where the employee is not normally resident in Great Britain and is being trained for a post outside Great Britain, where a seaman is recruited abroad, or where there is a positive discrimination in favour of a racial group currently under-represented in particular work. Nor does the Act apply to employment within a private household.

Once again, the major exception arises where it can be shown that being of a particular racial group is a 'genuine occupational qualification' for the job in question. The Act goes on to list the circumstances in which this may occur as being authenticity in entertainment, artistic or photographic modelling work, racial welfare work and employment in the service of food and drink to the public in a 'particular setting' for which a person of a particular racial group is required for reasons of authenticity (e.g. presumably, a Chinese or Indian restaurant).

It should also be noted that it is just as unlawful for an employer to discriminate on racial grounds against staff hired to him by an agency as it would be against his own permanent staff. Also, that it is unlawful for a trade union, or a professional or trade association, to discriminate against an applicant for admission, or in the matter of benefits or services.

As with complaints of sexual discrimination, complaints under the 1976 Act are handled by industrial tribunals, with the usual likelihood of prior intervention by an officer of

ACAS. If a complaint is upheld, the tribunal has exactly the same powers as it has in connection with sexual discrimination. The Commission for Racial Equality may conduct its own investigations into alleged discrimination, and may make recommendations to the Secretary of State for employment. It may also order employers to cease discriminatory practices, or bring actions before County Courts or Industrial Tribunals, as well as assisting individuals in complex or serious cases.

Time off

In certain circumstances, an employee is entitled to be granted time off from work, with or without pay. These are in connection with union activities, in pursuance of public duties, in pursuit of another job once a redundancy has been announced and for ante-natal purposes.

Time off for trade union matters

This right falls into two parts. First of all, under s. 27 of the 1978 Act, any employee who is an official of an independent trade union recognized by the employer must be allowed time off work by that employer in order that he may carry out any union duties connected with industrial relations between his employer, and any associated employer, and their employees, or in order that he may undergo training in aspects of industrial relations appropriate to those duties, or approved by the Trades Union Congress (TUC) for his own union.

The 'time off' to which the union official is entitled under this heading must be 'with pay', and the actual amount of time which he must be allowed must be 'reasonable' in the circumstances, according to the Code of Practice drawn up in 1978. The fine detail will be a matter for individual negotiation, and disputes will be handled by an industrial tribunal.

Section 28 of the Act also allows time off, but this time without pay, to employees who are ordinary members of a trade union recognized by the employer, in order that they may participate in trade union activity short of actual industrial action. Once again, the Code of Practice merely states that the amount of time thus allowed should be reasonable in the circumstances.

Time off for public duties

It is not at all unusual for an employee to have certain public duties to perform (e.g. as a magistrate or a local councillor), which have nothing directly to do with his work. In such cases, s. 29 of the 1978 Act allows him the right to time off from work, without pay, in order to perform those duties. The main public duties covered by s. 29 are those performed by magistrates, local councillors, and members of tribunals, health authorities, educational governing bodies and water authorities.

The amount of time allowed off need only be 'reasonable in all the circumstances', and the needs of both employer and employee must be balanced up. Disputes will, as usual, be dealt with by an industrial tribunal.

Time off during redundancy notice

Every employee with at least two years' continuous service who is given notice that he is to become redundant is entitled, before the redundancy notice expires, to take reasonable time off in order to seek new employment or make arrangements for retraining. He is entitled to payment of up to two-fifths of a week's pay, but it would seem that further time off without pay should be allowed where this would be reasonable.

Any disputes will be referred to an industrial tribunal.

Time off for ante-natal care

Every pregnant employee is, upon production of a suitable medical certificate, entitled to time off work, with pay, in order to attend for ante-natal care in a hospital, clinic, etc. This time off may not be 'unreasonably' refused, or else the tribunal may award compensation.

10 Trade unions and the law

The very mention of the phrase 'trade union' is guaranteed to provoke some sort of reaction, favourable or otherwise, from the industrial observer. The law relating to trade unions and their activities has changed radically from time to time in the past century or so, swinging first one way and then the other. The attempt to curb 'union power' by legislation has led to the downfall of at least one government, and at the time of writing a new Act (the Employment Act, 1980) has been introduced in order to exert greater control over emotive activities such as 'peaceful picketing' and social security benefits to striking workers.

What follows is a genuine attempt to explain, in outline, the law as it appears to affect trade unions and their activities. No political bias is intended or even felt by the author, who long ago became far too confused by the whole issue to be able to take sides. It is hoped that this chapter will be accepted on that understanding.

An historical perspective

In previous chapters, historical surveys have been kept to an almost indecent minimum, but on this occasion, the reader cannot avoid some history if he wishes to approach some sort of understanding of the current position.

In the earliest days, trade unions were actually illegal under the infamous Combination Laws, being regarded as a manifestation of conspiracy bordering upon sedition. In 1824 the Combination Acts were repealed, and it was no longer an offence simply to band together in an endeavour to improve the lot of the artisan. But the trade unions were far from being recognized in law, and officially they did not exist. This meant, for example, that they could not hold land, make contracts or sue anyone who injured them.

Under the Trade Union Act of 1871, trade unions were allowed to register themselves, in return for which they acquired certain special privileges, including the right to hold land and other property, and to bring and defend legal actions through the agency of trustees. At the same time, the registration documents required the unions to draft rules by which they would be bound, and in particular to declare the purposes to which their funds would be put.

The Conspiracy and Protection of Property Act of 1875 took the matter a stage further by enacting that henceforward, it would not be a criminal conspiracy to perform acts 'in contemplation or furtherance of a trade dispute', a phrase still in use today. But any form of violent behaviour during industrial unrest would still be punishable in the normal way, and picketing as we know it today remained a crime. The unions were further dealt a body blow by the decision in the *Taff Vale case* (1901), to the effect that a trade union itself could be liable in damages (i.e. a civil action) in respect of the misdeeds of its officers, servants, or agents, which in this particular case consisted of picketing a railway during a strike. This was despite the fact that the union had no official existence in law, except under the 1871 Act for the limited purpose of holding land.

Political dissatisfaction and the return of a Liberal government led to the Trade Disputes Act, 1906, which gave the unions the right to 'peaceful picketing', along with the right to immunity from legal actions for damages for inducing breaches of contract on the part of employees, where this was done in furtherance of a 'trade dispute' (i.e. calling workers out on strike). But the alleged political activities of trade unions were attacked by the House of Lords in *Amalgamated Society of Railway Servants* v. *Osborne* (1910), in which it was held to be no part of a union's legitimate activities to levy sums of money from its members which were then paid over to political party funds. A period of industrial unrest followed, and in the Trade Union Act of 1913, unions were once again allowed to participate in political activities provided that the approval of the members was sought, the purpose in question was incorporated into the union rule book, and the union was registered under the Act for that purpose.

In 1956, the importance of a union's own rules was re-emphasized when in the case of *Bonsor* v. *Musician's Union* (1956), it was held that a member of a registered trade union had the right to sue the union if he was expelled in a manner contrary to the union's own rule book. The next milestone occurred in 1965, when in *Rookes* v. *Barnard*, it was held that a union which threatens to call its members out on a strike which would be in breach of the contract of employment (because, in this case, of the continued employment of a non-union member) could be sued for the 'tort' of intimidation, notwithstanding the general exemption conferred by the 1906 Act. This was countered almost immediately by the Trade Disputes Act, 1965, which reversed the effect of the House of Lords decision and removed the threat of an intimidation action from the unions.

During the industrial unrest of the early 1970s, the ill-fated Industrial Relations Act, 1971, required all trade unions to register with a Registrar of Trade Unions, before they could enjoy those protections which they had hitherto enjoyed, and which were continued by the 1971 Act. Most unions simply refused to register, or even to recognize the National Industrial Relations Court designed to handle industrial relations cases, which merely succeeded in creating martyrs to the cause when it imprisoned certain union leaders for contempt.

The fate of the 1971 Act, and the government which sought to enforce it, is a matter of recent political history. We may now examine the provisions of the Trade Union and Labour Relations Act, 1974 (henceforth referred to simply as TULRA), which replaced the 1971 Act, and contains the present law.

The legal status of trade unions and employers' associations

Under TULRA, a 'trade union' is defined, in effect, as an organization of workers which includes among its principal purposes the 'regulation of relations between workers . . . and employers', or an affiliate or associate group of such organizations (e.g. the TUC). It seems that there can be in law a 'trade union' of self-employed persons, although in *Carter* v. *Law Society* (1973), it was held that the definition could not extend to a professional body such as the Society.

There are clearly two important tests to be satisfied before an organization will be classed as a trade union, and therefore entitled to the benefits conferred by the Act. The first is that the group in question must be an 'organization of workers', and the second is that at least one of the primary purposes for which it exists must be the regulation of employer/employee relationship. Thus, in *Midland Cold Storage* v. *Steer* (1972), the Joint Shop Stewards Committee of the Port of London which sought to persuade the directors of Midland Cold Storage to employ only dock workers in a container port by means of picketing incoming vehicles was held not to be a trade union because its sole purpose seemed to be to ensure that dock workers were employed by the firm being picketed.

The Act distinguishes between 'independent' trade unions and others, and the test of whether or not a trade union is 'independent' is whether or not it is under the 'domination or control' of an employer or group of employers, or free from 'interference', whether this arises from financial control or not. In view of the fate of the 1971 Act, its 1974 successor does not call upon unions to 'register', but in fact calls for them to undergo 'certification' by an officer of ACAS, which is in effect the process by which a union is declared 'independent', and hence, among other things, free to bargain for a 'closed shop' (see p. 269).

It should also be noted at this stage that TULRA recognizes the existence of separate 'employers' associations', who are in effect the other side of the industrial relations coin, being organizations of proprietors or employers, one of whose principal purposes is to regulate the relations between employers and employees. It also includes affiliate or constituent organizations of such bodies (e.g. the Confederation of British Industry (CBI)).

Section 2 of the Act goes to the heart of the question of the legal status of a trade union. No trade union may register as a 'body corporate' (e.g. a company) nor may it be treated as such. In other words, it cannot, by registering under the general law, acquire a full legal status of its own. This has already led to one unforeseen result, in *EETPU* v. *Times Newspapers* (1979), to the effect that a trade union cannot sue for a libel on its reputation, since it has no 'personality' of its own.

At the same time, the Act goes on to allow trade unions many of the benefits of possessing a legal status of one's own. They may, for example, make binding contracts in their own name, may hold property via trustees, may sue and be sued in their own names, and may be prosecuted in their own names. As will be seen later, trade unions are in any case immune from many such legal actions.

Employers' associations are afforded exactly the same special status, but in addition, they may be formed into 'bodies corporate' should they wish.

The Act also takes the opportunity to settle, for the time being at least, the problem of the legality of the purposes and objectives of a trade union. At Common Law, these purposes and objectives might well be in 'restraint of trade', and therefore void (see Chapter 3), although some observers believe that modern courts would take a lenient attitude. TULRA places the matter beyond all reasonable doubt by stating that the purposes of a trade union shall not be regarded as unlawful for being in restraint of trade, so as to make any agreement or contract unenforceable, or render any member of the union liable for criminal conspiracy. Despite attempts by Lord Denning to render unlawful any union rule which could deny an individual member the right to work, it seems that the principle applies even to union rule books, which will not be challengeable even where they result in a man being thrown out of work (e.g. by not having a union card in a 'closed shop' situation).

The organisation of trade unions and members' rights

In view of the power of trade unions, particularly over the working lives of its members, it is not surprising that TULRA seeks to impose some measure of control over the type of internal rules by which the unions are governed. Quite apart from the normal rules of contract and the principles of natural justice, both of which would imply that no member may be unjustly expelled from his union, the Act seeks to establish at least a framework for democratic and open government within each union.

We must examine the way in which the courts endeavour to uphold the 'rights' of the individual member. What effective protection does a member have against victimisation within the union, unfair refusal of membership, and so on? These points may now be examined in more detail.

Admission to membership

A trade union may apparently admit and reject whoever it likes, and it may be as exclusive as it wishes. By 1966, the Court of Appeal was making loud warning noises to the effect that it was unreasonably 'in restraint of trade' to refuse union membership to a person without good reason. But as we have already noted, the 'restraint of trade' argument no longer applies, since TULRA appears to apply even to the rules of a trade union, and to uphold them even though they are in restraint of trade. This is despite a spirited attempt by Lord Denning in *Edwards* v. *SOGAT* (1971) to resist any union rule which appears to deny a man 'the right to work', whatever that may mean.

The 1974 Act contains no provisions which will guarantee the admission into a union of any suitably qualified applicant. But the Employment Act, 1980, provides that in a 'closed shop' situation, the union may not 'unreasonably' withhold membership from an applicant, or 'unreasonably' expel an existing

member. The only other controls which exist are to be found
under the Sex Discrimination Act, 1975, and the Race Relations Act, 1976, which prohibit, in the context of union
membership, discrimination purely on the grounds of sex,
race, nationality, colour, etc.

Discipline

Once a member *has* been admitted, at least he is then party to
some sort of membership contract, which will, by law, include
union rules on the matter of discipline and expulsion. He also
comes under the protection of the 'rules of natural justice'
which each and every union is obliged by law to acknowledge.

In short, the member may only be disciplined (and ultimately expelled) in pursuance of and in compliance with, his
own union's rules. The one exception is presumably in the
case where the member fails to pay his subscription, so that he
is no longer contractually linked to the union anyway. Even
where the rules give the union, or its officials, a great deal of
discretion on whether, for example, a member's conduct has
been 'detrimental to the interests of the union as a whole',
the rules of natural justice still apply, and a member may not be
arbitrarily expelled without due process.

This means that, at the very least, the member concerned
must be fully informed of a complaint against him, be given an
opportunity to state his case, and be judged impartially. There
must also be some sort of appeals procedure, internal or otherwise, and the member may never be denied recourse to the
normal courts, in so far as they have the power to reverse or
modify a bad decision.

The closed shop

This is one of the most emotive areas of trade union operations,
and one which excites a good deal of criticism from opponents
of trade union power. Put at its simplest, it is a system whereby
no one may work in a particular job without holding a member-

ship card from a particular union. Clearly, such a system depends for its existence on the ability of the union to ensure that the employer observes it, either by agreement or by fear of the consequences of doing otherwise.

It is worth recalling at this stage that it is regarded as a 'fair' dismissal for an employer to dismiss an employee in compliance with a closed shop agreement, unless the member in question has a genuine religious objection to belonging to any trade union or objects on the grounds of some 'deeply held personal conviction'.

Any closed shop created after 15 August 1980 requires an 80-per-cent majority of those entitled to vote to actually vote in favour before it will be recognized by law. Also, after that date, no one may be dismissed simply for refusing to become a member of a union which has subsequently acquired a closed shop under a 'union–management agreement'. It will also be an 'inadmissible reason' for an employer to fire an employee because of his wish to join a union, or to take part in its activities.

Nevertheless, at Common Law, the closed shop is lawful. Nothing in any Act of Parliament renders it unlawful, and not even the 1980 Act, designed to curb the unions in certain of their powers, alters this situation. However, recent moves in the European Court of Human Rights suggest a possible remedy along the lines of the 'right to work' concept.

Collective agreements

When introducing the topic of written contracts of employment in Chapter 8, the point was made that many of the terms and conditions which will govern the contract of employment will not be a matter simply for private negotiation, but will in fact have been decided in advance, for *all* employees of that particular trade, in a 'collective agreement' between management and union. It now remains to place such collective agreements in a legal perspective.

The main question is, of course, whether or not, when the parties have finally made a collective bargaining, they are legally bound by it, at least for its stated period of duration. The answer to that question was fairly obscure until 1971, when under the Industrial Relations Act collective agreements were made legally enforceable, unless they contain a clause to the contrary. The result was that most subsequent agreements contained carefully worded clauses to the contrary. Under TULRA, Parliament came to terms with the situation, and reversed the presumption, so that, under s. 15, no collective agreement made in the future, or for that matter made before 1971 and still in force, will be presumed to have been intended to be legally binding unless (a) it is in writing; (b) it contains a clause to the effect that the parties intend it to be legally binding.

The parties may, if they wish, construct a collective agreement, only parts of which are intended to be legally binding. This will produce a document which is enforceable against either party in places, and totally unenforceable in others.

A 'collective agreement' is defined under the Act as being any arrangement or agreement which relates to any matter which might legitimately be an element of a 'trade dispute'.

Industrial disputes

In recent years, industrial disputes have been the most widely publicized aspect of the industrial relations scene, and have led to legal debates of the magnitude normally reserved for large wealthy estates. Reputations have been made and lost on the strength of major confrontations between management and union, and no observer of the industrial scene in the past ten years can fail to have noted names like Grunwick, Lord Denning and British Leyland.

The basic question can be put fairly simply, although the answer would take an entire book to explain in full. May a trade union or any of its officials be legally liable for any action taken against an employer, whether it takes the form of a strike, a picket or whatever? In order to begin answering that question, we must appreciate how many potential legal liabilities there are.

Criminal liability

First of all, it is possible that some criminal offence is committed. As we have seen, the mere act of forming a trade union is not a criminal offence, and has not been since the abolition of the Combination Acts. Under the Conspiracy and Protection of Property Act, 1875, however, it became, and remains, a criminal offence to assault or intimidate someone with a view to persuading him to take action, or refrain from action, or to 'persistently follow' him or 'beset' his house. Quite apart from these specialized offences, an unruly picket is likely to commit a variety of other criminal offences (e.g. breach of the peace, possessing an offensive weapon, assault, conspiracy, unlawful assembly, affray, malicious damage and obstructing the highway). There is no immunity from any of these offences simply because the occasion happens to be that of an industrial dispute. This is worth bearing in mind when commentators call for more power to be given to the police to deal with rowdy pickets.

In short, the criminal law has remained relatively neutral in the field of industrial disputes. On the one hand, it will not prevent trade unionists from peacefully following their own interests in the formation of unions and the presentation of claims to employers; on the other hand, in theory at least, a trade unionist who wishes to emphasize his point with a pick-axe handle, or by lying in the roadway, gets no special treatment. In the eyes of the law, he is as guilty as the man who behaves in such a fashion because he is drunk. Whether or not the criminal law will or should be used against striking unionists, is another matter. Nothing hastened the demise of the Industrial Relations Court more than the popular sentiment against it when it incarcerated a few picket bosses for contempt in 1972.

Civil liability of unions

Of far greater complexity is the possibility of civil liability. Without the intervention of some statutory protection, it is quite likely that a trade union (and its leaders) which called out its members on industrial action would face a variety of actions for damages from those who had been financially injured. The three most likely of these would be 'inducement to breach of contract', 'intimidation' and 'conspiracy'.

Space does not permit an excursion into the often fascinating history of the application of civil liability to situations created by striking unions. The position is now governed by TULRA, which distinguishes between the position of the union and the position of the individuals who control it.

Section 14 of TULRA states that as a general rule, trade unions are immune from all action in respect of civil wrongs, and that this immunity extends to members and office-bearers acting in the name of the union, assuming of course that they are authorized to do so. The two major exceptions to this general immunity arise where some wrongful action on the part of the union results in personal injury to someone, and in the case of a breach of duty in connection with the ownership, occupation or possession by the union of some property, either 'real' (e.g. buildings) or 'personal' (e.g. a car). In short, a union may still be liable if one of its drivers knocks down a pedestrian, or if a visitor to union premises is injured by a loose stair rail.

However, not even these exceptions apply where the action complained of was done in 'contemplation or furtherance of a trade dispute'. More will be written below about the unhappy history of that phrase, but it would seem that if the incident about which the plaintiff is complaining was in contemplation or furtherance of a trade dispute, then he is completely barred from suing the union or its officers. Was it really the intention of Parliament that, for example, the innocent pedestrian who is knocked down by a union bus carrying pickets to a factory should be unable to sue the union as employers of the driver (i.e. for 'vicarious liability')? Obviously the injured party may still sue the driver himself, but s. 14 does appear to prevent him from bringing action against the man's employers, as he would normally be entitled to do.

Exactly the same immunity is conferred upon employers' associations and clearly much will rest upon the definition of a 'trade dispute'.

Civil liability of individuals

Section 13 of TULRA (as amended in 1980) confers limited immunity upon all persons who engage in industrial action (e.g. shop stewards, members, regional conveners, etc.) in that it states that no action taken by *anyone* 'in contemplation or furtherance of a trade dispute' shall be actionable in a civil court simply because it induces another person to break a contract, or constitutes intimidation of the type which consists of threatening a withdrawal of labour.

Two points are immediately obvious upon reading the words of that section. The first is that the only civil liability from which the individual (as opposed to the union) is immune is that concerning inducing a breach of contract or intimidation. Any other type of civil wrong (e.g. the damaging of property) will still be actionable against the union, although from s. 14 above it would appear that the union would not be 'vicariously' liable for it, not even if it were done by a union official acting in the union's own name. The official, according to s. 13, would, however, be personally liable.

The second point is that an individual is apparently immune from the consequences of causing a breach of any contract, and not just a contract of employment, or a contract of employment to which his own union members are a party. In short, s. 13 grants immunity in respect of what has become known a 'secondary picketing', that is, picketing, etc., outside the premises of an organization or concern which has nothing directly to do with the dispute. In an endeavour to prevent s. 13 being used in such a way, Parliament passed s. 17 of the Employment Act, 1980, the overall effect of which is to limit the immunity conferred on union members by s. 13 to actions taken against the employer with whom there is a dispute, and to actions which directly interfere with the supply of goods and services in and out of premises owned by that employer. The union member will also be protected where he takes action to prevent or disrupt the supply of goods or services to some employer who is 'associated' with the employer in the dispute, where the goods or services are in 'substitution' for goods or services which would, but for the dispute, have been supplied to or by the employer in the dispute. 'Associated' employers will probably be limited in definition to those consisting of companies linked together financially.

But where the union members are picketing premises 'lawfully' under s. 15 of the 1947 Act (see below), they would appear to be still covered by the immunity conferred by s. 13, even if they indirectly cause some loss or damage to the employer which is outlawed under s. 17 of the 1980 Act.

More is written below about the separate 'right to picket', and it is merely used above as an illustration of the more general problem of 'secondary action'.

Trade disputes

Both ss. 13 and 14 are, to varying degrees, limited by the concept of a 'trade dispute', and one's definition of when an action is, or is not, taken in 'contemplation or furtherance' of it. Most of the test cases have been under s. 13, but it should not be forgotten that it is also important in determining when and if the exceptions to the general immunity of unions from the civil law may be invoked (see p. 272).

Section 29 of TULRA attempts a definition of a 'trade dispute' which in effect makes it a dispute between employers and workers, or between workers and workers, which is connected with terms and conditions of employment, physical conditions of employment, employment and dismissal of staff, allocation of duties, matters of discipline, membership or non-membership of unions, facilities afforded for unions, or negotiation machinery.

It seemed from *Torquay Hotel Co.* v. *Cousins* (1969), that this definition (and therefore the immunity from civil law which goes with it) would not apply where the action taken appears to have been actuated by malice or personal anger. Thus, the leader of the TGWU was held not to be entitled to any immunity when he succeeded in cutting off the supply of central heating fuel to an hotel (which was delivered by his own union's tanker drivers) in retaliation for comments about the union by the hotel manager in the press.

Similarly, in *BBC* v. *Hearn* (1977), it was held that a threat to cut off transmission of a television programme to South Africa by a union member whose union did not approve of the regime in that country had nothing to do with any likely 'trade dispute' as defined in s. 29.

There were many other such cases, and many cases in which the unions and their officers succeeded in showing that a 'trade dispute' was involved. In other words, the matter was one which could be ventilated in the courts, and each case would be treated on its merits. Lord Denning in the Court of Appeal showed himself to be particularly vigilant in ensuring that the definition of a 'trade dispute' did not become wider than Parliament had intended, particularly where 'secondary action' was concerned.

Then, in 1979, the whole position changed, as the result of the House of Lords decision in *Express Newspapers* v. *McShane*. The National Union of Journalists (NUJ) called a strike of provincial journalists, and in an endeavour to make it 'bite' harder, called for sympathetic action by the Press Association (PA). Disappointed by the response, the leader of the NUJ called for all PA 'copy', on all newspapers, to be blacked by NUJ members. The *Daily Express*, a national newspaper, had not been party to the original dispute, and sought an injunction to prevent the blacking. An injunction may only be granted against a threatened action which is unlawful, and the question therefore arose as to whether or not the union leader was protected by s. 13 of the 1974 Act, in that the call for blacking was made in contemplation or furtherance of a 'trade dispute'.

The House of Lords held that the test of whether or not an action is taken 'in furtherance of a trade dispute' is a purely subjective one, and that if the party taking the action genuinely believes that it will help his cause in an industrial dispute, and he does it for that purpose, then he is protected by s. 13.

The same point was made by the House of Lords a few months later, when in *Duport Steels* v. *Sirs* (1980), they refused an injunction against the leader of a steel union whose dispute was with public sector employers, but whose men were picketing private employers.

It would seem, therefore, that the courts of law, at their

highest level, have washed their hands of the matter, and feel that it is not their duty to act as umpire in the matter of actions taken during trade disputes. The courts are no longer the arbiters of what is, or is not, a 'trade dispute', and all that the unions and their leaders require to do in order to secure immunity from the type of civil liability mentioned above is provide some sort of reasonable evidence to show that it was genuinely believed that the action complained of would have the effect of assisting in a trade dispute. It was because of this attitude by the courts that the 1980 Act was passed, with its imposed limits on 'peaceful picketing' (see below) and its exclusion of 'secondary' and 'sympathy' action from the protection of s. 13 of the 1974 Act. In future, it will not matter whether or not such action is taken 'in contemplation or furtherance of a trade dispute' at all – it will expose the union member(s) to civil action for the simple reason that such acts are no longer protected by s. 13 anyway.

This is perhaps all very well when it comes to s. 13, or even the main part of s. 14, but it will be remembered that where an action is taken in contemplation or furtherance of a trade dispute, the union as such is granted immunity, under s. 14, from even civil claims arising from personal injury. It may be that the House of Lords did not intend their ruling on trade disputes to go so far as to deprive, for example, the innocent pedestrian mentioned above of the right to sue a union for the negligence of one of its drivers simply because the union decides, for itself, that the vehicle was being driven 'in contemplation or furtherance of a trade dispute'. But until there are further decisions, it is really only a matter of conjecture. Certainly, the law could hardly be regarded as being in a satisfactory state at the time of writing.

Picketing

The gulf between the theory and the reality of trade union law is perhaps at its widest when one comes to the subject of picketing. At Common Law, a picket is to be judged like any other assembly of persons, and the carrying of placards, shouting at passers-by, obstruction of incoming lorries and throwing of stones is no more lawful or unlawful than it would be if carried out by persons with no union motivation.

The point has already been made, but should perhaps be reinforced at this point, that in general, pickets have no immunity from the criminal law. Any rights or immunities which they may have, will come from statute.

Section 15 of TULRA, as amended by the 1980 Act, in fact gives them what might be described as a 'limited right' to picket, and by no means an all-embracing one. In fact, as the result of the passing of the Employment Act, 1980, s. 16, it will now only be 'lawful' to picket at or near one's own place of work, and even then the only persons who will be permitted to do this will be the members themselves, and their officials. In addition, an official may picket outside any premises of any employer who employs members whom he represents, provided that he is accompanied by at least one such member.

Both members and their officials will be limited in their activities to 'peacefully' persuading any person to work or not to work, and to 'peacefully' obtaining or communicating information. In addition, all action must be 'in contemplation or furtherance of a trade dispute'.

Again, the phrase, 'trade dispute', which was no doubt originally intended by Parliament to limit the occasions upon which picketing might lawfully occur, may now have become a free-for-all as the result of the *McShane* ruling (see p. 275). But even when one concedes that a particular event does arise in the course of a trade dispute, the pickets still appear to be limited to what has become known as 'peaceful picketing'. Indeed, the section uses the word 'peacefully' twice. The section certainly does not authorize or condone the violent scenes which have accompanied some pickets in recent years, and this is something else to remember when it is argued that 'the law against picketing needs tightening up'.

In short, the peaceful picket will only be protected by s. 15 from the consequences of unlawful action (e.g. trespass, obstructing the highways, etc.) which is 'peaceful' in nature. In recent years, our television screens have conveyed plenty of examples of unlawful action by pickets which is far from peaceful, and not even s. 15 will protect a picket if he indulges in violent or noisy behaviour. Thus, in *Hunt* v. *Broome* (1974), it was held that a picket had no right to stop a lorry entering a factory, and should therefore be convicted of obstructing the highway, and it has been asserted time and time again, usually at the level of the magistrates courts, that the police have the right to arrest pickets for a breach of the peace, or even when a breach of the peace is merely 'reasonably anticipated'.

One immediate effect of the new s. 15 will of course be to make 'flying pickets' unlawful, and this may well take much of the tension and violence out of picket situations. But if such people picket other premises than their own place of work in circumstances covered by s. 12 of the 1980 Act (see p. 274), presumably their actions will still be lawful.

The 1980 Code of Practice on Picketing emphasizes the importance of limiting the number of persons taking part in a picket, and ensuring that they are properly supervised. It also expresses the hope that vital goods and services will be exempted wherever possible.

Index

edited by Michael Molyneux
The Pan Guide to the Law   £3.50

An indispensable guide to the law and its effects on your
everyday life. In straightforward language this new handbook
explains what can and cannot be done by the citizen on his or
her own and gives guidance on when and where to go for
professional help on legal matters. Each section covers a
different area of law – in the home, at work, family matters,
the consumer, the motorist; the citizen and the police,
government departments, the courts, the ombudsman. Additionally,
advice on legal aid and a list of useful addresses and publications.

C. Northcote Parkinson and Nigel Rowe
Communicate   £1.20
Parkinson's formula for business survival

Peter Drucker says in his Foreword: 'This book, to my knowledge
for the first time, tackles all four elements of communication
(what to say; when to say it; whom to say it to; how to say it).
It makes the businessman literate and it gives him the competence
which he needs.'

'Will be read avidly by the professionals and the amateurs in
PR, but it is the individual businessman who will gain most from
it' DIRECTOR

R. E. Palmer and A. H. Taylor
Financial Planning and Control   £1.75

Today, more than ever before, it is essential that management
has a sound appreciation of the financial implications of its
plans and actions. Using clear, everyday language the authors
explain the nature of the assistance which higher levels of
accounting can provide in the planning and control of a modern
business.

'It really is excellent value and offers an intensely practical approach'
CERTIFIED ACCOUNTANTS JOURNAL

Charles Handy
Gods of Management £1.25

What sort of manager are you – and what sort of manager is your boss? Witty, imaginative, controversial and studded with real-life management case histories, *Gods of Management* has the answer.

'The gods of management are engaged in a great battle, the outcome of which could decide the future success of our nation ... Zeus, the dynamic entrepreneur ... Apollo, the god of order and bureaucracy ... A man with a lifetime's experience, Professor Handy has written one of the more stimulating books on management' FINANCIAL TIMES

Desmond Goch
Finance and Accounts for Managers £1.25

The art of accountancy is now the most important instrument of control in the management armoury. This comprehensive guide will enable managers – even those without formal training in business finance – to formulate trading policies, forecast future trends and effectively administer their departments.

Robert Seton Lawrence
A Guide to Speaking in Public £1.25

Here is a wealth of sound and practical advice, presented with examples both of great oratory and of the many pitfalls which the careful speaker can learn to avoid. This guide – highly recommended by many managerial and professional organizations – includes sections on how to: gain confidence; secure and hold an audience's attention; get people to *enjoy* listening to you; think logically; project your personality; cope with speaking at formal occasions; plus: developing children; the art of conversation; common speech faults and their cure; public speaking examinations.

Robert Taylor
The Fifth Estate £1.95

Are Britain's unions too weak or too powerful? Robber barons
or failed agents of social justice? Are they responsible for
Britain's postwar economic decline, or a constructive force?

Labour correspondent of the *Observer*, Robert Taylor examines
such questions, giving a highly readable profile of the trade
union movement, its history and structure. Revised and updated
to the May 1979 General Election, this will become the classic
analysis of the British unions in the late twentieth century.

'Invaluable . . . entertaining, informative and accurate' ECONOMIST

'Essential reading' SCOTSMAN

Alastair Mant
The Rise and Fall of the British Manager
£1.20

'Seeks to explain, in a vigorous style, why in this country we
"downgrade so many of the jobs that really matter" . . . Mant
argues that the business of making and selling things,
and doing these jobs well, has been submerged by the preoccupation
with "management", as if it was something quite distinct from
these humdrum activities' FINANCIAL TIMES

'What ails the British economy, he claims, is not the quality
of its management, but the fact that management exists at all'
NEW STATESMAN

'Managers and management teachers who are anxious to
explore new and more effective means of improving management
performance will not be deterred'
MANAGEMENT REVIEW AND DIGEST

Alvin Toffler
The Third Wave   £1.95

The First Wave was the agricultural revolution ; the Second
Wave was the industrial revolution ; the Third Wave is the
mightiest of all — the technological revolution, and it is upon
us now. In this controversial new perspective on tomorrow from
the author of *Future Shock*, Alvin Toffler describes the new
civilization being created around us — its lifestyles, jobs, sexual
attitudes, the family, economic and political structures — showing
us how to adapt to these changes and enjoy a startling, new and
fulfilling way of life.

'Provocative' FINANCIAL TIMES

'Brilliant passages . . . Toffler's energy is awesome'
THE TIMES EDUCATIONAL SUPPLEMENT

John Fenton
The A–Z of Sales Management   £1.75

A book for the sales manager determined to succeed. This
humorous yet highly practical book covers the ins and outs of
managing a sales force from Advertising to Zest, taking in all
the vital aspects : credit control, meetings and conferences,
decision making, sales forecasting, remuneration schemes, job
specifications, motivation, planning and control, leadership, expense
accounts and — last but not least — how to achieve consistently
good sales results.

How to Double Your Profits Within the Year   £1.50

A programme of improvements, applicable to all types of business,
to help you at least double your profits within twelve months.
Fictional but highly practical, the book is an extended memorandum,
an action plan, written by the MD of an imaginary company to
his top managers. It shows, for example, how you can choose
which customers contribute most to your profitability ; recruit the
right people ; improve production efficiency ; price for maximum
profit ; control your sales force. In the few hours it takes to read
the book, you will be convinced that the title's claim is a modest
understatement.

A Multilingual Commercial Dictionary
£1.95

Some 3,000 words and phrases in common commercial use are listed in English, French, German, Spanish and Portuguese followed by their translation in the other languages. The equivalent American expression is also included where relevant. Simple to use and invaluable for everyday reference, the dictionary covers terms used throughout banking, accounting, insurance, shipping, export and import and international trade.

edited by S. E. Stiegeler and Glyn Thomas
A Dictionary of Economics and Commerce
£1.50

An authoritative A–Z of the terms used internationally in the overlapping fields of theoretical economics and practical commerce. A team of expert contributors provides a formal definition of each word or term, followed by an explanation of its underlying concepts and accompanied by appropriate illustrations. Special attention is paid to such new and rapidly expanding subjects as cost-benefit analysis and welfare economics. And the vocabularies of banking, accounting, insurance, stock exchanges, commodity dealing, shipping, transport and commercial law are all included.

Russell Langley
Practical Statistics   £1.95

This book provides a simple description of the principles and practical application of statistics which will appeal both to the non-mathematician and to those who are more involved in the subject. It will be especially useful to students of such subjects as Physical, Life and Earth Sciences, Psychology, Medicine and Business Studies, who need a concise and straightforward introduction to the use of statistical method.

Reference, Language and Information

Management

☐ **Introducing Marketing**	Christopher, McDonald and Wills	£1.75p
☐ **The Effective Executive**		£1.25p
☐ **Management**		£2.50p
☐ **Managing for Results**	Peter Drucker	95p
☐ **Practice of Management**		£1.95p
☐ **A-Z of Sales Management**	John Fenton	£1.75p
☐ **How to Double Your Profits**		£1.50p
☐ **Finance and Accounts for Managers**	Desmond Goch	£1.25p
☐ **Gods of Management**	Charles Handy	£1.25p
☐ **The Managerial Woman**	M. Hennig and A. Jardim	£1.20p
☐ **Practical Statistics**	R. Langley	£1.95p
☐ **A Guide to Speaking in Public**	Robert Seton Lawrence	85p
☐ **The Rise and Fall of the British Manager**	Alistair Mant	£1.20p
☐ **Communicate**	C. Northcote Parkinson	£1.20p
☐ **Reality of Management**	Rosemary Stewart	£1.25p
☐ **Reality of Organisations**		£1.25p
☐ **Financial Planning for Managers**	A. H. Taylor and R. E. Palmer	£1.75p
☐ **Dictionary of Economics and Commerce**		£1.50p
☐ **Multilingual Commercial Dictionary**		£1.95p

All these books are available at your local bookshop or newsagent, or can be ordered direct from the publisher. Indicate the number of copies required and fill in the form below

Name

(block letters please)

Address

Send to Pan Books (CS Department), Cavaye Place, London SW10 9PG

Please enclose remittance to the value of the cover price plus:

25p for the first book plus 10p per copy for each additional book ordered to a maximum charge of £1.05 to cover postage and packing Applicable only in the UK

While every effort is made to keep prices low, it is sometimes necessary to increase prices at short notice. Pan Books reserve the right to show on covers and charge new retail prices which may differ from those advertised in the text or elsewhere